Stories for Saturday

Stories for
Popular Fiction Saturday

TRANSLATED BY
TIMOTHY C. WONG

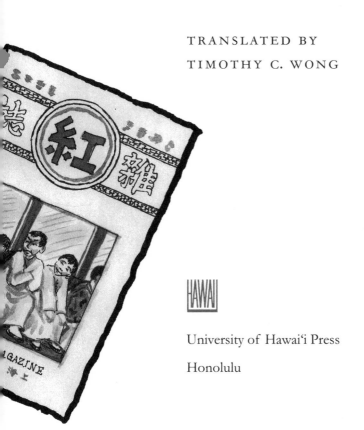

HAWAI

University of Hawai'i Press

Honolulu

© 2003 University of Hawai'i Press
All rights reserved
Printed in the United States of America
08 07 06 05 04 03   6 5 4 3 2 1

Library of Congress Cataloging-in-Publication Data
Stories for Saturday : twentieth-century Chinese
popular fiction / Translated by Timothy C. Wong.

   p.   cm.

ISBN 0-8248-2624-8 (hard cover: alk. paper)
ISBN 0-8248-2690-6 (pbk. : alk. paper)
1. Chinese fiction—20th century—Translations into
English.   I. Title: Twentieth-century Chinese popular
fiction.   II. Wong, Timothy C.

PL2658.E8 S85 2003
895.1'3508—dc21

                 2002153255

Designed by April Leidig-Higgins

Printed by The Maple-Vail Book Manufacturing Group

Contents

. . . .

Preface

. . . .

CONSCIOUSLY fictionalized narratives in China have always been labeled *xiaoshuo,* a term originally denoting "stories of minor consequence," to indicate the lesser status they were assigned in the pantheon of native literary genres. By the turn of the twentieth century, however, the combination of shaken cultural confidence and the need to become "modern" had brought about abrupt cultural changes. Especially after the reformer Liang Qichao's famous 1902 call to "renovate" *xiaoshuo,* the term was quickly understood to stand for Chinese equivalents of major fictional narratives in contemporary Japan and the West, narratives expected by writers and readers alike to carry out such serious missions as truthful self-expression and national reconstruction.

Because such expectations raised the status of all fictionalized writings in the eyes of both native and foreign critics and scholars, it has since been highly difficult to look at old-style *xiaoshuo* on its own terms—as predominantly recreational writings designed to give readers temporary respite from harsh or boring reality. Such writings, in the classical *wenyan* language, are part of a tradition dating back to at least the fourth-century ghost stories and the fifth-century anecdotes collected in such works as the *Shishuo xinyu* (New accounts of tales of the world). Later, when the tradition took the decisive step of adopting the vernacular *baihua* in imitation of oral storytelling, *xiaoshuo* flourished. From the latter part of the Ming dynasty (sixteenth century) to the turn of the twentieth century, the short stories and long narratives written in this more exhaustive language achieved high popularity among those who could read and who had the means to acquire either hand-copied or printed texts. By the 1920s, however, such people became the larger part of the populace in China's urban centers, especially Shanghai, the result of the development of public education and the introduction of cheaper methods of printing that also launched modern journalism. Nearly all of the authors represented here were newspaper reporters or editors.

It should be no surprise that the new readership would gravitate to what amounts to a modern extension of a tradition of escapist writings, especially at a time of anxiety brought on by astonishing political and economic reforms. As popular as such writings quickly became, however, they were disparaged as shirking or betraying the modernizing duties Liang had charged *xiaoshuo* to take up. Liang himself, feeling by 1915 that his call to make *xiaoshuo* into instruments for leading the masses to modernization had all but failed, bemoaned the seemingly unshakable dominance of old-style fiction. Other reformist intellectuals soon followed suit. In spite of their regular references to modernized actualities in the urban centers, fictional narratives of the time were considered, at best, to be remnants of a past that needed to be transformed.

By the 1920s, though, in spite of Liang's misgivings, the so-called May Fourth fiction—named after a 1919 student demonstration that turned into a national cultural movement—had come to the fore, openly and determinately attaching to fictional narratives the moral didacticism that premodern Chinese intellectuals had reserved for their official histories. At least in principle, the old "literati" had looked down on *xiaoshuo* for extending factual truth in order to provide escape. Now, under foreign influence, the fictionalizing had quickly become respectable, while the traditional aim of providing temporary respite "after tea and meals" had not. Still, even in a rapidly modernizing metropolis such as Shanghai, readers in consistently large numbers gravitated to the traditionalist and escapist *xiaoshuo,* which unabashedly labeled themselves as stories for Saturday, a day with a recently instituted afternoon of leisure, when a person could curl up with a magazine and forget for a time everything he or she had to deal with for most of the rest of the week.

When considering the texts alone, the leisurely disengagement from realities is not always immediately apparent. The traditional need to captivate the reader has always brought on the regular inclusion of facts, even as the facts are inevitably dressed up. Historians looking for descriptions of, say, urban life in the Shanghai of the 1920s, can readily find valuable evidence in the stories here; one or the other of these may actually evince a certain amount of social concern. In practice, the line between escape and engagement in any written narrative has never been hard and fast. On the other hand, *historical* evidence that the Chinese traditionally considered fictional stories as narratives of no great moral or political consequence is beyond dispute, and we should not insist, even from good intentions, that the "old-style" writings here be something that they are fundamentally not. It is this insistence, as a matter of fact, that has prevented us from attaining a more accurate picture of what really happened to the vibrant *xiaoshuo* tradition when China underwent cataclysmic cultural change in the first half of the twentieth century. While the temporal and intellectual distance between us and the China of that era continues to increase, the stories can still help us transcend the barriers of time and change by allowing us to experience vicariously, and hence to understand better, the preferred reading fare of so many urbanized Chinese on Saturday afternoons throughout the Republican period— "after a week of exhausting work," "with sunlight from the window," and "with the scent of flowers" about their chairs.

THE EFFORT TO PUT THIS book together took up my own leisure time for a number of years, during which I benefited greatly from the help and input of a number of colleagues and friends. In addition to Professor Fan Boqun of Suzhou University, who piqued what had been a passing curiosity on the subject and who has been sending me books on Butterfly-Saturday fiction since 1993, I want especially to thank Christian Bragg, David Y. Ch'en, Alice Chiang Meyering, William L. Hendrickson, Jeffrey C. Kinkley, Yan-shuan Lao, William A. Lyell, Sun Jingyao, Gang Xu, J. T. Wixted, Ai-hwa Wu, and Sharon Yamamoto. I am of course responsible for any shortcomings that remain.

For her general support and help in this and other endeavors in my life, the book is dedicated to Lib in the thirty-second year of our marriage.

T. C. W.

I. Scandal

· ·

STORIES PORTRAYING SCANDALS among the rich, powerful, or merely clever in China's major cities—what was called *heimu* or "black curtain" fiction—flourished after the 1910s, tied closely to the rise of modern journalism. Their aim was not muckraking or exposure, even though writers often insist (as do two of them here) that their stories are basically factual, and even though we can extrapolate much from them about China's social realities in their day. Far from answering any call to better the situations that allow the scandals to take place, these stories sought instead to provide what Perry Link calls "comfort" to their readers. The "unmasked corruption in high places," Link explains, suggested to readers that "even though the 'haves' may have money, they certainly lack virtue or happiness compared to us."[1]

The three *heimu* stories collected here, however, show that corruption and other immoral behavior actually permeated all levels of Chinese society in the early days of the Republic. Whereas General Li in "The Red Chips" is undeniably a member of the rich and powerful elite, Sanxin, or even Miss Zhou, in "The Confidence in the Game," are clearly not. And the Zhus' "Rickshaw Man"—a bona fide member of the underclass—proves in the end to be more avaricious and manipulative than the wealthy master and mistress he serves.

A telling characteristic of *heimu* stories is the absence of either untainted heros or unredeemed villains, a characteristic that contrasts directly with so much of the politically committed Chinese fiction in both the "modern" and the "contemporary" eras. In the stories here, the closest figure to a hero would be Chen Shoujing, the "slim, tall, thirtyish gentleman traveler" who unwittingly makes a fortune playing mahjongg for unbelievably high stakes; the reader is clearly led to delight in his unexpected gains. But he did not come to his riches as the result of any heroic deed; he was simply lucky. Depending on one's own sense of morality, neither does the distinction between hero and villain apply to Sanxin, the rake and con artist who triumphs in the end. The reader might well be glad that the Rickshaw Man profits from the adulterous couple. But, here again, the man does so much more from cold calculation than from any heroic virtue. Other than having the same occupation, he is in no way a Camel Xiangzi, the much-discussed rickshaw-pulling hero in the modern writer Lao She's novel *Luotuo Xiangzi* (Camel Lucky), published in 1936–1937.[2] Xiangzi struggles mightily in a social situation that dooms him to defeat. The reader's expected admiration of him leads logically to the deploring of the society that would not allow someone like him to thrive and prosper. The Rickshaw Man here is far less admirable, in spite of— really because of—his ability to milk the situation for personal profit. He's not a villain, since the reader is hardly expected to condemn what he does. But neither is he a hero, since he works around life's obstacles rather than rises above them.

What then do *heimu* stories do? Why were they read so avidly in their time? The first story in the section gives us a clear answer. Sanxin is someone who very much deserves what he gets, a profligate trapped by his own schemes. Were this a story about moral behavior, it would have ended with Miss Zhou going off with the four-and-a-half carat diamond. By extending the plot to Mr. Resourceful and the final con, the story reveals its fundamental concern: to surprise and delight the reader. This concern supercedes any ethical right or wrong, any true exploration of China's societal ills. Scandals may have the potential to arouse anger, to stir readers to political action. In *heimu* stories, however, they are recounted primarily to give vicarious pleasure, to make a reader smile while sipping tea on a Saturday afternoon. That they achieved such popularity in their time shows that the Chinese have always looked to their fiction for amusement, even as they have always sought truth or moral direction from other kinds of writings within their own cultural traditions.

Notes

1. See Perry Link, *Mandarin Ducks and Butterflies: Popular Fiction in Early Twentieth-Century Chinese Cities* (Berkeley: University of California Press, 1981), p. 20.

2. See the translation by Jean M. James, *Rickshaw* (Honolulu: University of Hawai'i Press, 1979).

The Confidence in the Game

. . . .

Zhu Shouju

On your finger, a diamond is really the tiniest of objects. But its demonic power is beyond all imagination. You may be the handsomest; you may be the smartest. Such qualities might have brought you status and acclaim in times gone by. These days, though, regale yourself as you would with the fanciest of clothes; if a diamond is not gracing that little digit of yours, all you can ever hope to attain is some label like "slick young man." Dress more plainly and you would not likely escape being dubbed a "poor fellow." Conversely, should your hand sport a diamond of even four or five carats, "slick" would instantly become "classy," and "poor fellow" would then be perceived as the scion of a wealthy household. Let's think about it. A four- to five-carat diamond is only slightly larger than a cherry pit, and not nearly the size of an almond. Yet it can actually determine a person's worth. And to an even greater extent than a man's, a woman's appeal is most intimately connected to these jewels. Is she pockmarked with missing front teeth? Does she have a face that brings on a three-day retch? Never mind! She becomes an instant center of attention once she puts on that glittery, sparkly diamond. Far from suffering nausea, those who see her will drool all over themselves. Psychologically, though, we can't say that every one of these people actually covets another's diamond. It's just that once in its presence, their attention is drawn directly to the gem, much as sunflowers to the sun or iron shavings to a magnet. Maybe physicists should look into the principle behind this.

Why am I not getting to my story, but going on and on with this bloated preface? Well, I have my reasons. Here in Shanghai, what's on the surface remains of paramount value. Time and again, people who do not have so much as a day's worth of food in the house are eager to dress themselves properly, in expensive finery from head to toe. They would rather exchange their winter furs for summer silks at pawnshops, claiming all the while that they are saving themselves the trouble of storage. People like that are known as embroidered pillows or, most popularly, con artists.

One such was Wang Sanxin, though *his* "pillow" was stuffed with much more than just straw. While his family did not exactly qualify as "well-heeled," there was always enough food on the table. On the other hand, he was not at all as well-off as he looked in full regalia. He wore a hat of silver-tipped mink, a fur-trimmed gown of dark blue silk with circular patterns, an embroidered vest of dark satin brocade, and dark green satin slip-on shoes with light soles. The attire was matched to a pale-complexioned face smeared regularly with Snow Blossom cream and adorned with two bushy eyebrows and a head of jet-black hair. What was most eye-catching about him, though, was the diamond on the ring finger of his left hand, a stone of perhaps four carats. Seeing that, who would doubt that he was heir to a family fortune of at least forty or fifty thousand?

No third person ever knew the origin of Sanxin's diamond ring. Of the two who did know, one was Sanxin himself; the identity of the other remained locked in Sanxin's heart. He never told a soul, and there was no way for anybody to find out. So we might as well say that only Sanxin knew. Because of that ring, Sanxin was able to close a number of deals. Some people would swear that the hat on his head and the clothes on his back were all obtained through the diamond. But since the ring continued to be in his possession, how on earth did he manage to acquire the hat and the clothes? *That* was the question that baffled one and all.

Armed with his impressive ensemble and the eye-catching diamond, Sanxin could not very well pass up spending three dollars an hour for a taxicab to show himself off a little during the New Year's festivities. The day was the fifth of this lunar year, when every family was feasting in honor of the god of wealth. Most of the pedestrians on the streets had a trace of ruddiness on their cheeks, as if in competition with the dark-faced immortal. Sanxin's cheeks, however, retained the color of Snow Blossom cream. He was not about to welcome the god of wealth in the ordinary way. The god other people were greeting was dark-complexioned. The human person he aimed to meet up with would be decidedly fairer.

That day, after dinner in some restaurant or other, he emerged to hail a cab for a spin around town. It occurred to him that he'd been spending quite a bit of money on taxis the last few days without getting anything out of it. He'd heard that "Pug-Nose" Mao Lin and "Tea Leaf" Xiao Lu had rented a room in the Hotel Europa; they were getting a large group together for dominoes. With the twenty silver dollars he had with him, he thought he'd go try his luck. His winnings could pay for all that taxi fare, or else he could just chalk up any losses as a business expense. So why not?

Having thus made up his mind, he ordered Ah Liu the driver to take him to the Hotel Europa on the boulevard. It was a familiar destination. Taking the elevator to the sixth floor, he knocked lightly three times on the door of room 99 and announced his name on cue. As the door opened, he saw that the place was already packed. He exchanged greetings with a few of the people he'd known well from similar gatherings. Most of the others he recognized as rather prominent folk— stockbrokers, managers, agents, and such. Having skimmed off money from everyone as part of their jobs, these people were there to redistribute their wealth. In that sense at least, they were living up to their fancy professional titles.

Then he noticed Xiao Lu, one of the hosts, presiding over a metal box full of chips. Mao Lin was seated next to the dealer to lay down the tiles. The dealer was a large fellow with a pockmarked face as red as a pig's lungs. Because he was having tremendous success, raking in a lot and giving out very little, he became extraordinarily exuberant. Because he was too occupied to mop up the sweat running down his brow, the pearly beads settled naturally into the flaws in his countenance. Too bad the temperature in the room was too high for the flow to stop; otherwise, it might have turned out to be a rare cure for facial pits.

After purchasing twenty dollars worth of chips from Xiao Lu, Sanxin positioned himself next to the gaming table. But he did not place any bets; he was waiting for the right time. It just so happened that the burly dealer, after winning for a while, began a bad run with consecutive losses. Taking advantage of the downturn, Sanxin threw down five dollars worth of chips on the upper tile, which showed a washout for all bettors when it was turned over. The people there grumbled about his impulsiveness costing them money. Sanxin well knew that especially among gamblers, there was the common tendency to blame somebody whenever money was lost. The best way to handle the situation was to ignore it. Or else, if disputants were hotheaded enough, an actual altercation would follow. For this reason, he kept his mouth shut, responding to all comments with a smile. He put down ten more dollars—and won. More success followed until he was up fifty against the big man. Then the dealer rallied, taking back twenty. The thought occurred to Sanxin that the thirty dollars left to him was gotten after expending much effort and suffering everyone's disdain; he was not about to give the money back. Thus deciding to beat a retreat, he cashed in his chips with Xiao Lu and got out of the place.

At the elevator shaft, Sanxin saw the counterweight dangling below; the car was still taking on passengers up on the seventh floor. He pressed the button and watched as the car slowly descended, coming to a stop in front of him. Sanxin stepped in as the operator opened the gate. Then he saw something flash before his eyes. Inside, there was nothing especially dazzling, just a girl of perhaps twenty. She had on a beige leather padded jacket trimmed with a border of silver and black, a skirt of dark, glittery silk, and a pair of patent-leather high-heel shoes. Her coiffure was styled into a bun. The tendrils over her temples did not require any eau de cologne or pomade to enhance their sheen. There was a diamond-studded hairpin on one side of her head, a pair of hoops with tiny diamonds on her ears. On one wrist was a gold watch, on the other a greenish "imported gold" bracelet. The name aside, this type of bracelet was actually combustible, costing less than a half-dollar to buy. Still, people who were eager to keep up with the latest fads were fond of wearing one. They liked the idea that something so cheap could look so bright and sparkly, especially on a person with whitish arms. (I need hardly mention that the girl's arms were like tender lotus roots in a shallow pond.) It was too bad that she also had on a pair of light-gray silk gloves that shielded all of her slender fingers from view. But her face was powdery and translucent, with shining eyes and gleaming teeth, a nose delicate as jade, and lips like cherries—in every way the very incarnation of an illustration from one of those books on ideal beauties. Even as Sanxin stared at her, she did not stop shooting glances his way. For it appeared that, in both age and appearance, Sanxin and the girl were a perfect match, neither one finding anything to dislike about the other. The attraction, as they say, was mutual and immediate.

Each pair of eyes locked onto the other; electric sparks flew in both. Good thing the wooden and expressionless operator was standing between them in the elevator, becoming a kind of porcelain insulation board blocking the passage of any direct current. In that way, the inevitable combustion which occurs when a negative yin spark meets a positive yang spark was avoided. Soon they were at street level. Sanxin let the girl get out before him. He was thinking that she was someone unfamiliar, someone he had not seen before in any of the pleasure spots he frequented. Maybe she wasn't a local. It would be hard to figure out where a local might be headed once she left the hotel. Then another thought occurred to him. The seventh floor was where they held those foreign-style banquets for the *filles de joie;* perhaps someone had just taken her there. But, no, he ought not to be thinking uncomplimentary thoughts about such a fine-looking person. From the way she carried herself, she was evidently from a prominent household. But he shouldn't be so hasty. He should see what type of vehicle she got into before jumping to any conclusion. If she hailed a rickshaw, for instance, he could then invite her to share the ride. That could turn out to be a great opportunity for a tête-à-tête.

Next to the Hotel Europa was an alleyway reserved for parking. Numerous automobiles, horse-drawn carriages, and taxis lined up there all hours of the day and night, Sanxin's rickshaw among them. A red sedan from a cab company was there as well. The driver inside had his feet propped up on the dashboard and his head resting on the opened window as he napped. It was difficult to fault the man for doing so. He had only five dollars to show for an entire day's work the day before. Feeling the itch last night, he'd gotten himself into a round of dominoes with his fellow drivers. Not only did he lose all the money in his possession, but he also wound up six dollars in arrears. That he forfeited an entire night's sleep in addition goes without saying. Because he was on duty today, he had to take the car out, but fortunately for him, his passenger had gone inside for dinner, allowing him to catch his forty winks. Anyway, by his napping for an hour, the company would be getting three dollars of income, certainly a nice profit in view of his recent loss of eleven dollars plus a night's sleep after a whole day's work. But his sweet dreams were less than half over when they were interrupted. Opening his eyes, he saw that it was his woman passenger. He stretched his arms back to open a rear door for her and gave his eyes a quick rub. Then he started up the motor.

Watching the woman get into the car, Sanxin could not help letting out a silent cheer. This time, he assured himself, he would surely snare his prey. Still, there he was in a rickshaw and she in an automobile. Not only would that make her impossible to tail, but she might also form a bad first impression of him, making it difficult to get to first base. No, he would not give up his quest merely on account of some motorized vehicle! He jumped into a cab of his own posthaste, barking at Ah Liu behind the wheel to hurry after the red car.

It was just after ten o'clock. The night was very young, Sanxin was thinking. If he could just catch her and get her to a theater, he need not worry about an opportunity for a chat. It would be perfect if he could get her to the Rainbow District for a movie, where he might get to fondle her in the dark. What's more, with his knowledge of smatterings of different foreign languages, she might welcome his ability to fill her in on parts of the plot. Then it would be even easier to get close to her.

Although he had the details mapped out in his head, the girl seemed bent on going against them. She did not take any circuitous cruise, but headed directly west. Her cab turned at the New World Cinemas and then went south along the racetrack straight to Linyin Road in the foreign concession area beyond the West Gate. It stopped at the front entrance of a spacious two-story row house. The woman got out to rap at the door as the driver turned the car around and, with a few honks of his horn, sped off to find his companions for yet another round of dominoes.

When he saw the cab he was tailing come to a stop, Sanxin told his driver to follow suit about two and a half houses back. He watched as the cab door opened, and the girl walked out, head held high; then it slammed shut again. Sanxin could not help feeling distressed that she never looked back, seemingly oblivious that anyone was following her. He got out of the cab to examine the door of the house under the street light. On it was a small brass plaque, engraved in black with Residence of the Zhou Family of Xuancheng. So this really was a prominent family! Sanxin could not help talking pleasure at his own prescience. So what if the girl had yet to show any interest. As the old saying went, "The cure for a proper woman is an ardent man." Besides, she did make eyes at him. It merely remained for him to put out a little; the rest would happen on its own. But since she had already gone inside, he shouldn't be waiting around like a dope right then. Tomorrow evening he'd be back to stake her out.

Having thus settled on his course of action, he took the cab home. At dusk the following day, Sanxin did indeed turn up at the door of the Zhou residence, where he kept watch for over two hours. Not only was there no sign of the girl; the front door did not open even once. Anyone else standing out there all that time would surely have lost patience and gone off. But Sanxin had learned from his experiences over the years. He had developed a remarkable maturity. Sure, he had to be on his feet out there for a long time, but he remained unfazed. The neighbors, though, must think it strange for a well-dressed man to be standing under somebody's eaves like that. Several came out to stare at Sanxin, causing him some discomfort. There had to be a back door to the house, he thought. Perhaps she went out the back way. In that case, wouldn't it be pretty stupid of him to wait out there like that? He wandered down a little alley off to the side to explore. Sure enough, pasted on the door of the first house was a red slip of paper with Zhou Residence, Rear Entry written on it. The door was ajar, with the glare of lightbulbs beyond it. Inside, there was the sound of crackling oil and the pervasive aroma of meat sizzling in a pan. This had to be the family's kitchen. Sanxin felt his stomach gurgling as he stood there. He had started out without any dinner. Even though he had been so intent on his mission that he'd forgotten about the need for food, the smell of the cooking made the roundworms in his belly cry out against their unjust neglect. The cries became so formidable that Sanxin could hardly ignore them. Too bad he did not know the Zhou woman well as yet, he was thinking. Otherwise, he could have been a drop-in guest and shared in the family's gastronomical delights.

The alley dead-ended, much like the intellect of an illiterate. Sanxin went all the way down it before realizing that he had to retrace his steps. The mouth of the alley was next to the front door. He had been standing across the street, so how on earth could he have missed her had she actually gone out? Perhaps she left earlier, or else she was not going anywhere that day. With nothing in his stomach, he could not very well remain there. He might as well get home, have some dinner, and come back earlier tomorrow. With enough determination, a steel pole can be ground into a needle. He need not doubt that, in time, he would succeed.

Sanxin kept up his watch four days in a row, getting to his post earlier each day. On day four, he was there right after lunch and waited until nine-thirty at night without catching so much as a glimpse of her. His inner resolve began to waver: This was one needle that might never be ground. He would come back again the next day, bringing along some kind of snack so that he need not go home for sustenance. If nothing came of it, then he must have been mistaken in his calculations. Maybe this was the house of her relatives; she might have gone back home after an overnight stay. If he went on looking for her here, then his effort would become a big joke in the history of his amorous adventures.

Now, Wang Sanxin was a man of determination. He got up bright and early the following day, just as he'd planned. Then he spent thirty cents at the Wing On Company for a box of tea snacks and went back to the side of the street across from the Zhous, where there was a little store selling cigarettes and dry goods from Beijing. The proprietor had gone away on business and his daughter was manning the counter. While hanging around the last three days in order to carry out his noble resolve, Sanxin had become acquainted with her, occasionally going in for cigarettes and casual conversation. When she saw him there once more, she thought that the plainclothes police-man had come back again. "You're even earlier today," she said as she greeted him with a dimpled smile.

Sanxin nodded as he returned the smile. "I have something to leave with you," he said, handing her the box of snacks for safekeeping even though he had no intention of venturing beyond the immediate environs of the Zhou residence.

This time, the old adage that all good things come to those who wait finally came true. He had been there since early morning. Around five in the afternoon, he saw someone who looked like a servant come out of the Zhou house to get rickshaws. The man hailed five in all, lining them up in front of the house. Sanxin's heart throbbed even as he feigned nonchalance with the shop girl. Who were the people across the street, he was asking her. Why would they order so many rickshaws? The girl was not at all dense and had by then guessed what Sanxin was up to. She gave him the straightforward answer that she knew he was looking for. "The Zhous moved here only last year, so we don't know much about them. I heard that the head of the house-hold works for the government in Beijing. His immediate family in-cludes quite a few women—daughters and concubines, all really pretty. They are fond of going out for movies and other kinds of amuse-ment. I don't know why they haven't left the house these last few days. The rickshaws mean that now they are about to go out again."

Before she finished, seven or eight females in heavy makeup emerged from the house, looking like flowers draped with brocade. It goes without saying that the group included the someone who had occupied Sanxin's every thought for an entire week. Seeing her now, he could not contain himself and bounded out of the shop, no longer interested in what the shop girl was telling him. The larger women sat alone in the rickshaws; the slimmer ones shared. That girl was paired with a fourteen- or fifteen-year-old. As she was getting in, her gaze drifted in Sanxin's direction until she caught sight of him. Her face instantly took on a startled expression. She shot him a glance, and then another. Sanxin never bothered to acknowledge her eyes with his own. He was too occupied with getting a rickshaw for himself, to go after the entourage as if his life depended on it. He didn't hear the shop girl calling after him about the snack box he was leaving behind.

As they sped along, the girl turned her head again and again to look at Sanxin—unmistakable evidence of her interest. Sanxin's joy knew no bounds. The pullers ran extremely fast, and Sanxin momentarily forgot he was in a rickshaw. Instead, he felt he was flying on a cloud, chasing after a coterie of immortal maidens. Only when they reached the entrance of the First-Class Fragrance Restaurant did he regain his orientation. Realizing that the women were going in as a group, he quickly paid his fare and followed them upstairs. They had evidently reserved a private room. A placard with The Family Zhou written on it was hanging on the door. The rooms immediately adjoining had also been spoken for. Fortunately, the hour was still early, well before the arrival of the dinner crowd. Well acquainted with the waiters in the main dining hall, Sanxin was able to get them to slip him into a room right next door. He ordered his meal, all the while listening to the scattered sounds of happy chatter from the other side of the wall; he could not tell which of the birdlike chirps came from *her*. All he could do as he ate was wait for the women to finish and leave the restaurant—whereupon he tagged along as before. This aroused the suspicions of those in the girl's entourage. One after another they turned in their rickshaws to look at him. The most suspicious of them was the girl's young seatmate, who was aware that she was turning to look at him time and again. Now she was saying something to the girl, who Sanxin could see was shaking her head. Obviously, the younger girl was asking whether *she* knew the person following them and was getting a negative answer. He smiled to himself at the thought that most young ladies nowadays loved to meddle in someone else's business, even while worrying that someone else might meddle in theirs. How ludicrous they were!

Soon the rickshaws arrived at the Second Theater, coming to a stop in front of it. Sanxin could not help letting out a moan. Business at the place had really picked up the last few days, and the women undoubtedly had reserved seats. Having come unprepared, all he could hope to get after queuing up would be a hard seat high up among the rafters; he would not even be able to have eye contact with them. What was he to do? Well, since he was already there, he would make the best of the evening. He was acquainted with a number of the functionaries at the theater. Still, he got the expected answer as to available seats: There were none. He walked around on the second level, from where he saw the women filing one by one into the seats of a reserved box up front. Sanxin was beside himself and urged one of the ushers to think of something. But while people like him might have done all they could to accommodate customers during bad times, the bustling business they were now enjoying had given them inflated opinions of themselves. The man kept shaking his head. There was nothing he could do; Sanxin ought to get there earlier tomorrow. At his wit's end, Sanxin could only say, "I don't want a seat anymore. Just tear off a ticket stub for me." The man did as he was asked, and Sanxin found a square foot of space for himself among the hired help. He was indeed far away, but there was nothing cutting off the line of sight between him and the reserved box with the women seated inside. That girl had no inkling that Sanxin would be situated up where he was, and even though she looked around again and again, her gaze never turned in his direction. Unable to call to her, Sanxin could only agonize in silence.

Things remained that way for over an hour before a minor opportunity presented itself. The girl, having had too much tea, needed to visit the restroom. She was leaving her seat by herself! At last, thought Sanxin with glee. He would wait for her by the ladies' room. Before she could go in, he would invite her to come by herself for a performance the next day. But alas, even before she started off toward her destination, her young partner from the rickshaw suddenly told her to wait up; she, too, was going along. Seeing all this, Sanxin could only curse his luck.

Nevertheless, what was transpiring was not really unlucky for him after all. For even though his location was remote, anyone going from the reserved box to the ladies' room had to pass by it. The two women, their heads down, were talking to each other as they walked along. When they got to where he sat, nothing in the world could have made him forgo the chance for personal contact. He let out a loud cough. Startled, the girl turned and could not help betraying a bit of elation on seeing him. She smiled broadly, as if to say that she was delighted to find him. Sanxin felt extremely fulfilled at this. He was particularly glad that the other girl, who was walking very fast, had gone on ahead without noticing the exchange; no one else could know what passed between them. It was only after the two girls were on their way back that the younger one saw him in his seat, wedged between two old, unwashed amahs. She chuckled, then said something to her companion, who turned around to look again at Sanxin, flashing him another smile and a quick wink. Sanxin was in seventh heaven. The misery he had been feeling for the past hour or so quickly vanished into the clouds.

Now that the girl knew his location, she kept looking up at him, her eyes full of tender feelings. Sanxin could tell that she was still inexperienced, that it would not be difficult to win her over. It was just that there were too many people around her; he would be wise not to be too rash. For the moment, there remained the chance of getting to her when the show was over. If he somehow failed to take advantage of it, his only recourse would be to play stakeout detective again tomorrow—in which case, he could not guess how many days would go by before he'd get to see her again. After the performance, however, he'd have to rub shoulders with the crowd, and with everyone looking on, he couldn't very well speak freely. He would be forced to hand her a written note and hope his luck would hold out. He did not know whether she could read, but from all indications, she should not be illiterate. Anyway, he'd at least make the attempt and then see what would happen.

So he took out a cigarette wrapper and scribbled the following message on it with a pencil:

Please come here by yourself for the matinee tomorrow. If you are not interested, then don't bother. Otherwise, do not miss the appointment under any circumstances.

The message was brief and simple. He crumpled it into a ball and hid it in the palm of his hand. When the show was over, he stationed himself at the top of the stairs, where the girl quickly spotted him. She deliberately let her companions get ahead while she lagged some distance behind. Sanxin could hardly contain his joy. Then, noticing that she carried a fox-fur muff, he knew what to do. He waited until she drew near before walking down the stairs alongside her; then he slipped the balled-up message surreptitiously into the muff, his fingertips brushing against her jadelike wrist as he did so. She made no sound. Sanxin would have encouraged her to say something, but that younger girl up ahead was looking back and urging her to catch up. At that, Sanxin lost his nerve. He kept silent as he made straight for the front entrance, pretending to wait for a taxi, while keeping his eyes fixed on the girl's every move. He watched her come down the stairs, take out the note, flatten it out, and read it under a light; then she stuffed it nonchalantly back into the muff before any of her companions noticed. Sanxin could only be impressed by her cool composure. Since she did not throw the note away, he was sure she would not reject him. Anyway, everything would come out in the wash the following day. As she got into her rickshaw, he saw her roll her eyes flirtatiously at him before going off. The happiness this brought Sanxin is beyond anything I, the storyteller, have ever felt; I cannot therefore describe it to you.

First thing the next morning, Sanxin went to the Second Theater to reserve a couple of seats, then returned there right after lunch. He also bought generous quantities of melon seeds, pastries, and fruit. How pleasant it would be to munch and chat together, once the girl showed up! His anticipation was so keen that he never expected to have to wait and wait. From twelve-thirty to four o'clock—a couple of lifetimes—he waited, before he concluded that she was not coming. That in itself might not much matter. He had clearly written on the note yesterday that she should not bother to come if she was not interested. But wasn't she interested in him after all? The thought that all the emotional turmoil of the last few days was going for naught was just too much to bear. He was becoming greatly distressed, when suddenly from behind him came a fragrant breeze. He spun around and saw the girl, standing outside his reserved box with a grin on her face. For Sanxin, that moment was like coming upon a rare treasure. He jumped up quickly and escorted her to her seat. When he asked her why she was late, she only smiled. Her fragrance invaded his nostrils in waves, working like an anesthetic. He had a whole slate of questions ready for her, but now nothing escaped his lips. To tell the truth, Sanxin was, as the old Shanghainese saying goes, like a soft clay Buddha in a jar of hot water. He was already falling to pieces.

THEY REMAINED THERE from four o'clock until the play ended. It was not an especially long time, but long enough for them to have had a good conversation. Sanxin learned that she was the eldest daughter in the Zhou family. The girl with her yesterday was her youngest sister. She had another sister living in Beijing. The other women were all her father's concubines. Little wonder they all seemed so coquettish, with their shiny hairdos and powdered faces. Sanxin noticed that she seemed less than experienced when she talked. Then he remembered how difficult it was to get her there. He knew he could not just let her off his hook or she might be gone forever. So he decided to abandon his false mask of propriety and asked her directly to get a room with him at the Hotel Europa afterward. Miss Zhou replied that she wouldn't go to the Hotel Europa—there were many who'd recognize her. They might tell her father, and then there would be hell to pay. Sanxin suggested several alternatives, all of which she vetoed. A place was either too shabby or too likely for her to bump into someone she knew. But these were the most prominent hotels in Shanghai, Sanxin thought, even though none seemed satisfactory. The only other possibility would be Paradise Villa on Bubbling Well Road. He didn't know if she'd be willing to go way out there, but he made the suggestion anyway. Miss Zhou appeared to be somewhat persuaded. "Let's just do that," she said as she flashed him another smile.

The Villa was a place frequented by persons of status and wealth, as its extraordinarily steep prices indicated. For an overnight stay, including food, the tariff always exceeded twenty dollars. Sanxin of course knew this, but in the discussion, his sole concern was to secure Miss Zhou's assent. Cost was not something he remembered to take into account. Now that she'd said yes, however, he naturally began to think about what he must spend. Whatever that would be, since he'd asked her, he had to grin and bear it. It's like going out to catch rare crabs with a golden hook: You had to put up the capital. He then thought of the great distance between where they were and the Paradise Villa. It just would not look right for them to go by rickshaw. No way could he save the three-dollar cab fare. As long as he had to spend all that money, he ought to do it right. So he asked an usher to get him a taxi from the company next door and to have it wait for them at the theater entrance. When the play ended, they got into it together and ordered the driver to head toward the Paradise Villa.

As to the propriety of getting a room at a hotel under those circumstances, it does not really matter whether or not you readers understand. I'm not going to take the trouble to explain it for you. In any case, the two of them had a scrumptious meal, then confessed to each other the anguish of their passion in recent days. "That diamond ring on your finger is really rather impressive," said Miss Zhou to Sanxin as she leaned against a pillow. "Won't you take it off and let me have a look?"

As filled with happiness as he was at that moment, Sanxin could never have refused the request; he slipped the ring right off. Taking it in her hand, Miss Zhou examined it over and over before asking Sanxin how many carats the diamond weighed. Sanxin actually did not know. His answer was that it was roughly four-and-a-half carats. "Then it could be worth one thousand eight hundred dollars?" she wanted to know.

"A good guess," said Sanxin. "Even at four hundred dollars a carat, it would be worth that much."

Miss Zhou nodded, then quickly slipped the ring on her own finger. Smiling, she asked Sanxin whether it looked good. The question made Sanxin's heart skip a beat. He was concerned that if he answered yes, she might very well then have just asked him to let her keep it. That would be catastrophic. As for no, it was more than the fact that he simply could not bring himself to say it. There was no reason in the entire universe for someone to put on a diamond ring and then disapprove of its looks. In the current situation, he could only swallow hard and tell her that it looked fine.

Luckily for him, Miss Zhou did not respond to the remark. She merely pressed her powdered cheek against his. "Are you cold?" she asked as he shook his head. This should have been their supreme moment, their time of sheer ecstasy. For Sanxin, however, the inner happiness that should have filled his being had left him, along with those four-and-a-half carats, settling now into Miss Zhou. All he had left was a wildly beating heart.

Miss Zhou became greatly animated. She prattled on and on about one subject or another. Sanxin did not know where she found so much to talk about. Of all she was saying, however, not a word touched upon the subject of the diamond ring. In his anxiety, Sanxin could manage only vacant responses. The ring was securely around her finger; he didn't dare tell her to take it off. As if in a trance, he waited for her to return it to its rightful owner. Neither of them made a move until long after midnight. "*Aiya,* it's gotten late," Miss Zhou exclaimed with a glance at her watch. "They'll be questioning me when I get home. I still have lots to talk to you about, so let's just keep the room another day. I'll see you here again in the evening. You have to take me home now. I live so far away and it's so late. The way back is frightful."

When he heard all this, Sanxin saw another twenty dollars fly out the window. But she had the diamond ring, which she might return to him at the next meeting. This, therefore, was money he could not avoid spending. He also heard her asking him to escort her home. What could he have done but tell the bellhop to phone for a taxi to do just that? The taxi came shortly thereafter, and Sanxin got into it with the girl for the long trip outside the West Gate. All along the way, he said nothing. He was still thinking she might just return the ring to him when she got home. How really wonderful that would be! But she was oblivious to his thoughts as she left the cab, merely reminding him not to forget their appointment. She knocked on the door, smiling at him again before going into the house. With eyes wide open, Sanxin watched as she took the four-and-a-half carats in with her. The door slammed shut, leaving him alone on the roadside with the cab. The scene was not unlike that of a week ago, when he'd tailed her to that very spot.

Sanxin returned to his own house with a heavy heart. He kept his left hand hidden in his sleeve, as if it had committed some sort of crime; he did not dare let his wife see it. Luckily for him, she did not notice a thing. In any case, she could never have imagined a wise veteran like him suffering a setback like that. The night passed quickly, and Sanxin had no choice but to go to the Paradise Villa the next evening and wait for Miss Zhou. A dark fear continued to gnaw at his insides. What would he do if she simply went off with the ring and never showed up? It was a good thing then that Miss Zhou proved to be a woman of her word: She was there before it got dark—even interrupting his dinner—and treated him with great affection. The diamond ring was indeed on her finger. She acted as if she'd forgotten about it, however, making no reference to it at all. In spite of his deep anxiety, Sanxin could only carry on with her as if nothing had happened. This rendezvous was identical to that of the night before. Around one-thirty, she again wanted Sanxin to take her home, as well as to hold on to the room for another tryst the day following.

The same story repeated itself for nearly a week. The ring aside, Sanxin's total expenses now exceeded one hundred dollars. Poor man. In the very beginning, he was spending the money he had won. By the second day, he was already digging down to where it hurt. After that, he became completely broke and had to pawn his dark brocade vest and his mink hat for the necessary funds. It was fortunate for him that the weather was cooperating. The February temperatures remained mild, and so he could get away with wearing a gown and a small chapeau without anybody suspecting anything. Still, this little adventure of his was turning out to be the costliest of his life. But even though he now felt regretful and resentful in the extreme, the diamond ring was still in the girl's clutches. He had no choice but to continue expending capital to keep her happy. None of this bothered Miss Zhou, who asked to see him day after day without so much as thinking about returning the ring. At his wit's end, Sanxin now sought out a friend of his, a Mr. Resourceful, for a solution to his problem.

Mr. Resourceful let out a guffaw when he heard about all that had transpired. "I never thought I'd see the day when you, thirty years a midwife, would wrap a baby butt-side up. This woman's a real schemer. She saw that you were rather openhanded when she got hold of your ring. She thinks that she can get more out of you, not minding getting together with you day after day. To her, you're a steady bank account. She never suspected that you'd turn out to be someone with zero reserves. Now that things have come to this pass, there is no way out for you except to use her own scheming against her. But don't ever, under any circumstances, let her see through to what you'll be doing.

I have a friend in town who's a jewel merchant. He told me the other day that there is now a kind of pseudodiamond made from chemicals. While new, the stuff is indistinguishable from the real thing, losing its coloring only with time. It's not cheap, either, retailing for ten dollars a carat. Didn't you tell me that your diamond weighs four-and-a-half carats? Well, then, let's make a chemical diamond of a little over six carats and set it onto a ring." Then he gave Sanxin the details of the plan. "You'll also need to have seven hundred dollars in bills available at a moment's notice. If you can't come up with that amount, I'll lend it to you for the short while we'll be needing it. If we carry out the whole plan, as greedy a female as she is, there is no way she can help taking the bait. When everything's over, don't forget you'll be owing me a few gourmet foreign meals in posh restaurants."

Sanxin clapped his hands together in delight upon hearing this. He begged this Mr. Resourceful to go with him into town, find the jeweler friend, and set up everything according to plan. All that happened subsequently will be revealed as the rest of the story unfolds.

Three days later, Sanxin again had dinner at the Paradise Villa with Miss Zhou. They had just entered their room to relax and chat when the bellhop brought in a name card. "Someone here to see Mr. Wang," he announced. Sanxin gave the card a once-over. "Do you know who this person may be?" he cheerfully inquired of Miss Zhou. She saw the name Huang Hucheng on the card, along with Huang-Hu Company, Jewel Merchant in small print in the right corner; she admitted that she was not acquainted with the person. "The man owns a jewelry firm which does a lot of business," Sanxin said. "Even my wife buys from him regularly. This is about the diamond ring I gave you the other day. It belongs to my wife, who was letting me wear it for fun. A day or so ago, she saw that it was missing and demanded to know its whereabouts. I almost let the cat out of the bag then, so I had no choice but to ask the boss of this company to get me a ring with a slightly larger stone. If it suits your fancy, I'll just make a present of it to you. Let me take that smaller one back to my wife to save

myself a lot of explaining. I've been meaning to tell you all this before. Now that he's here to look for me, I guess he's got the goods
with him." At that, he nodded to the bellhop. "Ask Mr. Huang to
come in."

Miss Zhou was quickly impressed by Huang Hucheng's resplendent attire and by his elegant demeanor. He surely looked like the
head of a jewelry firm. Once in the room, he showed unusual deference to Sanxin, repeatedly inquiring about his health. He also wanted
to send his regards to the young madame at the Wang residence, asking why it had been so long since she had been to see them at the
store. "It's the New Year's holidays," smiled Sanxin. "She's been busy
playing games for petty stakes or going to the theater. She simply
hasn't the time to go shopping for jewelry. Have you got the stuff with
you?"

"I've got it here! I've got it here!" Huang Hucheng repeated as he
fished out a small, brocade-covered box from his pocket. He handed
it over with the cover open. Sanxin took out the ring to inspect it with
Miss Zhou. The "diamond," large as a fingertip, dazzled the eyes with
its sparkle under the lights. The other stone on Miss Zhou's hand not
only appeared smaller; it also seemed to be less brilliant. Huang Hucheng then took out an invoice, showing that the stone weighed 6.2
carats and had a value of $2,480. It took Miss Zhou no time at all to
remove those four-and-a-half carats and to return them to Sanxin
without waiting for him to ask. Then she put on the new stone, which
glittered and glowed as if on fire. Huang Hucheng put in a few words
of praise as Miss Zhou's countenance betrayed her joy.

"Now that you've decided on the purchase, I must beg your for-
giveness concerning an unpleasant matter," said Huang to Sanxin.
"Because our company has benefited from doing so much business
with your wife in the past, we should not be concerned even with
a sum of twenty or thirty thousand, much less ten percent of that
amount. But this is the beginning of the year, and the first entry on
our ledgers. Also, this is not a transaction with the young madame

herself. Then, too, speaking frankly, this piece of merchandise is not from our company, but is something taken on consignment from another firm. We've had to put down some deposit money on it. Even so, I cannot presume to ask you to settle the entire amount right away. But please remit a thousand dollars to me first, so that I can begin to take care of my immediate expenses. As for the remainder, I can easily put it on the young madame's account and bill her at the proper time."

Sanxin appeared to take offense at this. "Is it possible that you distrust me?" he asked, the anger evident in his voice.

Huang Hucheng tried to be conciliatory. "I would never, never dare do that," he said. "As I was saying, the merchandise is not ours, but taken on consignment from elsewhere only after we paid a deposit. If you don't believe that, then consider why I would be asking for only a thousand for something worth over two thousand dollars."

This calmed Sanxin down. "In that case, just wait a while," he said. "I'll go home and get you the thousand dollars." He rushed off, telling Miss Zhou to stay put. A half-hour or so later, he was back with a fistful of paper currency. "It's late right now, and the banks are all closed," he said to Huang Hucheng. "I have no more than seven hundred dollars cash in the house. I simply cannot come up with the whole amount tonight. So how about just taking seven hundred for now? Come back tomorrow. I'll withdraw another three hundred from the bank for you."

Huang Hucheng kept shaking his head. "I must beg your pardon," he said. "My firm is strapped for cash at the moment and we cannot advance the difference. The choice is clear: If you want to take the merchandise, you'll have to put down the thousand and not a dollar less. If you're short right now, I'll have to take the diamond back. We'll see about the deal on another day."

Sanxin's face showed hesitation. Without saying anything, he looked over at Miss Zhou. Having listened intently to the exchange, Miss Zhou was thinking that she would not give back the ring in a million years, now that she had it in her possession. Recognizing Sanxin's problem with the seller, she interjected a solution. "No problem," she said to him. "The pair of diamond earrings I have on cost five hundred dollars to buy. Just tell him to hock them for three hundred, and then redeem them for me tomorrow." As she spoke, she unhooked the diamond-studded hoops from her ears to hand over to Sanxin. Sanxin then handed them over to Huang Hucheng, telling him to get to a pawnshop.

Huang Hucheng was not shy. He went off with the jewelry, returning with four hundred and fifty dollars. He turned the pawn ticket and the cash over to Sanxin, who then took out three hundred to combine with the seven hundred he had with him for the thousand-dollar total, which Huang Hucheng accepted. As for the invoice, Sanxin struck a match and burned it up. Taking out the one hundred fifty that was left, he asked Miss Zhou whether she needed any cash. "Fifty dollars will be enough for me," Miss Zhou said. "You keep the hundred and the pawn ticket with you. That way, you won't have to go through much trouble tomorrow getting my earrings back."

From that day on, the Paradise Villa never saw another trace of Sanxin. Miss Zhou did show up quite a few times to look for him there. Some time afterward, she went searching around the various theaters without knowing what she would say to him if she found him. At the very time she was doing that, Sanxin was dining tête-à-tête with his wife. "Diamond earrings are the rage right now," his wife was saying. "I want to get myself a pair to wear around."

"That's easy enough," said Sanxin, smiling. "I've had my eye on a pair costing four hundred fifty at a jeweler's. Too bad I only have a couple hundred on hand right now. Wait until I scrape together another two hundred fifty. I will definitely get them for you to put on and show off."

— *1922*

The Red Chips

. . . .

Feng Shuluan

There was much jostling in the unbearably crowded first- and second-class cars on the Beijing-Fengtian rail line for the run from Tianjin to Beijing. A slim, tall, thirtyish gentleman traveler with a southern accent had just gotten on and was looking all around for a seat without finding one. The many foreigners with their leather luggage and uniformed soldiers with their sabers and rifles were taking up most of the seating space, and he was timid about asking them to make room. He hesitated for quite a while before noticing a couple of men with a small leather satchel seated at the very front of the second-class car. He went over to confer with them in a low, deferential voice. The two were willing and moved the satchel underneath their seat, leaving perhaps a foot of space for him to finally sit down. He then exchanged introductions with them. The one who was in his fifties, with a few barely perceptible whiskers, said his surname was Wang, and he was called Danting. The other was perhaps over twenty, with a darkish complexion and a strapping build. He said he was Li Fubiao. In turn, the man announced that his family name was Chen and that he was Shoujing to his friends. The train had already sped away from the Tianjin station as the three seatmates started a conversation.

"How did today's train get so crammed with people?" Chen Shou-jing began.

The question brought smiles from the other two. "When is it *not* like this on this run?" they said together. Then Wang Danting added, "Mr. Chen, you don't usually come this way, do you?"

"I have never been here before," Shoujing had to admit. "This is the first time."

"From your accent, Mr. Chen, I gather you're from the south," said Danting. "Why didn't you take the Tianjin-Pukou express? Wouldn't that have been both faster and more comfortable?"

"I heard that the half-price tickets for officials are not accepted on express trains," said Shoujing.

"Ah! No wonder," said Danting. "What agency should we congratulate you for working in?"

Chen Shoujing was not sure he caught the drift of the question, but Fubiao jumped in to explain. "He was asking you which government office you work out of."

"I'm not on any kind of official business," Shoujing hastened to say. "I'm going to visit friends." Then he put the same question to the others.

"I'm with the Foreign Office," said Danting, as Li Fubiao took out a calling card. Three or four titles were listed on it, the most important being Inspector, Investigative Bureau, Military Police. Shoujing was decidedly impressed.

The tenor of their conversation again shifted. "It's gotten difficult to do our jobs these days," said Danting. "I needn't mention the other problems. Just the fact that we can never get our salaries is frustrating."

"Isn't that the truth!" said Fubiao. "We've had to remain in debt to people we never borrowed from before."

"The Military Police is in much better shape, after all is said and done," said Danting. "The people upstairs are concerned about troop unrest. They have to find ways to keep the organization going. Were it another governmental bureau, you could agitate all you wanted about getting paid. It would all be for naught."

On hearing this, Shoujing's heart half sank. "So, working for the government in Beijing amounts to just this," he thought. "Why did I bother to come?" Then he had another notion. Since he was already there, he might as well proceed boldly as planned, give things a try, and see what happened.

Seven o'clock approached; they would soon be in Beijing. "Where will you be staying?" Danting asked Shoujing.

"I haven't decided," Shoujing replied. "Probably in an inn for now."

"In that case," said Fubiao, "why don't we go together to the Golden Stage? It so happens I have to escort a friend there."

Shoujing assented, and almost the next instant, they pulled into Beijing station. Danting headed for his own house while Shoujing went off with Fubiao to the first-class car to meet a woman. The trio arrived at the Golden Stage together. Fubiao settled the woman in the spacious room 52; Shoujing took number 36, a small room, for himself.

The following morning, two visitors came separately to the gate-house of a huge residence on Nanchang Street. The first, a man, came in a rickshaw. His accent was southern. He handed a calling card over to the gatekeeper. Without bothering to get up, the keeper glanced at the name on it: Chen Shoujing. "The master has not yet gotten up," he said.

Shoujing put on an obsequious smile. "I came from Hangzhou."

"Wherever you may be from, I can't very well announce you before the master gets up," said the keeper.

A servant reclining on a bed alongside also chimed in. "You're talking too much. Just get out of here! Come back in the afternoon."

"What time in the afternoon?" Shoujing asked, managing to maintain his decorum.

"No earlier than four or five o'clock," said the keeper.

Just then another visitor arrived, in a horse carriage. The driver came ahead to the gatehouse and announced that his passenger was a woman, here to see the master. At this, the gatekeeper hurried out to receive her. Quite astonished, Shoujing tagged along after him. The female visitor, sporting heavy makeup and a bouffant hairdo, was seated regally behind the window of the carriage. She turned her face at the sound of approaching steps and wound up looking straight into Shoujing's eyes. She was none other than the woman who had been on his train, the one staying in the same Golden Stage Hotel.

"The master's still asleep," the gatekeeper announced to her as well. "Where are you staying? In a while, when the master wakes up, he can contact you by phone."

The woman nodded and smiled. She ordered the driver to pick up a large basket of canned goods, along with several wrapped items, to hand over to the keeper. "A few gifts, local products from home," she said.

Uncomfortable dallying there, Shoujing hurried off. "The woman's behavior is rather odd," he thought to himself. "For her to be paying a call here, too, she's got to be a relative of some kind. In that case, why was she asking just for the master and not for his wife?"

That evening Li Fubiao came again to the Golden Stage, also stopping by Shoujing's room to visit. Still bothered by what had happened in the morning, Shoujing told him of the encounter with the woman at the Li residence on Nanchang Street. He also asked who she might be and whether she was related to General Li.

Fubiao answered with a guffaw. "They are related, as far as that goes—and very intimately," he said. "Since you went there as well, you, too, must have some connection with the General. So let me introduce you to this 'cousin' of his." He then took Shoujing by the hand and led him to the woman's room, where she was combing her hair. "This here is the 'kissing cousin' of General Li. You can call her Fourth Sister," he told Shoujing. Then he turned to the woman. "Mr.

Chen here is a friend of the General's. So don't treat him like a stranger."

Fourth Sister let out a chuckle, then lapsed into Shanghainese. "What*evah* do y'all *mean* by 'kissin cousin'?" she protested. "Ah just don't *git* it. Y'all tryin to *bull*shit him or some'in?" She invited Shoujing to sit down, ordered tea to be made, and offered him a cigarette. Only then did Shoujing begin to understand the situation: Fourth Sister was no relative of General Li's.

Shoujing stayed on for another couple of weeks after that. His main task every day was to return to the General's residence to try and see him, but he was not able to get so much as a glimpse. On his second visit, he received a message through the gatekeeper to wait around for a few days. He was also asked where he was staying. Because of this, Shoujing not only did not dare give up, but actually felt a bit encouraged. After that, however, nothing more came of his daily visits. He routinely left a calling card each time and then merely sat in the parlor, waiting.

About two o'clock one afternoon, Shoujing was having a casual conversation in Fourth Sister's room. They had seen each other often since Fubiao's introduction. Restless and far from home, Shoujing was glad to have this means of relieving boredom. Quite unexpectedly, the bellhop brought in a houseboy who explained that he'd come from the Li residence on Nanchang Street. He took out an envelope from his breast pocket, and Fourth Sister asked Shoujing to open it for her. The envelope was addressed to Fourth Sister, Room 52, The Golden Stage Hotel, and the name Li was given as the sender. Shoujing found no message inside, just a check for a thousand dollars that he handed over to Fourth Sister. "The master said it's for you to use as you please," the houseboy informed her.

"Your master doesn't really think much of me, does he?" said Fourth Sister with a smirk. "Can I be so hard up for money that I would accept this pittance? You might as well take it back." The boy would not think of complying. "I'll be going over to your place soon, and then I can handle the matter," she said sternly. "So just take it back." Then she pulled out a five-dollar bill and handed it over. "You've had to come a long way. Take this for cab fare." The houseboy tried to refuse again, but finally muttered his thanks and departed with the check and the cash. Fourth Sister began to mumble to herself. "How could he have done such a thing? No one can be bought off so cheap."

Shoujing found it inconvenient to ask questions. He knew that Fourth Sister was due at the Li house for dinner at six that evening. "So then the General must be home for the occasion," he thought. "Why not take the chance and get over there? Who knows? Perhaps I can finally get to see him. Waiting around like this, my funds will soon dry up."

As for General Li, he had been thinking hard about what to do ever since his houseboy returned and reported that Fourth Sister had refused the check. There was one relatively good course of action: He would get together a foursome for mahjongg and reward her with the takeouts from the kitty. Just then Fourth Sister arrived, and he explained the idea to her. Quickly he ordered his houseboy to invite over his usual gambling companions—Cabinet Minister Wang, and Party Chiefs Lu and Chang. In short order Chang and Wang were there. Lu's family, however, reported over the phone that he'd gone to Tianjin. General Li was extremely disappointed about being one person short. Still, he could not very well call the whole thing off. He hurriedly ordered that General Ma or Director Gao be invited by phone. Either one would be fine as long as he was at home and could come at a moment's notice. The houseboy went off and returned shortly, announcing, "The Gaos said the Director has also gone to Tianjin, while General Ma's family reported that he is away in Tangshan." General Li could hardly contain his frustration. Just as he was getting to the desperate stage, the gatekeeper brought in another calling card. On it was the name Chen Shoujing.

Instantly he saw the answer to his problem. He ordered that Shoujing be asked into a small study and seated. "Please wait while I meet with him briefly," he said to Chang and Wang. "I'm certain our game will be on." Sure enough, barely seconds went by before he led in the unknown guest and introduced him to the two. "This is a native of my hometown, a family friend, Chen Shoujing," he said as both Chang and Wang nodded their acknowledgment. The interior room had long since been readied with mahjongg tiles and table, chairs, tea tables, tobacco, tea leaves, and chips. After taking his place, Shoujing saw that there were three stacks of round ivory chips—red, yellow, and white; the reds were worth the most, the whites the least. "How much is each pot worth?" he wanted to know.

"Never mind asking," said General Li. "Just play."

"The table stakes here must be considerable," Shoujing thought. "I would guess each pot to be worth a hundred dollars. But since he said not to worry, I don't suppose it would matter much if I came out a bit short." He therefore set all concerns aside.

They played four rounds before breaking for dinner. Shoujing was not losing. When the game resumed, Shoujing unexpectedly won one or two deals. When everything was tallied up, he had won seven red chips and ten or so white ones. Thinking that he ought not to appear petty in such company, and that at any rate, he had come out ahead, he announced, "Since my winnings are paltry, I'll just pass them on to the help to divide up."

"That's too generous," said General Li. "Just let them have the white ones." As he spoke, he took out a checkbook, tore off a check, and scribbled an amount on it; then he added his signature and handed it over to Shoujing, who saw that the kitty had over ten red chips remaining. General Li then signed and passed another check to Fourth Sister for them. No longer coy, she quickly accepted.

The following morning, Shoujing, thinking he might be short of travel funds, took out the check he had won. He noted that it was to the Bank of Communications, but, because the amount was written out in a foreign language, he could not make out what it was. "Seven red chips—that's probably equivalent to seventy dollars," he thought.

Fortunately, the Bank of Communications was located next to the West Moat, not far away. He walked over to get the cash.

The clerk there looked at the check over and over. "Do you want it in bills or in silver dollars?" he asked.

"Silver dollars would be fine."

"Do you have a car?"

Shoujing became annoyed. "What's it to you whether I have a car or not?"

"Without a car, can you carry away seven thousand silver dollars by yourself?" said the clerk, smiling.

Shoujing was stunned. How could he have known that seven chips were worth so much money? Quickly he changed his tune. "I'm staying at the Golden Stage Hotel," he said. "I was expecting that your bank could get someone to deliver the money there for me."

"That's possible," said the clerk. "Only, you'll have to pay the transportation costs." Shoujing assented. Sure enough, a mule cart was hired in order to get all those silver dollars to the Golden Stage.

That very evening, Fourth Sister began packing to leave. When Shoujing asked her why she was in such a rush, she answered that once she had her money, Beijing was not a place to dally in.

Her words touched a chord in Shoujing. "These last two weeks have cost me over a hundred dollars just for daily necessities," he thought. "Even had I gotten a government job here, my salary would not have been more than a hundred dollars a month. So why don't I take my seven thousand home to the south, where I can stake out my own livelihood?"

The next day, the names of both Fourth Sister in room 52 and Chen Shoujing in room 36 were wiped off the guest registry that hung opposite the entrance of the Golden Stage Hotel.

The author said that this news story was spread with great excitement from the north to the south during the fall of 1921. It is, moreover, absolutely factual.

— 1922

Rickshaw Man

. . . .

Zhang Biwu

The following story was once told by Ah San, the Zhu family's rickshaw puller, to several people.

Altogether, it's been three years since I was hired on as the rickshaw man for the Zhu family. During this time, without counting the monthly salary I was regularly paid, my earnings have not been at all paltry. Why, just last month, I took leave for a few days to return to my home village to buy over ten *mou* of land in preparation for the future. When I get old and can no longer pull the load, I'll just go home to the farm and take my ease.

People have asked me how on earth I, a mere rickshaw puller, can manage to save up all that. They seem to think that the money came as the result of shady activities. Actually, I have never robbed. Nor have I ever stolen a thing from anyone. I have not fallen in with thugs, never made so much as a cent from blackmail. All the money I have has been most willingly handed over to me by the young master and his wife in my household. Sometimes, when I pretend to decline what they offer, they are even willing to come off their high horses, to smile at me and insist that I accept! The fact is, after taking them around for three years, I know all about the places each of them go to. It so happens that the master is unwilling for the mistress to know the places he visits, just as the mistress is very concerned about him finding out her habitual whereabouts. So each one buys my silence, telling me to hold my tongue no matter what. With a situation like this, I am often able to borrow from them beyond what they tip me. Because they rely on me, they can hardly refuse. Also, when I say "borrow," I never actually have to worry about repaying. So I wind up with quite a wad of income each month. After three years of this, it's easy to see how I can afford all that land.

I may be raking in a lot of cash. But, to be honest, the job also takes up a good bit of energy. After lunch each day, I have to first take the master out, and then the mistress. After that, if it's not pulling him here and there, then it's taking her this place or that on the run. Can't even think about heading home before two or three in the morning. Had heaven not blessed me with two strong, swift legs, I'd never be able to earn all that money, even with it there for the earning. Still, I can grab all the sleep I want in the morning, unlike the pullers in other households who have to pick up the living room and mop the floor. This privilege also came after talking with my master and mistress and getting them to agree. I would say in general that I am in a very special situation. I don't know if you can find another rickshaw man like me in all of Shanghai.

My young master is in textiles. After lunch each day, he leaves home in the rickshaw to go to some association or trade office. Sometimes he even goes to the factories. Anyway, I know that the places are all legitimate, and I don't have to mention them because they're boring. In the evenings, nine days out of ten, he fools around in brothels. That's when I get meal tickets, almost every time. When he comes with three or four buddies all on a high, they will want to continue the fun elsewhere. Where they decide to go then varies greatly, and my two legs are usually in for it, running him hither and yon while I huff and puff and the sweat pours down like rain.

I'll never forget the night I pulled him behind his friends in several rickshaws to the gates of a large, imposing house in Zhabei, on the edge of town. He got right off and rushed in with the others. From the looks of the place, I guessed it to be an uppity household. Then came several other rickshaws, all very classy, with bright electric lights. The passengers were without exception young and female, each one gorgeously dressed, but definitely not like whores. So I became even more sure that this was a party and the women were invited guests. The pullers of the ten or twenty rickshaws parked outside got together and talked. Only then did I learn from the others that the family living there was not at all rich or prominent, that the house was nothing more than a huge pleasure den. My young master and his friends came for a good time, and the girls were purposely called to give it to them. "Don't tell me that girls from good homes would actually run to a place like this to do these kinds of things," I could not help thinking to myself at the time. "The building looks so impressive, but such shameful things go on in there that it's really rotten to the core."

Then I thought of my young mistress. No one can deny she's attractive. With her slim figure and pretty face, there can be no better match for the master. So then why does he continue to sneak around and carry on like this away from home? He really doesn't know what he's got.

The master also goes regularly to one other place. He stops by at least once each evening. A beautiful woman lives there. At first I thought it was another of those establishments. But my master seemed to be the only man going in. Later I found out the truth from the old amah there—that the girl is my master's beloved concubine. Because of my mistress's temper, she didn't dare move into the house and so is living there. But one night I got the time wrong and took the rickshaw there at midnight instead of at two in the morning, as the master had instructed me. I noticed that there was another hired rig already waiting at the door. A man came out, jumped in, and was quickly towed away. The man did not look at all familiar. For sure he was not a friend of my master's. So why was he leaving the place at such an hour? Then the answer became obvious, and I couldn't help getting upset about the wrong that had been done to my master. It also occurred to me that he would be coming along soon, since the man was in such a hurry. Sure enough, the master arrived very shortly afterward. Were I following my own heart, I would've told him what had happened. But the matter was not simple. I was concerned that telling him would bring on a heap of trouble, so I kept my mouth shut. Later on I came up with an idea: I would use what happened to cow this little woman. Several times after that, I asked for cash from her and got it each time in the amount I wanted. No way she would dare refuse me. That's how she became one of my principal money trees.

The young mistress at home is a restless sort who never wants to stay still. All year long, she hardly spends a single day in the house. Whether it be in the heat of summer or the cold of winter, she has to be out every single afternoon. I am of course her regular means of transportation, so I know every place she goes. She never tries to cover up her "proper" trips—to the theater, the amusement park, Western-style restaurants and night clubs—so I'm not secretive about them, either. But there's this one place which she tells me time and time again to never *ever* even *hint* about in front of the master. To make sure I continue to keep her secret, she has rewarded me with money several times over. So I have never breathed a word to the master, and, up to now, he's been completely hoodwinked. The place I'm talking about is not large, with just one all-purpose room off to the side. It is looked after by an amah who answers to no one but the mistress. When my mistress goes there, I always see this good-looking man going in and out. The man is neither relative nor friend, but sneaks around and does one kind of hanky-panky or another with her. The way the mistress treats him, though, is extremely warm and kindly—ten times better than she treats the master.

Ever since I've known about the relationship, I've thought it was strange. The master is surely not worse-looking than this man. So why does the mistress go on with this kind of thing? Her own parents and her in-laws are all upstanding people. How can she do this to them? I've also thought a lot about the master's habitual fondness for fooling around with someone else's women for the sake of having a good time. Who would have guessed that his own wife would be seduced by another man and be giving that other man a good time? Isn't this simply proper retribution? When that man carries on like that with my mistress, on the other hand, how can he be sure *his* own wife is not carrying on in the same way with some other fellow? Thinking like this frightens me. Good thing my wife does not live in Shanghai, and she is not beautiful. Otherwise—*ha-ha!*—I would never be comfortable about being away all hours of the day and night pulling a rickshaw.

I am simple by nature. I never feel right inside when I see the master and mistress doing these things in secret. I really wish I could expose the one to the other, and ask each to behave. If I do that, however, my sources of funding will immediately be cut off. So, for the sake of the money, I might as well control my urges. It's none of my business, anyway.

Even though I say that to you now, there was one time when I nearly had to let the cat out of the bag. I was eating lunch in the kitchen one day when the mistress's personal maid burst in all in a dither to tell me that I was wanted. Quickly, I put down my rice bowl and went out. The mistress was seated on the sofa, anger all over her face. The master, head down, was at her side. "Where does your master actually go every night?" she shouted out upon seeing me. "You have to know. Say it right away and nothing will happen to you. Otherwise, you will be kicked out of here this instant!"

I didn't know what to do when I heard this. If I came right out with the truth, I thought, the master would be upset at me for sure. Who's to say? He might even fire me. Besides, he gave me money to shut my mouth up, and I shouldn't squeal on him. One more thing: I had something on the mistress. Even though I didn't say anything, she probably wouldn't dare fire me. I also saw the master signaling me with his eyes. So I decided to keep the faith and said that he usually went to the Association and the Trade Company and sometimes he played mahjongg. The mistress pressed me for more, but I stuck to my guns and merely repeated myself. She could do nothing with me, and so she turned back to the master to carry on the argument. Me, I went back to my lunch.

Afterward, when I took the master out, he praised me to the sky, even rewarded me with five dollars. Then he took out a ten-dollar bill and said that it would be mine if I gave him all the dope about the places the mistress visits. With that pretty green flashing before my eyes, I was truly tempted to tell him. Lucky for me I quickly decided not to. After he learned the facts, I said to myself, the master would surely start another row with the mistress. Whatever happened then, I would wind up the culprit. I'm the only one who knew where she'd been; she'd definitely figure out that I talked and would never let me get away with it. It's not a big deal to get fired. But wouldn't it be a darn shame to give up a big-money job like this so easily? By the time I thought of all this, the ten-dollar bill had become poison; I'd made up my mind not to touch it. "Don't tell me you don't know where the mistress goes," I said to the master in response to the offer. "She usually just goes to movies and wanders around the amusement park. It's rare for her even to gamble." Besides these places, he wanted to know whether there were hush-hush destinations. I answered that the mistress always rode in my rickshaw when she went out and that I had never taken her any place to be quiet about. I even added that since the master was used to sneaking around himself, he shouldn't suspect others of doing the same.

He laughed at the remark. "You're a real devil, but I do enjoy you very much," he said. "You can still have these ten bucks as a reward."

As I took the money I quietly became aware of my good fortune. I had gotten it anyway, without having to reveal anything to him.

Now I could go claim another reward from the mistress, as I did later on, when I found an opportunity. "Ma'am, a huge calamity was about to come down, but I was able to ward it off for you casually," I said to her. When she asked, I told her in detail about what transpired with the master and how I responded. At that, of course, she, too, repeated how great I was. "It's just that the ten bucks never reached my hands because, for your sake, I could not tell him the truth," I said. "Now that I think about it, I am a little sorry."

"Forget about that." She smiled. "For helping me out like this, I'll be giving you lots of chances to make money." She fished out two tens as she was speaking and began by handing one of them to me. "You can consider this one a consolation prize for the ten dollars you lost because of me," she said. "This other one is presented to you for lying on my behalf."

I was overjoyed to receive the two bills. "Ah San, Ah San," I silently mouthed my own name. "You lucky son of a bitch! Only because you turned down those first ten bucks are you able to squeeze out thirty from them in the end. Had you been too greedy, been dazzled by the money early on and told on the mistress, another twenty would not have come to you now. Had you gotten her mad at you, your rice bowl would probably be smashed to bits. The old saying's right on: There's money all over the land, if you only know how to get it. How nicely put! From now on, I must be more tight-lipped than ever about their separate affairs. You won't hear me let out so much as a peep!"

Zhang Biwu says: In a place like Shanghai, wouldn't you agree that the Zhus are not really unique?

—*1923*

II. Love

• •

IN EARLY REPUBLICAN CHINA, even as Western narratives such as Dumas' *La Dame aux Camélias* were becoming known to the public at large, stories dealing with romantic love were relegated to the category of pastime fiction. The label "Mandarin Ducks and Butterflies," which was quickly applied to all stories written for leisurely escape, originated in fact as a term of disparagement for such tales of personal romance as Xu Zhenya's (1889–1937) *Yuli hun* (Jade pear spirit), published in 1912. In a troubled era when serious authors were writing for national salvation, the implication was that love stories, which often involve at least quiet personal opposition to general social norms, distracted readers' attention from pressing national needs. It did not help that many of those who set the intellectual agenda for the time saw the overall repudiation of China's cultural traditions as one of those needs.

To a greater degree than any other category of stories classified as "Saturday" fiction, the love stories are heavily traditional. C. T. Hsia tells us that *Yuli hun,* which began the love-fiction published in newspapers and magazines during the period, is a product of the "sentimental-erotic tradition of Chinese literature."[1] While he does not really justify adding the "erotic" label to the fiction, his explanation of the sentimental bent of such early Republican stories gives us much insight into all three of the examples gathered here. The "sentimental-erotic tradition," Hsia writes, "stresses the close linkage and ultimate identity of the three faculties without which no one can be called a lover: *qing* (capacity for love or feeling), *cai* (literary talent), and *chou* (capacity for sorrow). Thus Xu Zhenya writes of the hero of *Yuli hun* that he was, to be sure, a man of talent and a man of feeling, but he was a man of sorrow as well."[2]

Even Chinese readers in current times would find "The Bridal Palanquin" to be unbearably maudlin, just as they would any of Xu Zhenya's writings. But their counterparts in the 1920s were evidently quick to identify with Huiyun and Jueping, who are attracted to each other because of their mutual capacity for love and sorrow, and because of their common literary talent. He is quickly impressed by her "graceful" and "subtle" writing style; she, in turn, finds that each and every one of his sentences stirs her "to the depths of her soul." Her death, and then his, could be taken to be a protest against the custom of arranged marriages of the time. But their own lack of rebellion ultimately betrays the author's greater concern to milk the plot for all the "feelings"[3] it can stir up in the reader.

The heavy sentimentality in "Palanquin" is not found in "For the Love of Her Feet," which is more indebted to the vernacular fiction that flourished after the sixteenth century. The narrator's intrusive commentary throughout, set off here by parentheses, betrays the story's ties to an important native tradition.[4] "Feet" is a happy story because it features a Horatio Alger kind of hero, one who is ultimately rewarded for his talent, his effort, and, yes, his sentimentality. Published just two years after "Palanquin," it is a love story that shows a lighter side of China's storytelling tradition, a side that better suits those who do not wish to become so saddened by what they read at leisure.

Written much later but by one of the major authors of "Saturday" fiction, "So Near, So Far" is interesting as a later development of the Chinese love story. C. T. Hsia praises Xu Zhenya's venture into epistolary fiction as a means of exploring "the subjective world of hero and heroine" in love. But here the two exchanging letters are married and parents of a child on whom they both dote. The love they express to each other in letters, while deeply felt, would be much closer to the Western concept of agape than of eros. Was such a story possible because the difference between the two has never been stressed in China's own traditions? How else could such strong sentiments be awakened in a plot that features conjugal unity rather than destructive passion?

Notes

1. See "Hsu Chen-ya's *Yu-li hun:* An Essay in Literary History and Criticism" in the special issue on "Middlebrow Fiction" in *Renditions,* nos. 17 and 18 (spring/autumn 1982): 213–214.

2. *Ibid.,* p. 214. I have changed Hsia's romanization from Wade-Giles to pinyin for the sake of consistency. The Chinese ideographs in the original have also been left out.

3. In his highly influential preface to his translation of Goethe's *The Sorrows of Young Werther,* published in 1922, the then advocate of romantic literature Guo Moruo (1892–1978) quotes Werther's declaration that "My feelings alone are my most precious treasure, only they are the fountainhead of everything, all power, all happiness, all misfortune." See the translation by Kirk A. Denton in Kirk A. Denton, ed., *Modern Chinese Literary Thought: Writings on Literature, 1893–1945* (Stanford: Stanford University Press, 1996), p. 206.

4. See my article "Commentary and *Xiaoshuo* Fiction" in *Journal of the American Oriental Society,* vol. 120, no. 3 (November/December 2000).

The Bridal Palanquin

· ·

Yan Fusun

A bridal palanquin is covered with multicolored silk and is resplendent with sparkling red lanterns and flower patterns in different hues. It is an extremely eye-catching conveyance, with its mixture of color and light. As it rides along on the shoulders of its bearers, the painted bells on its corners jingle continuously. With the pipes and drums of the band leading the way, it floods the ears with joyous sounds, making young girls clap their little hands and giggle with delight. Which one among them would not wish in her heart of hearts to grow up quickly and choose a husband, so that she could have the good fortune to sit regally inside a fancy contraption like that, with attendants and guards shouting everyone out of the way as it makes its way across town? How nice it would be for the lucky young lady riding on her way to win the admiration of the bystanders. Alas for these lovable, romantic, naive maidens who do not understand the sorrows of life. Ever optimistic, they consider the ride to be the same as the one the kitchen god takes on New Year's Eve: Once the happy day arrives, the palanquin will fly them straight to heaven. Never does it dawn on them that as long as there is heaven, there also has to be hell. The shape of a palanquin is oblong. Sideways, it is identical to a coffin. For those among them who will be giving up a lifetime of happiness once they get to their husbands, entering the palanquin will be like entering a coffin—to be buried in the yellow earth where they will never be resurrected. The bustling attendants who escort them from their parents' homes can thus be considered members of a funeral procession, and the music of pipes and drums will then be heard as the mournful notes of a dirge.

Take the daughter of the Yu family, which owned a business renting out palanquins. She was only seventeen, but was wise enough to have decided long ago that the conveyances were ill-starred. Sometimes, when one came back from a rental, she would scrutinize the insides and invariably find traces of bitter weeping. On each such discovery, she would not be able to restrain her feelings and would shed her own tears in sympathy. Or else she would then sob alone in her room. "Most of the women in the world are doomed to lead unhappy lives," she would sigh. "How very pitiful they are. My father ought not to use such a cursed means to help carry out their fate, to transport people's daughters to the depths of hell where they receive the sentence of a slow death from the devil himself. Within the last several years, he's done that to quite a few. How really inhumane he's been!"

The sounds of her weeping reached her neighbors, who collectively thought that Yu Huiyun over at the shop must have gone mad. Alas, Huiyun's sensitive and fragile heart, long soaked with her bitter tears, could not but betray its grief. She was after all a bright, educated girl. How could you simply say that she was crazy? Ten years before, her father did take leave of his senses for a while. At the time Huiyun was a girl of just seven, but he would not wait. He asked someone to make a match for her with Lan Puren, the eight-year-old boy from the Lan Shun Xing Butcher Shop on Long Street. Lan Puren was then a winsome and lively lad who had caught her father's eye. What pleased him most about the entire transaction, moreover, was the betrothal gift of two-hundred dollars from the boy's family, which, ever since, had satisfied him as an appropriate price for the sale of a daughter. He managed, however, to spend all of the money in less than three days. His initial eagerness to match his daughter with someone can therefore be explained by this immediate gain, which he squandered in the blink of an eye. Right then, he even asked himself with some regret why he had never had a few more daughters. Then he blamed his wife for being useless. Alas, Huiyun was not at all insane. It was her father's behavior at the time that can be called insane to a disturbing degree.

As editor of the paper *The People's Will*, Luo Jueping had published many of his own writings over the preceding two years. Among writers and aficionados of fiction, he was making a bit of a name for himself. Readers were fighting to read anything he wrote as soon as it appeared. In terms of age, he was a promising young man of no more than eighteen. His forte was crafting sad stories, weaving a sense of lingering grief into all of his writings, which were deeply moving. His love stories in *Star Weekly* showed his skill in conveying emotion with every sentence. His pen could reveal love or hate, or a woman's touching innermost feelings. His readers were invariably moved to tears. At the end of the year, for a special issue on love, the magazine advertised for external submissions and received a draft manuscript from someone signing the name Huiyun. The style was graceful, the expression subtle. It described with great effect and detail the pain of a girl forced to marry against her will. Only later did he learn that Huiyun was the daughter in the Yu family shop, which rented out bridal palanquins. By then he was becoming thoroughly impressed. After that he saw an exquisite photograph of her in a catalogue of women writers, and, touched by her ethereal appearance, became even more attracted. Before long, he was exchanging letters with her. On Huiyun's part, she considered Luo Jueping to be among the very best of fiction writers of the day. She usually shed tears over his love stories, which were always tinged with sadness. What was so unusual about his writing was that each and every sentence seemed to stir her to the depths of her being. For a long time now, she had taken him to be the only person who understood her. Whatever anguish she felt but could not quite express, he was able to express deftly in his writing. Each time she received a letter from him, she alternately fretted and rejoiced, as if she had just gotten hold of a great treasure. Her father, however, retained strict control of her; she was not usually allowed to venture out. So even though she and Jueping had now known each other for a year and a half, their relationship was maintained only through correspondence. They never once met in person.

On one occasion, Jueping opened a letter from Huiyun to find tear stains all over the pages. Each one of her words, so full of anguish and pain, pointed to her frustration with life and her wish to leave it. Upon reading the letter, Jueping was taken aback. He had considered Huiyun to be a happy young girl; he had only to look at her high-spirited face in the catalogue photograph to recognize her joie de vivre. What in the world made her go down the path of such melancholy? Hard as he tried he could find no immediate answer to the question. After that, he exerted much effort before learning Huiyun's painful story.

Her intended, Lan Puren, turned out to be a lazy, pleasure-seeking sort. Having recently taken up with indolent companions, his character had slowly deteriorated. Time and again, he had absconded with money from his father's business, spending it on lavish parties or in brothels. His father had been thrifty and hard-working all his life, managing through much effort to set up his grocery business. He had also purchased a house and some land in his home village. When the thefts were discovered, the old man shook with anger at the thought of having such a son as a reward for his own scrupulously honest life. That very night, he spat up a mouthful of phlegm and died, thus taking immediate leave of his unfilial offspring. Lan Puren was of course overjoyed to jump just like that from the position of heir to that of boss. Aside from other advantages, he could now do whatever he wanted with his inheritance without anyone saying anything about it. During the funeral, his mother and the workers in the shop who had benefited from the old man's kindnesses were weeping and wailing around the coffin. Though he carried himself with the cool confidence of someone who had just come into money, Lan Puren nevertheless shed a crocodile tear or two in front of the assemblage. But as he looked upon his father's pale, ashen face, he could not help laughing to himself. "While you were alive," he thought, "you would never willingly give me a red cent. But now you're gone with nary a whimper. The money you've struggled all your life to accumulate can never be in the coffin with you. Every bit of it is now mine, to do with as I please, and you won't be able to do a thing about it. As tightfisted as you were in life, what did it bring you?" At this point, Puren examined his father's face once more. He seemed to see the old man's dull, round eyes pop open slightly, as if he were responding with a sigh.

After the funeral, he was on the verge of liquidating the estate so that he could indulge himself and play the big shot with his friends. But his philandering in recent years had been extremely taxing on his health. It so happened that the spring weather caused boils to break out all over his body. At first, he merely felt some aching in his joints. Before long, however, the abscesses all burst. Then he also broke his nose. Dripping blood and pus, he emitted an unbearable stench, to such an extent that everyone treated him as if he were a pariah and wanted to stay far away. Because no one else was willing to risk contamination to care for him, his mother had to stay by her son day and night. She sent for a doctor and filled prescriptions, busying herself each day from dawn to dusk, not sparing any effort on his behalf. In her mind, what her son had done in the past had been an aberration. Once he got well, he would change. It would not be difficult for him to start life anew.

One evening, on her way to Rainbow Temple to fill a prescription, she stopped for a reading with the well-known fortune-teller Squinty Wu. She wanted to know what was in store for her son, what could be done to bring about a miracle cure. Wu was eager to please his new client. He gave her some of his mumbo-jumbo, telling her that the stars of good fortune were shining on her son in the current year. If she could quickly get him married, she would fend off the evil spirits and his illness would then go away by itself. Naturally, she was excited to hear this kind of talk. She immediately contacted the original go-between to inform the Yu family of her decision. She selected the fourteenth of the second lunar month, a propitious day, for the wedding, and expected to welcome her new daughter-in-law into her home at that time.

Jueping's reaction upon learning this news was nothing short of bizarre. Ever since he had begun corresponding with Huiyun, he had been as enthusiastic as she was, never missing a single day. After that time, however, he ceased all communication with her. Even more strangely, he went as far as to resign his editorship of both the *People's Will* and *Star Weekly*. No one knew where he was hiding himself. When Jueping's letters stopped, Huiyun was at first puzzled. Then, after she learned of his two resignations, she felt that something inexplicable was happening and wondered what it could be. Some told her he'd died. Others said he went abroad. From then on, though, Huiyun could no longer read those lingeringly melancholic stories that touched her to the very core. She had lost someone who really understood how she felt. It was like losing a chunk of her soul. For days on end, she was unable to stop weeping.

On the fourteenth day of the second month, Huiyun's father picked out a most elaborately decorated palanquin. He told people that it had been used in the weddings of many girls from prominent and wealthy families, all of whom prospered in their husbands' homes and all of whom enjoyed happiness without end. Everyone agreed that the good fortune was the legacy of the palanquin, that Huiyun was indeed blessed to be able to ride in it that day.

A couple of weeks earlier, when her future in-laws set the date for the wedding, Huiyun had started a chain of thought. Her prospects of finding happiness throughout life had long ago been settled by her father, in no more time than it took for a smile to cross his face. It was as if she were a criminal, someone already condemned to suffer the death penalty. She was awaiting the autumn executions, passing the bitter days left to her in a prison cell. The announcement of the wedding date was tantamount to an announcement that autumn was here, that she could no longer avoid the beheading. That she had borne her pain in silence and without rebelling was all for the sake of keeping her father's word. Now that the time had come for her to face her fate, what was there left for her to say?

On the day of her wedding, her father brought out all the wreaths and decorative brocade he had not rented out, and covered every nook and cranny of the shop with clusters and layers of silks and flowers. In the colorful glow of the bridal lanterns, the place took on a sparkle that dazzled the eyes of the onlookers. The lanterns were of varying shapes, each with a cleverly auspicious appellation: "Prosperity, Posterity," "Hoary-Headed Harmony," "Twin-Star Togetherness," "Mandarin-Duck Mischief." The large variety added to the excitement of anticipation.

The crowd of well-wishers knew only that Huiyun's father had been flourishing these last few years. His present business had expanded tenfold since its early beginnings, and the frequency of his contacts with relatives and friends had likewise increased. Today visitors were coming to him in an unending stream; his house was packed with wedding guests. They well knew that the groom was infected with a life-threatening disease, that receiving a bride into his house was intended to boost his spirits. Nonetheless, their congratulatory notes uniformly included flattering comments. They all said that Miss Huiyun was a lucky girl indeed. As Mr. Lan had now passed away, she could help to manage the family's finances after the marriage. Puren might have some unknown ailment, but, as long as there was money in the family, they considered her blessed. A bit of illness never hurt anybody. "That Yu girl surely has good karma," the group of old women, there to catch the excitement, were saying. "How fortuitous for her to be born into a shop with bridal palanquins. Without too much ado, everything's already there for her to have as fancy a wedding as she pleases. How grand! The display of even a middle-class wedding would be less elaborate. What's more, the palanquin she'll be riding in will be one that exactly suits her fancy. It's commonly said that if the ride pleases a girl on her wedding day, everything else will also suit her fancy. Her new husband's family, moreover, runs a butcher shop. Whatever else might happen, she needn't worry about having good, fresh meat on the dinner table. The girl's set for life, marrying into a situation like that."

By this time, Huiyun had long since put on her red gown for the ceremony. She was sitting stiffly by herself, waiting for the propitious hour to get into the palanquin. As human voices mingled with the music blaring around her, her mind began to drift. It was as if she were entering a state of semiconsciousness, or her cowed soul, after all that battering, were leaving her body. She recalled the love her mother lavished on her in childhood. Too bad she had died so early. Her father had coveted the bride-price and was willing to go against reason in deciding his daughter's lifelong fate. Today she would go to her place of execution. There was no escape. If her dead mother somehow learned of this, she would surely be shedding heartbroken tears in the nether regions. This last thought seemed to trigger her own tears, which rolled down drop after drop. She then considered the dreadful days she would be living through once she entered that family. How could she bear it? The surge of grief quite overwhelmed her. Greatly shaken, she fainted away.

Many rushed over to help, and then slowly she was revived. Lowering her head, she gave a sudden start at the sight of her own bright-red costume; for a moment, she thought it was soaked with fresh blood. At the same time, the different voices offering congratulations grew louder, pouring into her ears along with the music. Her heart seemed to be pierced with a shiny dagger that then slowly hacked her insides to pieces. Each time someone said something about her happy covenant, her inner self vibrated like a plucked zither. "Covenant." The word reminded her of "convent," a place a woman entered to become a nun—to leave her family and her worldly ambitions, content to be cut off for the rest of her days from those who loved her. Her father was going to expel her from her home, to a place where she would not see the light of day as long as she lived. In getting married like that, what would be the difference between herself and someone who chose to enter a nunnery? Then she had another thought. She was not about to "enter" anything. Rather, she was about to be "interred," her soul condemned to suffer hell's most painful tortures. But what sin had she committed? Why was a woman like her fated to make a home for herself in the bowels of hell? Thoroughly distracted, she allowed her imagination to wander in most bizarre directions, quite beyond her control.

In no time, she heard the music start up once more, followed by the rapid beating of gongs. "Hurry! Come see the bride get into the palanquin!" some children shouted. Strange as it seemed, Huiyun was somehow able to put aside her pain. Her eyes were dry throughout the sacrifices to her ancestors. Her father stole a moment to whisper in her ear: "A daughter is always brought up for someone else. Don't you take things too hard. When you get to your new home, take good care of your husband. I am hoping that the union will bring you both luck, that he will quickly get over his illness. Fortunately his shop has been bringing in some money these last few years and you will not need to be concerned about material necessities. Your father's foresight a decade ago has not turned out badly at all, has it?"

Huiyun was completely dry-eyed as she forced a smile and thanked him for his good intentions. By now she had become very calm, as if she had reached some kind of decision that cleared the gloom before her eyes. She betrayed no trace of sadness and appeared to be a different person altogether. On hearing her thanks, her father broke into a smile. "You're an educated and reasonable person," he said. "I knew that sooner or later, you'd understand everything in your heart."

At the propitious hour, Huiyun showed neither shyness nor hesitation. She strode to the palanquin in large steps and got right into it. The bearers took it up and sped away. All those who gathered to watch along the route voiced their admiration. At their arrival, the Lan family was preoccupied with the groom, whose illness had taken a turn for the worse. He had lapsed into a coma. The paper "palanquin horses" had long been in place in the rear courtyard. But on this day the house was relatively empty and quiet, with no sounds of celebration. Only two female attendants came to the door to greet the bridal palanquin. When they lifted the curtain, they received a horrible shock. The lovely girl inside, dressed and made up to be gorgeous as a flower, had somehow slit her own throat with a paper cutter; she had been dead for some time. The newspapers reported the extraordinary happening the following day; the story brought repeated sighs from its readers. Most remarkably, Luo Jueping, who had long been missing, soon resurfaced in the pages of *Star Weekly,* his name again set in bold type.

Jueping had admired Huiyun in his heart. He only gave up his own hopes of a future with her after learning of her distressing situation. From the unrelieved melancholy in her writing, he could see that she would soon come to a tragic end. Concluding with regret that it was beyond his power to remove her curse, he had made up his mind to leave Shanghai, to make a clean break by ceasing all communication with her. Not long afterward, he saw in a Shanghai paper the sad news he'd been expecting. It was then that he rejoined the Star Society, to summon all his skills to craft a love story he titled "The Person in the Palanquin." In it, he described Huiyun's sorrows with penetrating insight. When he got to the tragic parts, he was actually shedding a tear for every word he set down. Never could he bear to read the whole story through to the end. His motive for setting everything down was to give vent to Huiyun's resentment toward life. Written with his heart's blood, the masterly story was his way of repaying his dead soulmate. But Jueping was himself a man of great sensitivity, one who marched to the beat of his own drummer. He had an extremely delicate constitution, owing to his overconcentration on books and on matters intellectual since childhood. From the time he learned of Huiyun's tragic demise, he would become greatly traumatized each time he reconsidered his own long piece about her. Soon after, his mind began to lose touch with reality. He would laugh or cry without apparent cause. Gradually he lost control of himself, behaving as if he was suffering a nervous breakdown.

In the winter of that same year, Jueping's mother, who was advanced in years and eager to see grandchildren, arranged for him to get married. By then, Jueping's illness was worsening by the day. He had lost all sense of perception and was unable to carry on normal functions without help. Like a puppet, he was dependent on others to pull the strings. On his wedding day, in his new ceremonial robe, he approached everyone with a vacant grin. When he saw that the nuptial scroll in the bridal chamber contained the line "Blessings and Wisdom Mutually Adorn," he ripped it to bits, insisting that a bit of soul lurked within the word "wisdom"— *hui,* as in Huiyun. Then, when the bridal palanquin arrived, the sight set off the old tenderness in his brain. In an instant, he cried out and vomited forth a half-basin of blood and then lost consciousness. When he came to, he was lying on a perfumed bed in a bridal chamber, wondering whether he'd been dreaming. Somehow or other, his energy level suddenly increased several fold. He rushed headlong downstairs in spite of the efforts of many who tried to restrain him. He ran to the receiving room, where he saw a deep patch of red on the floorboards of the palanquin—no doubt the last remnant of Huiyun's bloody suicide. Then he looked around the outsides. A burst of color flashed before his eyes. All that crimson appeared to him to be Huiyun's blood. As he struggled with the grief in his heart, everything turned dark. Once again, he fainted away.

His mother was beside herself. She quickly sent for a doctor to give him an emergency injection, but by the time the man arrived, Hui-yun's limbs were turning cold. When she was told that nothing could be done for her son, she began to wail. Wagging her finger, she railed at the bridal palanquin, spitting out hatred with every word: "My son's death is all your doing! You are nothing but a damnable curse!"

— 1921

For the Love of Her Feet

. . . .

He Haiming

The store selling medium-priced leather footwear was located next to a large amusement park, so that the men and women entering and exiting the park each day had to pass by the storefront. Nearly everyone inside could see the bustle. The store consisted of two and a half stories, with an interior layout as follows. The upper story was made up of offices for the manager and the various bookkeepers; it also served as a storage area for a certain amount of stock. The lower story was the shop, with the commotion of a bevy of clerks making sales. The remaining half-story was the basement, which housed the only factory for the enterprise.

An apprentice named Ah Fa, who had just completed his initial training, worked in this factory. He was only seventeen but had already labored in the basement for three years.

Three whole years! For a young man, shouldn't they be as precious as gold? Wasn't it regrettable to have to spend them in an underground factory? And yet, the skill of putting together shoes by hand had undeniably been acquired there, so that the time did not seem to have been expended in vain. It's just that the fervent spirit of youth could never actually be shut up in any dungeon. The two street-level windows never stopped flashing with light, letting in sights of the outside world for him, as if to keep him enticed.

The daily routine of his life, on the other hand, was utterly monotonous. He was a very tiny person in a very tiny place, using his very tiny hands to do a very tiny job. Whenever he looked around, his tools and the workbench next to him all appeared so small. In his seemingly detached world of limited sunshine, everything was miniaturized according to scale. Still, he was able to leave this workspace in spirit, to uncover those little eyeballs that so rarely encountered direct sunlight, to peek semiconsciously out a street-level window time and time again. But would this limited line of vision possibly allow him to see everything in human society? Could it show him the kaleidoscopic world he imagined existed outside his half-buried environment?

The reader ought to know that according to practice, basement windows of this sort were situated at sidewalk level along the thoroughfare. The line of vision of anyone looking out from them was exactly at the shoe level of passersby. Hence, the result of Ah Fa's close observation of human society outside his domain was the sight of different feet—large, small, long, short—as well as shoes of varying styles for both men and women. The sidewalk outside his window, moreover, was a place everyone entering or exiting the amusement park had to pass. So the foot traffic there was far more dense than anywhere else. Bedazzled by the colorful variety of what he saw, he gradually developed a certain expertise at what had begun as curious observation.

"All these feet," he secretly mused. "What sort of people do they belong to? Why is it that they gad about like that, so thoroughly unrestrained? Can they just be running around outside all day long? Ah, I, too, have a pair of feet. Why then do I have to confine myself to this little bit of space all the time, without being able to make a single spontaneous move?" His thoughts thus led from the unfettered feet of others to his own confined ones, making him feel the sharp pain of lost freedom. Then his mind began to stir once more. "Don't those feet constantly go in and out of that park next door? The people go to seek amusement day in and day out, never tiring of doing so. I've only been there once myself, during New Year's. Ah, feet! How unlucky for you to be at the end of my legs! I'm really rather sorry for you." As if to mock him, the music from the park, carried by the wind, came through the window in waves, the clear and pleasant notes making the itch in his feet all the harder to bear. He so wanted to pick them up and rush right over there. But this dungeon of a basement was watched over by a foreman as if he were a prison guard. No one could escape using just a pair of feet. So even though he had long since flown off in his imagination, he still had to pretend to focus on the work in front of him, to do it over and over. The stitch after hempen stitch he was applying to the shiny black leather of a pair of women's shoes seemed also to be sewing up the inner chambers of his heart. Who was there to know his pain, or to comfort him in his depression?

The greater his suffering and vexation, the more he liked to peek out the window, as if searching for the comfort he craved. For a long, long time, he found nothing at all. But looking out like that did add to his powers of perception. He was actually able to identify the feet of a good number of men and women who frequented the park. Among them was a pair belonging to a female, which he never tired of looking at, and which he could never erase from his mind. It is reasonable to suppose that any cobbler would naturally have a heightened ability to judge the aesthetics of feet. This particularly feminine pair was neither too large nor too small, too fat nor too thin. They were perfect in size, and the pair of black leather pumps they had on complemented them well. The flair they displayed when they walked made them especially attractive. No one other than a gorgeous young woman could possibly have feet like those, he thought. After that, in order to substantiate his hypothesis, he once actually hurried over to the window to look up when he saw the feet passing by. Indeed, she was as he imagined. Too bad she was walking past so quickly he was only able to catch her profile. Still, that one glance erased all questions regarding her appearance.

From that day on, he was no longer satisfied just looking at her footsteps. Several times he was able to escape the notice of the others and, boldly yet carefully, stole glimpses of the woman with the beautiful feet. He put together the various profile angles to form a mental portrait, which he kept locked in the inner recesses of his heart. She was lovely beyond compare. Fortunately, the girl liked to visit the park day after day. Thus, he had regular opportunities to catch sight of those feet, which drove out all of his other desires, including his interest in looking at anything else around them. Each day, his eyes waited hungrily for this particular pair of feet. Seeing them time and again, he developed an inexplicable obsession: He had to look at them constantly. On any given day when the feet came around later than usual, his heart would be at his throat in his longing for them. Whenever they suddenly arrived as he was thinking about them, a wild feeling of joy would come over him and a smile would instantly appear on his face. Sometimes, as the feet left the park to return home, he would hardly be able to bear seeing them go. He would then suppress the urge to bid them good night and promise to see them again on the morrow. When the feet would stay away for an entire day, his disappointment would know no bounds. He would go about with a heavy heart, worried that the girl could have perhaps fallen ill. In sum, each time he saw her yielded a feeling of gladness, each time he did not, a feeling of woe. His moods swung between the extremes of joy and sorrow. Caught in this emotional turmoil, he had no idea what to do. He began by falling in love with a pair of feet and ended up falling in love with the whole person. His opportunities varied by the day, however. Mostly, he saw the feet, far less often the person. Chances for seeing the feet came easily, those for seeing the person came rarely. In the abstract sense, he did indeed become enamored of those feet.

But in terms of actual feelings, how could he have helped extending this love to include the one to whom the feet belonged?

After pondering the matter for an extended time, he came to realize that he had fallen hard for this girl. How wonderful it would be if he could exchange names with her, or escort her to the amusement park. And, thinking ahead another step, if they were to get married, that would be better still. He would then be able to watch over her feet all his life. At this thought, his face felt a little feverish, and he was embarrassed enough to chide himself. "Aren't you going too far?" he muttered. "She looks like a person of means, the daughter of a wealthy family, while you, with your ragged clothes, are no more than a pauper of a cobbler. How on earth could you match up with her? *Ai* . . . What is it that has made you so poor ever since you were born?" (*The same thought sequence has turned the determined into successes, the crafty into criminals, and the cowardly into suicide victims.*) Then another thought occurred to him. "Not so. She and I are the same sort of people. Our ages are similar. So why can't we be married? I may be relatively poor right now, but who's to say I won't become rich in the future? There are many in the world who overcame a destitute childhood to end up tycoons. Everything is the result of what one does. It doesn't seem to be all that impossible for me to become wealthy. So, fine! From now on I resolve to be an earnest, hardworking young man, to advance my position so that I can marry this girl in the future and have a fulfilling family life with her. Otherwise, it's useless to go on fantasizing as I have day in and day out."

Making up his mind at that moment, he indeed strove to succeed with extraordinary determination. He showed an exceptional eagerness for learning, rushing to handle every task. He mastered all the required skills to near perfection. On his time off from his job, he regularly attended night classes to advance his academic knowledge. Through it all, he was happy to be able to see those feet outside the window every day. Looking at them each time, he would resolve once again to strive harder. It was as if they were actively encouraging him.

Eventually, thanks to the strenuous effort he expended for their sake, he attained his goals.

For a businessman, time never passes so easily. For a storyteller, however, a decade can go by with a mere stroke of the pen. The Ah Fa after that time was no longer the earlier Ah Fa. From the young apprentice he had been, he became one of the successful people in the world of industry. At first, the manager in the store noticed his excellent work and sent him to another town to be foreman at a branch. Then, when the manager's position opened up there, he was promoted to fill it. Business boomed during the next several years, allowing him to save some money. He then quickly became a stockholder in the enterprise. Toward the end of the period, the business was greatly expanded and was reorganized into a limited corporation issuing stock. In this way, he became an important founding member of the firm. At the elections to fill the firm's various posts during its establishment, he was voted by the stockholders into the position of vice-president in charge of managing the main store. In this way he again returned to his original location.

What we must settle at this point is whether, through all this, he had forgotten the person whose feet he had been so infatuated with as a youth. Even as he was being transferred out of the main store, he could not help having lingering regrets about the move: He would miss those feet. But business came first (*those words constituting a fundamental principle for his major accomplishments*), and he could not very well have remained in the basement just for those feet outside the window. To go out and take care of proper business, moreover, was clearly one very good way to eventually possess those feet. So he had determinedly gone on his way, not daring to tarry. There was more and more work at his post each day, and he was getting older and older each year. Eventually, as we might expect, the infatuation he first felt as a lad gradually faded. There were times, however, when the memories did come sneaking back, memories he had some trouble brushing off. But other than laughing at himself, there was nothing he could do about them. How ludicrous, to lavish such fantasies on nothing more than a pair of feet!

Now that he had returned and was successful, he lived with several shareholders in a large hotel. Venturing out in daylight, he felt a flutter in his heart when he saw the feet of so many women. That first night, he could not get to sleep, as various thoughts came back to him. The image of those feet from the past, long embedded in his brain, seemed to reappear with stark clarity before his eyes, like a movie film placed in the light of a projector. All he had to do was shut his eyelids and they would be there. Evidently, the first love of one's youth cannot ever be forgotten. In pondering the past, his thoughts went as follows: "Why are those feet still in my head? Why do I still love them? Could I still be as naive as I was as a young man? Since I'm not able to free myself from them, I ought to exhaust all means, to plunge myself into the mass of humanity in order to seek them out. And yet, realistically speaking, that would be an impossible task. Too bad I was such a dope then, wallowing in my own infatuation without bothering to find out her background or address. If I were to look for her now, where would I begin?"

Then one evening, having finished his work, he rested alone in his hotel room, stretched out comfortably on a sofa. The image of the feet was again welling up in his mind. It happened that he had left his door open. Since the sofa was directly opposite it, his line of vision was unconsciously directed outside the room. Even though a swinging door was still in the way, he could see out the unobstructed area beneath it. The feet of various hotel guests went past from the corridor outside, reminding him of what he saw out the basement window years before. Yes, uncanny coincidences do indeed happen. For, in a flash, he again caught sight of *those* feet.

Having looked at them so many times, he had long known by instinct their exact width and length, how they were pointed at the toes and rounded at the heels, as well as the way they moved either in a hurry or at a leisurely pace. Should you ask him to explain this knowledge in detail, he wouldn't of course be able to do so. But encountering them again suddenly was like rereading an old book: Instantly he was certain of what he saw. One thing about them had not changed, moreover: Even now, those feet had on shiny black shoes. For a former cobbler, the ability to determine the size and style of leather footwear was of course unerring. In addition, there was one other feature that made the feet easily identifiable. The bone at the second joint of each big toe jutted out at a sharp angle. Here was a truly remarkable encounter, and he wasn't about to let this rarest of opportunities pass. So he rushed out after her.

It was all right. She had not gone far, only to the table at the corner of the corridor. What's more, she was standing right there, turning her head to ask a bellhop where room 107 was, and learning that it was upstairs to the west. As she nodded her thanks, her face became distinctly visible from a distance. Surely she had to be the one. Her attire was even more gaudy than before, even though it had been ten years and she was now a woman of twenty-five or twenty-six. Could she still be single? Why wasn't she wearing a skirt? Why was she dressed like the teenager she'd not been in years? Looking again, he saw a girl by her side, someone much younger but made up with so much powder and rouge that she appeared to be a prostitute. What were they doing together? Who were they looking for in the hotel?

Befuddled for the moment, he called the bellhop over after the two went off, and asked who they were. "They're both call girls," the young man replied with a smirk. "The younger one is Hibiscus Blossom; the other is Old Number Five. She tells people she's the older sister. But she's really the well-known courtesan Spring Hibiscus Number Five." How had she come to this? He wanted badly to find out everything from her. So he went back to his room and filled out an order for the bellhop to bring her there.

In short order she arrived, Hibiscus Blossom in tow. He invited her to sit down, then greeted her by announcing, "We haven't seen each other for a very long time."

She searched her memory for a time without coming up with any-thing. "We've met before . . . somewhere," she responded vaguely.

"It's something that happened quite some time ago," he said with a smile. "It was I, though, who was acquainted with you, not at all the other way around. As to what I recognize in you, I'm afraid it's just those feet of yours—not you as a total person."

She thought this exceedingly strange. "How is it that you recognize my feet?" she immediately asked. "Perhaps you're playing with me . . ."

"It's all true," he said. "You'll understand after I explain."

He then recounted all that had happened years ago, as if he were telling her a story. At the end, he let out a sigh. "I had no idea I would see you here today, not to mention finding you in such straits," he said. "Just talking about everything grieves me deeply. (*We shed tears on reading these words.*) Now that I've told you all about me, can you tell me about yourself?"

She and Hibiscus Blossom were both dumbfounded at the story, and she, especially, was deeply moved. "How in the world," she thought, "could there be such a single-minded fool? He fell in love with my feet, then extended that love to all of me. At least he appears to care a lot for me. So why not bare my soul to him?"

Thereupon she laid out in detail for him all that had happened to her over the past ten years. Her father, it turned out, died when she was little, leaving her to grow up with only her mother. Until she was fifteen or so, she had attended school. But she had always been fond of going to the amusement park, even at the cost of neglecting her studies. Then she was charmed by a slick young man, to whom she lost her virginity. Her mother became so upset she took ill and died. Thereafter, she descended into the world of prostitution. After be-coming a veteran in the trade, she began to get into the business side of it as well. At present she was an assistant in the organization. In retrospect she could see that everything was the consequence of her early attraction to the amusement park. (*Those who are similarly addicted today ought to take note of this.*) And yet, had she not gone there so often during those years, she would never have left her footprints so deeply in his mind. The whole thing was a kind of karma, something ordained by fate.

Hearing all this, he could only let out sigh after sigh. Then he took on a very serious air. "Our meeting today is the result of your feet acting as our go-between," he said to her. "From what you tell me now, your decade of misfortune also came about because of your fun-loving feet. For my part, though, what success I enjoy today has been given to me by those same feet of yours. If not for them, I would not have accomplished what I have. So I should give great thanks to them in appreciation for the good they have provided me for ten years, for motivating me to get better and better. After all, your feet are nothing but an appendage of your whole self, and I can't think of any appropriate gift to offer them. To get them a few pairs of shoes, for example, would hardly be sufficient. So I have no choice but to go from feet to person, to express my heartfelt gratitude. What are you in need of right now? Please tell me without hesitation. As long as it lies within my powers, I am willing to provide you whatever you ask for."

Old Number Five pondered for a while. "I would never guess that these feet of mine would lead to any good; they have only taken me to dissipation and ruin," she frankly admitted. "Now, after meeting a caring person such as yourself, I'm overwhelmingly ashamed of what I've done. To think someone would strive so hard for the love of my feet. Even though I have my own heartaches, I could never seek to profit from you the way I've always sought to profit from my ordinary customers. For the sake of what you have felt for my feet, I beg you to allow all of me to become your dependent. Since you have loved them so, you won't be able to bear seeing them wander about in the world forever, without ever having a place to call home. So please take me in. You can make me your concubine or maidservant . . ." (*These were not words of gratitude, but words of love.*) Tears were running all over her face by the time she concluded. (*How could she not shed them?*) She looked up at him, waiting for a reply.

He could not help being moved by this unexpected request, which he quickly agreed to grant. "These last few years, I have been so occupied with my work I have not even taken a wife," he told her. "In my heart, I have of course wished for a day like this. You may have betrayed your own feet, but they have not betrayed me. They have made me a success in my profession, and you will be marrying me only because of them. So, in the end, your feet are a boon to you. From now on, may you keep them under control for my sake, so that I can be close to them each and every day. Then may I redouble my efforts and renew my resolve to strive for even greater success in my work. Your feet have now taken you through the gate of good fortune to a peaceful and happy existence. You have no reason to grieve anymore."

As they were thus agreeing to marry, Miss Hibiscus Blossom prudently slipped away to return alone to the brothel. "Fifth Sister is going to get married," she proclaimed to everyone there. "I heard the groom is Zhao Fa, the Vice-President and Manager of China Leather Goods." Another decade after that, another news item was spread around. "Zhao Fa has become a tycoon. In consultation with his wife, he has bought out the large amusement park, turning it into a department store for Chinese products. Footwear produced by the China Leather Goods Company is on display in the basement. Most remarkably, Manager Zhao's office has been located there all along. He said that a person should never forget where he comes from." (*He achieved his current success only because he was always mindful. All of you who work for a living should take Zhao Fa as a model.*)

— *1923*

So Near, So Far

· ·

Bao Jianxiao

Ling Zhuoru, a journalist in the editorial room of the *Times*, called himself a nocturnal animal. He did all his work at night, usually arriving at the news office after it got dark and not starting for home until dawn.

A free spirit, he was nonetheless dedicated to his job. Each day he would scrutinize the drafts of the articles one by one, deciding which to reject or print, which to bring out in bold or reduced type, which to put on the front or back pages. There was also the matter of subtitles below the headlines. Some were necessary and others whimsical, put in to catch the readers' attention and perhaps inject a bit of humor into otherwise somber and boring news accounts.

Now and then Zhuoru would write a piece of social commentary on his own. It was always something spontaneous and timely, unlike so many such pieces that could have been published last month or next month, or pieces on academics, art, or literature, which would not be affected by delays. The commentaries he wrote were all based on the crucial news of the day. As a journalist, he considered it his natural responsibility to express views on matters of national import.

For all these reasons, he could not but bury himself from dusk to dawn under a pile of paper in the editorial room, living a life of red pencils and black ink, scissors and paste. He was, moreover, a combination of boldness and fastidiousness, never relaxing even after the type was set and the galleys made up. Only when the presses began to rumble did he feel a sense of relief. At first light, after all, the papers had to reach the hands of the readers; any delay would put the operation behind.

So Ling Zhuoru never set out for home before the first light of day, never before the sky to the east had already begun to pale. Wouldn't this kind of life—up one long night after another—be draining on him? At thirty-something, he still had the vigor of youth. Yet walking out of the office this time, he did look somewhat worn down.

Because of his tight budget, he could not afford taking taxis, and so he started for home in the pedicab he hailed at the curb outside the entrance. At that hour the street lamps were still lit, throwing their faded, depressing light on the pedestrians. Vegetable vendors on their way to neighborhood markets were out in droves, riding in rickshaws loaded fore and aft with baskets full of greens in varying hues. One little cart had in it a couple of shaved pig carcasses, heads missing, fresh from the slaughterhouse and about to satisfy a horde of carnivores. The pedicab went past a small house alongside the road, from which dim lamplight was visible. The whimpers of an infant at the breast and a mother's loving pats and sleepy lullaby that emerged would have been enough to touch anyone's heart.

Ling Zhuoru, you see, had a twenty-six-year-old wife as well as a daughter not quite three. When he heard the sounds from that little dwelling, he naturally thought of his own. He was only renting the front apartment in someone's three-story building to house his family. But even a place like that had not been easily gotten. He had exhausted every effort, accumulated a ton of IOUs, and paid out not a little cash before he succeeded.

Even though the place took up only a part of one story, it was bright and open. The balcony in front was nice for catching a breeze or looking out into the distance. The bathroom in back had all the fixtures. It was just that there was no kitchen. But then the family was not large and they could make do with a stove and a few cooking utensils placed next to the sunny area at the top of the stairs. Though the furnishings were spare, the apartment was neat and orderly and included a small desk and bookshelf. Suffice it to say that their little haven was adequate to accommodate normal daily living, including eating, sleeping, and studying.

Ling Zhuoru's wife, Shen Xiaoyin, was a senior high school graduate. While a schoolgirl, she had been considered pretty. For almost four years now, she had been married to Ling; their much-beloved angel of a daughter, the delicate and precious little Peipei, was not yet three. In addition to the three of them, there was Goldie, a servant girl hired from the countryside, who had just turned twelve.

At a time when those who worked in the cultural sphere were so poorly compensated, Ling Zhuoru's salary was not really sufficient to maintain the family. So his wife had made up her mind to find a job in order to supplement their income. As a good, educated wife, she had hoped to keep up a decent front both inside and outside the home, to not appear shabby. Their little daughter, especially, ought to be well-dressed enough to look pleasant. But with the current high cost of everything, her husband simply could not take care of such matters himself. His wife, therefore, had had to act boldly, to seek out ways and means on her own.

Through her efforts as well as through the strong recommendation of a former schoolmate, she had landed a job as a bookkeeper for a certain firm. This, though, brought on difficulties. First, what was she to do with Peipei? She definitely could not bring her to work. But if she left her at home, Goldie could never manage. Have Peipei's father take care of her? That would of course be best. But her father usually slept until the afternoon after returning in the early morning. Having worked hard all night, he had to have time to recover. How could she bear to have him bothered? Second, she had always been the cook.

Even though Ling Zhuoru slept on till later in the day, she had always been able to have a solid meal ready for him when he got up. Who would fix the food for him now? Twelve-year-old Goldie could never take on the responsibility. Nor could he cook for himself. Shen Xiao-yin was again thrown into a quandary.

To Ling Zhuoru, getting food was not a problem. He only ate one meal—lunch—at home, and all the others at the office. If he had to, he could just buy anything cooked, some bread, and muddle through. The problem with the child, however, was clearly serious. Even though he could get up in the afternoons and play with her, what would they do with her in the mornings? With her mother away, caring for her would indeed become a problem; therefore he thought that for the sake of the little one, he would rather his wife turn down the job.

His wife did not agree, however. It didn't matter that she had put forth so much effort. But she had asked a favor and gotten the opportunity only through someone's kind recommendation. If she were to give it up after all this, how could she face that person? Getting a job in such times was no easy matter. If she didn't take it then, she could never bring herself to ask for help again. She was nothing if not determined. Within three days she'd found a nursery school not far from their home. What made it so satisfactory for her was the fact that the place was run by another former classmate, someone who later specialized in childhood education in teacher-training school. There could be no better solution. So the matter was settled: Peipei was to go there in the mornings and be picked up in the evenings.

On the way to work each morning, Shen Xiaoyin took Peipei to the nursery school and brought her home at nightfall. At first, the child was shy about the unfamiliar situation, but she adjusted in a couple of days. The problem of Ling Zhuoru's meals was also solved. She began by teaching Goldie the proper proportion of water and grain to cook rice. During the winter she would fix dishes the night before, and in the summer, in the mornings. Sometimes she'd buy a bit of ready-made food as supplement. It was only one meal, after all; she always came up with a way to provide it. A few days of experimenting and everything began to go smoothly. She was able to go off to work free of worries about home.

As a young couple, they should have been sharing a bed. But each day Ling Zhuoru never got back much before sunrise. If he even puttered around a little, bright daylight would be upon them. His wife had always risen early; she could hardly have done otherwise since all youngsters seem to follow the same pattern. They never fail to wake up at the crack of dawn and to be utterly unwilling to go back to sleep after that. They would squeal and coo at you, tell you things, or else start to gurgle some tune. If you tried to ignore them, they'd scratch your nose with their little hands, or pucker up their tiny lips to kiss your cheeks. Peipei, at least, always behaved that way. So I ask you: Could her mother have been able to remain in bed through all this?

Whenever Ling Zhuoru came home from work and got into bed, his wife would be about to get up. So even though we can say that they shared a bed, there was little substance to the sharing. They were more like the Orion and Lucifer constellations, which never come into direct contact with each other. Still, young couple that they were, they could not very well toss aside their natural feelings for each other. Sometimes Ling Zhuoru would want his wife to dally a few moments before jumping up. But just to enjoy those moments, she would first have to take Peipei elsewhere so that they would not be interrupted. As she was being carried away, Peipei would invariably want her mother to remain with her. Once she began to cry, her mother would become distraught. Whatever romantic mood they might have been in would by then be dissipated.

After some time, his wife bought a twin bed and moved it into the room. "Peipei and I can sleep together on the smaller bed from now on," she said. "When you come home, just get into the larger one. It's more convenient that way, more comfortable for you."

The idea of sleeping in a separate bed from his wife bothered Ling Zhuoru. But since she had gone this far, he could hardly object. Then a thought occurred to him: Why couldn't they switch? It wasn't as if the beds were divided by some kind of iron curtain. Getting the smaller one was rather like annexing a satellite nation or gaining another colony. Nothing was wrong with that. "You two go ahead and take the larger bed," he said. "I would rather be in the little one. After all, there are two of you and I am by myself. That way, I won't be disturbing your sleep when I come home."

So the matter was considered settled. When the person on the smaller bed came to the bigger one on occasion, the person there did not really object. The territorial boundary was, after all, not so clearly defined. But from the time his wife took her new post on the larger bed, he on the small one had even fewer opportunities to invade. Just think about it: Everyone at her job had to sign in by the start of the work day at eight. The list was taken away after fifteen minutes. Tardiness was duly recorded; salary was deducted from occasional transgressors, demerits given to habitual ones. No matter what, therefore, she had to be there on time each morning.

To make sure, she was up no later than six, getting dressed, dressing Peipei, eating breakfast, fixing her husband's lunch, and getting Peipei to nursery school—all before getting herself to work. Were she like those so-called modern young ladies of Shanghai, just combing her hair and washing her face in the morning would take as much as three hours. Then again, the distance from her house to her office was considerable. When the tram or bus became overly crowded on occasion, she would have to get a rickshaw. Even then she might run into traffic jams on the way. The pressure on her was quite extreme.

There were days when Shen Xiaoyin was up a little after five. At that hour in the winter, the sky would not even have brightened and she would have to turn on the lights. Sometimes Ling Zhuoru would already be home. But he was nothing but a bookworm, hardly any help. Sometimes he would already be asleep by the time his wife got up. She would tiptoe around, not daring to speak above a whisper, concerned that her husband not be disturbed. She knew that he would be exhausted from a night of hard work. Peipei would be stopped short in her singing with a "Hush! Don't wake your father!"

Ling Zhuoru came home early from the newspaper one day, at about four in the morning. It was at the onset of winter, around the end of the tenth lunar month, when the air had gotten more and more nippy. Having been out in the cold night wind, he was inevitably a bit stiff and numb. He had a key to the back door and usually let himself in that way after tiptoeing lightly up the stairs to his apartment on the third floor.

The heater was not lit. But coming in from the wintry blasts outside, he could immediately feel a flow of warm air caressing his cheeks and his limbs. A bulb of just ten lumens was turned on in the room, but to him everything appeared exceptionally bright. He let out a breath. Back now in his happy little nest, he seemed to have purged what he had just been writing about—the Soviet-American cold war, the atrocities of the hot struggle between Nationalists and Communists—from the recesses of his mind.

His wife, he saw, was sleeping with the covers over her face, a mass of wavy hair laid out like loose clouds on the snow-white pillow. In her arms she held Peipei tightly; Peipei, her cheeks red as apples, hugged her mother around the neck, her head nestled into a space next to her mother's. He could not restrain himself from lightly kissing his wife's hair, and then Peipei's face. Neither of them awoke. His wife merely turned her head ever so slightly, and Peipei pursed her lips; they were both fast asleep. He had an impulse to flip over the covers and join them. But to stick his icy body into their warm little world would surely startle them out of their sweet slumber. In less than an hour, they would have to be up. He'd better not disturb them.

He quietly took himself to the other bed. In almost no time, he could hear Peipei's high-pitched chatter even as he was drifting off. His wife, too, must already be up and about. Peipei left her bed and was about to go visit her father when her mother stopped her with "Don't wake your dad!" It wasn't long before the room fell silent and he sensed that they'd both left.

By the time Ling Zhuoru woke up, it was already past noon. At about two he had his midday meal, with Goldie waiting on him and clearing away the dishes afterward. This was the daily routine. His leisure time followed, the usual time for him to rest, smoke, read, or write letters. It occurred to him that he had recently had very little opportunity to converse with his wife, and he deeply regretted the situation. Then a different thought came. Other loving couples have had to be separated, to spend a considerable amount of time apart from each other. But the two of them were living together, or at least appeared to be so. Those who had to be far away could communicate through letters; lovers who were apart could at least write love letters to each other. "Haven't my wife and I done that in the past?" he thought. "So why shouldn't I give it a try?" Then he picked up a pen and began to write:

My love!

When I returned in the wee hours this morning, I felt a warmth engulfing me as soon as I entered our home and thought about the preciousness of familial love. I came up to your bed, saw that you were fast asleep, and kissed your hair and Peipei's face. Funny, neither of you seemed to have felt it. I didn't want to disturb you, to stick my icy body under your warm covers. So I very quietly and stealthily crept into my own cold bed.

I don't dare hold any resentment toward you, or any jealousy toward Peipei. In my heart, I am simply sorry that I, a man, could not take care of you, but must make you run out at dawn, not to return before dusk. You've had to rush off no matter the weather or season, to sign in here and sign out there. And darling little Peipei has had to have her upbringing put into someone else's hands. This has saddened me. As the ancients put it, life's joyful fulfillment consists of "looking after one's wife on the one hand, and raising one's children on the other." This may seem to be common sense on first consideration. But as I think about it now, to be able to do that is to be truly blessed.

Your Zhuoru

He put the note in an envelope and wrote "Dear Xiaoyin" on it. Then he sealed it and put it on the small desk. "When the mistress gets home, let her see this letter," he told Goldie before leaving the house.

By the time Xiaoyin got home, darkness had already descended. The days being short in early winter, the streets were already lit up everywhere. She had to prepare dinner as soon as she got home. Peipei's eyes clouded over and her eyelids were beginning to droop right after she was fed. In the middle of this, Goldie suddenly remembered. "Ma'am! When the master was leaving, he said there was a letter for you on the desk."

"Where's it from?" She had Peipei in her arms and was speaking with divided attention.

"No. The master wrote it to you. I saw him write it," said Goldie.

Xiaoyin was a bit baffled. She quickly put Peipei down and ran over to the desk. Sure enough, there was the letter, placed squarely on the top. The "Dear Xiaoyin" on the envelope was unmistakably Zhuoru's handwriting. She became apprehensive. They lived in the same place, slept in the same room. Why had he written her a letter? Was it something important, something he didn't care to say to her face? Was that why he had written it? Her hands were trembling as she ripped open the envelope, took out the sheet inside, and read it through without taking a breath. Nothing important was in it. Was it maybe his way of venting his spleen after his affections were ignored? It was kind of funny, she thought, for him to get his bookish dander up like that. Why write some letter and scare the daylights out of her? Yet she could not help reading it over, and then over again. She folded it and put it back into the envelope, but then took it out to read it once more. All told, she read it seven times. She might have laughed at her husband's weird behavior at first, but the words in the letter somehow came to touch her heart—each, in fact, burning an indelible mark into it.

"What are you looking at, mommy?" Peipei was wagging her mother's knee back and forth.

"I'm reading your daddy's letter." She reached out to pick her up and place her on her knee.

"I want my daddy. I want daddy to carry Peipei!" the child shouted out.

It was not easy to calm her down and get her to fall asleep. After that, Shen Xiaoyin looked the letter over one more time before settling herself under an electric light and taking pen and paper to write a reply:

Zhuoru, my husband,

I am touched by the letter you left me. Because both of us try to fulfill all our duties at work, we are like Yin and Xing, the rival concubines of the Han Martial Emperor: We seem to avoid each other even though we live under the same roof. I am greatly saddened by this. When you returned in the wee hours, coming in from chilling winds of winter, Peipei and I were already in the sweet realm of deep slumber. Considering your cold and our warmth, I feel that we were really too selfish. By caressing us without waking us, you showed your selfless love, and I am moved to tears.

Your letter said that I live too hard a life, rushing off at dawn and not returning till dusk. The truth is my life has not been at all hard. We both do our jobs; our consciences are clear. We are good to each other. There is great happiness in all this. We are moreover still young, not dependent on anyone. So what is so bad about having to suffer through some difficult days? For Peipei's sake, I was somewhat concerned in the beginning. Now I see that the nursery school is a good one, and the people there all adore her. So I don't worry about that anymore. Do you want me to be some contented housewife, a woman who

spends her time in her room primping? I don't think you could ever hold me in
such low regard. You said that you don't dare become jealous of Peipei. What
a dope you can be! I could never take love away from you to give to Peipei. I
adore Peipei. I also adore you. Oh, husband of mine. When you say things like
this, you break my heart.

Your loving wife

She, too, slipped her letter into an envelope and placed it on the
desk—exactly where Ling Zhuoru had placed his, so that upon his
return, he could spot it at a glance as soon as he came near. Of course
there was a sense of absurdity in the idea of two people in the same
house corresponding in writing. Still, what they were conveying to
each other were words from their very souls.

As it was getting light, Ling Zhuoru came home. As usual he tip-
toed up the stairs and gingerly pushed open the door to enter. Concerned about waking his wife and daughter, he even shut the door
without making a sound and then removed his hat and overcoat.
Normally he would then proceed to warm his stomach with rice
gruel and various condiments laid out for him by his wife. Today,
however, he was immediately thinking of the letter on the desk. Had
she seen it?

Going over, he saw at a glance that the letter seemed to be resting
exactly where he'd put it, completely untouched. Hadn't his wife seen
it? He did charge Goldie to tell her about it as he was leaving. Then
again, she had perhaps read it already, then simply put it back in its
old place. Ling Zhuoru, it should be explained, was a little near-
sighted. Also, he and his wife had used identical envelopes. So it
wasn't until he held the envelope in his hands to examine it that he realized she had written back to him.

His wife's written words comforted Ling Zhuoru greatly. He downed
his rice gruel and, as usual, went over to the other bed to gaze down
at his sleeping family before turning in himself. What an overgrown

child he had been! How ludicrous, to contend with his daughter for his wife's affections! At that moment, however, his smile was one of happiness, with no trace of irony whatsoever.

Because they barely met face to face in the mornings or evenings, the two of them wrote to each other regularly. Even though the exchange of letters did not occur every day, they relied on pen and ink to convey their thoughts, to pose questions, and to ask after each other. That desk became for them a kind of post office, and young Goldie their official messenger.

What did they write about in these letters? Did they simply dwell on matters romantic? While the letters could have been gathered together and edited into a book of love, there weren't all that many romantic things to say. Since the two were a family, they had to write about different domestic matters, especially at a time of increasing economic pressures in their daily lives. If in the past a man could just rely on his wife to run the household, he could hardly do so at present. The rising price of rice had brought banner headlines in the economic section of the newspaper. And there was no denying the general concern over the inability to get rationed coal.

The problem of having to queue up to buy rice brought on another exchange of letters between them. Ling Zhuoru's job at the newspaper entitled him to rice rations. But the allotment was very small. Delivery, moreover, was regularly postponed, so that a long time would go by before he could get what was coming. The rice they had was just about gone. However clever she might be, his wife could not fix meals without the staple. She knew a place that sold rice, five *sheng* per customer, and was thinking of taking off work the following morning to get in line.

When Goldie informed Ling Zhuoru of this, he wrote a letter to tell her to stop. His general opinion was that getting into an interminable line of jostling people would be too hard on her. He had seen many fragile young women sandwiched between men in yellow uniforms who might be soldiers. The men deliberately pushed against them, so tightly that they could hardly breathe. Whoever would be on your back would likely take the opportunity to "feast on your bean curd" as the Shanghainese say—sniffing at your hair with his nose and snuggling against your neck. What's more, you could still come home empty-handed, without a grain of rice to show for the good many hours you spent in line. That often happened.

His wife's response was also very reasonable. In these times, it was all but impossible to buy rice even if they had the cash; their money, moreover, was limited. At the moment, the rice in their house was nearly gone, and she was anxious about having to fix meals without it. The cafeteria at work had already closed down owing to its inability to purchase rice or meat. A man from the office who usually ate lunch in restaurants had gone out the day before and, after walking several blocks, could not find a single one open. All had posted a sign on the door saying Temporary Stoppage of Business Due to Stove Repairs. Since she couldn't get home during the day, she had to carry her lunch to work and heat it up on the company's stove. Actually, they could have Goldie get in that line, but that could end up as disastrously as when the cartoon character San Mao tried to purchase rice that way.

But the arguments did not change Ling Zhuoru's mind: He did not want her to try to buy rice. With a bit of humor, he reiterated his opinion:

The poet Tao Yuanming refused to bend his back and bow down for a job paying five dou of rice, and posterity has admired him for this. For only a tenth as much, you would stand up straight and stiff for several hours. Even though you won't have to bend over, you will surely be complaining about your aching back when you get home. Confucius himself had to go without meals when he was in the state of Chen, but he didn't die of starvation. We surely won't have to worry about eating regularly. We are not particular about our food. A small amount of rice like that can be gotten on loan from my colleagues. I have long ago written out the request. So please. Forget your idea.

Meanwhile, his wife happened to hear about a pregnant young woman in the neighborhood who suffered a miscarriage from having been squeezed so hard standing in a rice line. There was also the story of the soldier trying to maintain order in the same situation, who ended up shooting and killing a destitute woman. Since her husband could manage to borrow the rice, she ought not to endanger herself and give him another cause for worry. So she gave up her plan.

Before long, a curfew was imposed on the district, though it hardly affected the two of them. From eleven at night to six in the morning, all street traffic was cut off. Ling Zhuoru had to be at work at 6 P.M. and did not start for home until the sun was about to come up. Whenever he finished work early, say by 4 or 5 A.M., he had a pass from the office to get home. It hardly mattered if no transportation was available right away, since it would be only an hour or so before the curfew was lifted. It was not much bother to have to wait till after six.

His wife was not even up sometimes when he got home at six. Or else, she would be running about getting Peipei dressed, combing her hair, and washing her face, before dressing herself and doing all the morning chores. What little time together they could salvage was fleeting and precious. As she scurried about taking care of this and that, they could not say much to each other. So the two of them continued to wield the pen as before, to exchange letters as before, to communicate their feelings through their family post office as before.

Good news did arrive, in spite of everything. The editor in chief of the *Times* became concerned for Ling Zhuoru, thinking that the unrelieved nocturnal work was too hard on him. But newspapers in China followed the inhumane policy of publishing on Sundays. In order to give Zhuoru some relief and to soothe his spirits, Associate Editor Li, who had no family living with him and who usually slept in the office, was asked to stand in for him every Saturday night. This would allow him to get home early enough to have a weekend break.

Now no matter what else, they no longer needed to write to each other on Sundays. Saturday nights would become honeymoons, each moment treasured and appreciated.

Even though Ling Zhuoru went to the office on Saturday afternoon, he got home between nine and ten at night, before the curfew. Since Shen Xiaoyin was off work the next day and Peipei was not going to the nursery, they could all sleep in in the morning. Each time her mother had urged her to get to bed, Peipei had stubbornly refused: "No! Wait till daddy gets home!" He now came in with expected sweets as well as other goodies, so that she was not disappointed. Then he took her in his arms and bounced her on his knee, enjoying a father-and-daughter time together.

For this day, the smaller bed had been moved to a different position, away from the now reopened territory of the larger one. Since it had gotten past Peipei's bedtime, Ling Zhuoru asked his wife to go on to bed with her. He was used to staying up all night; he would not be able to fall asleep much before twelve. He would use the quiet time to read and write something.

By the time the little clock struck midnight, Peipei had fallen into a deep sleep, and his wife was about to join her. Ling Zhuoru changed and got ready to turn in. As he eased himself into the gentle warmth of the bedding, an intoxicating sweetness seemed to overwhelm him. "We are far luckier than the stars Aquila and Vega, the Cowherd and the Weaving Maid," he told his wife as he embraced her. "They only get to cross the Milky Way and be together once a year. For us, it's once a week. Aren't we much better off?"

"Shhh!" his wife warned as she entwined a tender arm around him. "Don't wake Peipei up!"

It was only on Saturday night, however, that they could enjoy such connubial bliss. All other days, they still communicated by writing. Their letters, put together, now made a huge pile. None were ever discarded. Not only were they all kept in a cardboard box, but each one was also numbered at the top. Even though the letters required no stamps and were not marked as registered or express, they had taken up a considerable amount of stationery.

One day Ling Zhuoru counted all of them. There were more than a hundred. The two had said everything to each other in those letters. Some of them were wordy, others terse; some melancholy, others joyful. Some dealt with major events in the world, others with personal matters suitable for the privacy of home or bedroom. There was every variety.

"These hundred-some letters could make up a book about this period of our lives," said Ling Zhuoru, smiling.

"A book? What shall we call it?" said his wife, smiling back.

"Ah, I've got it," said Ling. "We can entitle it 'So Near, So Far.' " That would be perfect. You and I are but a foot away from each other, but there were times we might have been a world apart. That's why these letters exist. Interesting, don't you agree?"

Promptly, he wrote down four words on the cover of the box: So Near, So Far.

— *1949*

III. Gallantry

. . . .

IF "SATURDAY" STORIES as a whole were considered "old-style" in their heyday, those dealing with martial gallantry—*wuxia*—show us most clearly why. For, to a greater extent than all the others, *wuxia* stories follow the old formula of making the wildest fantasies seem credible by surrounding them with recognizable fact. The stories, including the three collected here, greatly exaggerate the capabilities of the martial arts, now displayed through cinematic magic in "kung fu" films: Combatants in a sword fight can leap at will to the top of a mast; a person can fly with the wind and transport people and goods as he does so; a young woman can scamper over rooftops and, undetected, enter and exit the heavily guarded house of a fierce warlord. But even in the 1920s, when the three selections here were published, most Chinese readers did not question these feats any more than their grandparents did the similar feats in the narrative *Sanxia wuyi* (Three heroes and five gallants),[1] published in 1879 and usually pointed to as the immediate predecessor for the vernacular *wuxia* fiction that followed.

Two major reasons for this come quickly to mind. Most obviously, because fiction in China originated with the interaction of fantasy and fact, *wuxia* stories can be regarded as one fairly natural result. The martial arts do extend human physical capabilities to fantastic lengths. If practitioners are not really superhuman, they are at least extraordinary. While there is no evidence any of them levitate, much less fly, real martial artists have been known, for example, to smash bricks with their bare hands. It is stretching the imagination only slightly to depict the best of them as people who *can* fly, or at least leap to the top of a building or a mast with a single bound. Remember here that the Chinese reader is seeking recreation and not really factual or philosophical truth. Then again, these stories feature relatively realistic accounting of time and place, in direct contrast with a true fantasy such as the Ming dynasty's *Xiyou ji* (Monkey), which portrays a humanoid Monkey who is able to traverse "a hundred and eight thousand leagues" with a single leap and who is sealed under the Mountain of Five Elements for five hundred years.[2] Unlike the *Xiyou ji,* all three of the *wuxia* stories collected here account for the passing of time in realistic terms. In "The Windmaster," the seventeen years Mengxiang spends away from home is carefully calculated, as are the days Gongmei, in "Thistle Gate," spends traveling and in the robbers' lair and Zhu Zhenyue, in the excerpt from *Marvelous Gallants,* spends on the river. Especially in Zhu Zhenyue's case, the calculations are coordinated with the actual time it would take to go from Xi'an to Changde by land and water. Without doubt, the mention of the specific time (the Xianfeng period of the Qing dynasty) and the actual places (Whitefish Cliff on the edge of Hunan province, White Horse Pass near Changde) where the events occur clearly increases the credibility that is one of the story's chief concerns.

This increase is necessary, since the fantasy in *wuxia* stories go well beyond the exaggerated abilities of the heroes. Both the Windmaster and the unnamed woman in "Thistle Gate," for example, have secluded and well-furnished safe houses that should tax our credulity as much as they vicariously fulfill our desires. The ability to present fantasy in realistic or factual terms was what made the *Sanxia wuyi* so popular in premodern China. The stories here, having clearly evolved from the tradition the *Sanxia wuyi* established, may appear too fantastic to suit modern tastes. The undiminished popularity of "kung fu" novels and movies in modernized countries around the world—including the United States—should assure us, on the other hand, that the tradition is alive and well even among increasingly skeptical and technologized readers.

Notes

1. For a description of this work in English, see Lu Hsun (Lu Xun), *A Brief History of Chinese Fiction,* trans. Yang Hsien-yi (Yang Xianyi) and Gladys Yang (Beijing: Foreign Languages Press, 1964), pp. 360–364. See also James J. Y. Liu, *The Chinese Knight-Errant* (Chicago: University of Chicago Press, 1967), pp. 117–120.

2. See Arthur Waley, trans., *Monkey* (New York: Grove Press, Inc., 1958), pp. 75–84. See also the translation by Anthony C. Yu, *The Journey to the West,* vol. 1 (Chicago: University of Chicago Press, 1977), p. 173–175.

On the Road to Thistle Gate

. . . .

Cheng Danlu

A caravan of four or five mule wagons hurrying along on the road to Thistle Gate had just reached a desolate stretch. The round red sun was disappearing into the bowels of the western hills, where darkening woods dominated the landscape. The trees were lined up on either side of the travelers, as if to greet them and send them on their way. In the last wagon sat a young student, impatiently asking his driver whether they would reach the station on time.

"We won't make it," the mule driver said after looking down the road a piece.

"What are we to do, then?" The student was full of anxiety.

"No problem about that," said the driver. "If we don't get there, we can spend the night in a village. There are four wagons ahead of us. If they stop, then we stop; if they want to rest for the night, then we'll rest for the night. With so many people along, what have we got to be afraid of?"

"When will we be getting to Thistle County, then?"

"Another ten miles or so, you'll be able to see the marketplace. You can count on getting to Thistle Town safe and sound sometime tomorrow morning."

"How is it that we still have that far to go?" mumbled the student to himself. "By my calculations, we should've gotten there today at the latest. God in heaven, you've got to make it possible for my father and me to see each other again."

Just then they heard a jangling of bells, followed by a whoosh. An arrow shot out from among the trees, spun about, and dropped to the ground. All the drivers, having seen this before, knew that highwaymen were about to arrive. They simply followed the long-standing procedure and one after the other, jumped down to hide themselves behind their vehicles. Then came the roar of hoofbeats as four horses, each with a strapping rider, flashed to the scene like the wind, galloping around the now immobile caravan. The occupants of the first three wagons were experienced traders who knew what to do. Hearing the bells, they immediately scrambled down from their seats, then stood respectfully to the left of the shafts, making not a sound. The valuable cargo in the wagons was under the care of a professional armed escort. The man was not really blessed with earthshaking martial prowess; the firm he worked for simply had an "exchange agreement" with the chief of the brigands. When the escort encountered them, he'd simply flash them a secret signal, and they would not proceed with the robbery. Whenever these highwaymen happened to pass by the firm and be short of travel expenses, the firm would play host and provide them proper hospitality, including bountiful banquets. At their departure, they would receive money for the road.

Let us not digress, however, but get back to the mounted robbers. As they were galloping about, the escort was already passing them the signal, so that the three front wagons were left untouched. In the fourth wagon sat a middle-aged man who had never before ventured far from home. Because of his total inexperience, he did not alight from his vehicle beforehand. Only when the robbers were upon them did he think of doing so. He had been sitting shoeless, his legs folded. As he was getting out of his seat, he reached down with one hand to fetch his shoes, an action that violated a rule of the road. In less time than it takes to tell it, a shot rang out and he tumbled backwards; for upon seeing him reach down, one of the robbers fired first, assuming that the man was grabbing for a pistol. The bullet entered the man's chest and was immediately fatal. After this regrettable happening, his money and possessions were taken.

Now, the one occupying the fifth wagon was the aforementioned student; he could only tremble in fear, with no idea of what to do. The robbers seized him, tied his hands behind his back, and put a kerchief over his eyes. Thus restrained, the student could only let his captors do with him as they wished. They lifted him up onto a mount, and he became a veritable blind man on a sightless horse, oblivious of his destination. The crunching of fallen leaves as the hooves trampled them suggested to him that they were entering the forest. The group went on for an hour or so before the galloping stopped. Someone took him down from the saddle, then led him inside an entrance so low he felt he would bump his forehead if he walked standing straight up. Someone told him to duck, and he lowered his head as they started on a long, winding path. Only when he was told to do so did he dare straighten up. They went on another ten paces or so before someone shouted "Stop!" Still blindfolded, he was anxious and depressed. He did not know where he was and thought he must be in the lair of fierce outlaws, where prospects for a happy outcome would be extremely slim. Who would have guessed how completely wrong he was? The melodious sounds of female voices flooded his ears. "Hey, look!" someone said. "This young man's not at all bad looking. Our mistress may be impressed when she sees this one." Said another, "Our mistress has unforgiving standards. We can't count the attractive men she's already looked over. Not a one has managed to catch her eye. I'm afraid Rolling Dragon and Climbing Tiger have again put out a lot of effort for nothing."

All the talk about "our mistress" made the student fear he'd been taken to some perverse nunnery where he'd be a pawn in such sexual shenanigans as described in the story "Jade Dragonfly." The thought made him shudder even though it was not cold. As he stood there quite unable to control his trembling, he heard someone near him whisper, "Hush! The mistress is coming!" Instantly, everyone fell silent. The only sound was the *clip-clop* of leather soles approaching them from an adjoining room. No question, it had to be the mistress.

Ooh! How utterly amazing! The place turned out to be neither robber's lair nor nunnery. Rather, it was a three-room suite with extraordinarily sparkling adornments. Oil lamps hung from the ceiling, sending forth light in all directions. Under their glow, the smile of the beautiful woman there appeared even more fresh and alluring. Her eyebrows seemed to bend down like willow branches in the spring. She looked older than eighteen but just a bit younger than twenty. She was dressed like one of those fashionable models on a calendar, with a form-fitting embroidered jacket, a short skirt, and long silk stockings. She leaned back on the sofa with her legs crossed to one side; her patent-leather high-heels sparkled in the lamplight. At her side were four maids-in-waiting, each different in size and shape, all uncommonly attractive. How, oh how, had he gotten into someone's boudoir? By now, of course, the kerchief over the student's eyes had been removed. He looked around without seeing signs of the highwaymen who had abducted him. He saw only the people and objects described above. How could he stop from marveling?

"Why aren't you on your knees before the mistress?" one of the maids shouted at him. "Don't just stand there craning your neck at everything!" Only then did the student realize that the beautiful woman was not just the head of the household but the chief of the robbers. He immediately knelt down.

"Ma'am, I beg you to take pity on my misfortune, and, out of respect for Heaven's sustenance of all life, release me to rejoin my loved ones," he said, as tears rolled down his cheeks.

The beautiful woman snickered. "This boy has a way with words. More than likely, he's from an educated family." She ordered the maids to help him to his feet and untie his hands. Indicating a chair, she told him to sit down. Then she directed her bewitching eyes on his face until he lowered his head in embarrassment. "From your accent, you must be from the south," she said. "What's your name? What made you rush all the way here? Are you trying to get into the government bureaucracy? Rather than that, you might as well aspire to be a robber, because our standards are much higher than those for officials."

The student bowed down to her. "I'm a native of Shanyin in Zhejiang. My family name is Xu. I am called Gongmei. All along, I have been studying in Nanjing. It's not because I want to be an official that I was headed to Thistle County. It's because my father is an administrative official there."

"So your dad's an official," the woman interrupted, before he could finish. "Why does he bother with a job that brings about so much evil? Better he be a robber, so he could do some good and bolster his karma for his next life." She flashed him a look and a smile as she spoke, revealing her straight white teeth. Gongmei was too frightened to respond. Just then, a young manservant came in to ask that the mistress attend to some business outside. "Take good care of Mr. Xu," the woman told the maids as she departed.

That casual order was taken very seriously. The maids brought tea and snacks and attended to the student's every need. They also whispered back and forth about how truly fortunate Mr. Xu was to have caught the mistress's eye. To become consort in that place would be even more glorious than to be named the top scholar at the national examinations! For his part, Gongmei could only knit his eyebrows, unable to tell anyone of all that troubled him. He did privately ask one of the maids the mistress' name and how a fine woman like her came to her present circumstances. The maid shot him a look of disgust. "So you think what we do is low-class? Actually, there's no occupation that's superior. At the very least, it's much better than working for the government, like your father! As for my mistress's name, I shan't reveal it to you just now. In a while, when she gets back in here and decides she really does like you, she'll be telling you herself. I needn't tell you now."

"The mistress is no pushover," another maid advised him. "Those who do as she wishes will live; anyone who opposes her will die. She considers all that she's put together here sacred. In a while, when she finishes her business and comes back to talk with you, you'll have to go along with how she feels. Tell her that every other occupation in the world is inferior to hers. If what you say pleases her, it'll be your great good fortune."

Even as they were speaking, the beautiful woman reentered the room, having settled whatever had caused the interruption. She was all smiles as she spoke to Gongmei. "Let me tell you, no business is more fairly disposed of than mine. A while ago, one of my men killed a traveler. This violated one of our laws. We take money and goods from those who pass our way, but the first law is not to take lives. An exception is made only when someone opens fire on us in opposition. Then we won't hesitate to shoot him dead. Even though this particular killing was not so much intentional as it was the result of a misunderstanding, the person involved is nevertheless partially culpable. This very night, I've sent someone to detain Climbing Tiger on White Cloud Mountain. A number of our people spoke up on his behalf. But I adhered to principle and acted according to the letter of the law, which does not allow for personal sentiments. You should know, Mr. Xu, that laws among outlaws are especially sacred and inviolable. We are not like those corrupt officials in the world who either break or manipulate laws for gain. Does your dad do anything like that, Mr. Xu? You ought to be able to say."

At the the mention of his father, Gongmei could not help breaking into loud sobs. "Why are you crying like that?" the woman hastened to ask. It was then that Gongmei tearfully related the details of why he had embarked on his long journey, a journey that put him on that road to Thistle Gate.

Xu Jinglian had been the magistrate of Thistle County for a good number of years. A Provincial Graduate, he had labored in government circles without giving up his intellectual pursuits. The people under him benefited from his administration; they all agreed that he was an honest official. Habitually inclined toward kindliness, it was all but inevitable that he be more of a bookworm than an astute administrator. Then again, it was the warlord period, a time when those in charge of the military regularly sent out official directives to the magistrate's yamen to "borrow" pay or provisions for their troops. Fawning, obsequious officials would take the directives as opportunities to squeeze the fat out of the hides of the common people. The greater part of what they collected went to the warlords, while they padded their own pockets from the small amounts left over. Jinglian alone appeared to be poisoned by ethical concepts. He would rather oppose the warlords than harm those in his charge. Never mind that directives for provisions fell on him like snowflakes. He would only respond with words of conscience that were out of step with the times: "The people are destitute. How can I demand anything from them? The storehouses are empty as well. To borrow goods from them is even less possible. I only inform you, therefore, that I can supply nothing on your list."

How can an answer like this not provoke the ire of those warlords above him? One of them, the powerful General Zang, pounded his desk at Xu Jinglian during an audience. "Because you did nothing about the provisions, you have failed our troops," he shouted. "What do you think your punishment should be?"

Jinglian did not flinch. "My responsibility is to the people," he replied. "I do not deal with military matters."

This made General Zang furious. "You don't think I can 'deal' with you, then?" he shouted. Immediately, he summoned his guards, who clapped chains on Jinglian and hauled him off to prison that very day. Then he passed Jinglian's seal of office to a military officer. Eager to follow his superior's wishes, the latter trumped up every imaginable charge. He accused Jinglian of overspending five thousand dollars of public funds and proposed that he be prosecuted for repayment in order to replenish the public coffers. Alas for Jinglian! Overwhelmed by his incarceration and with nowhere to turn for help, he was certain that death awaited him. His wife wept her heart out as she wrote a letter to inform their son Gongmei, telling him to hurry to Thistle Gate and see about saving his father. A student in Nanjing at the time, Gongmei was overcome by the news and nearly fainted away. But the matter required immediate attention. He dared not dally before setting out. Hurrying to the Hankou Station in the eastern sector of the city, he boarded an express train for Tong County. There he hired a mule wagon bound for Thistle Gate, never expecting to be waylaid that very evening. His own life, he allowed, was not worth much. How, on the other hand, could he not weep at the prospect of never again seeing his father?

The foregoing was related in Gongmei's words. The account was in fits and starts, interrupted here and there by sobs. It should have been divided into little sections, each separated by ellipses to indicate teardrops. That would only be appropriate, given the lachrymose style of the narration. Your author, however, has decided for the sake of convenience to write down everything in the conventional manner, to delete all those little dots, which would have taken up too much space on the page.

The beautiful woman silently mulled over all that had been said to her. "What, in your opinion, ought to be done now?" she coolly inquired of Gongmei.

"Ever since I received the news, I have been in a dither," he answered. "I just want to grow wings and fly straightaway to Thistle Gate. I hope the mistress will take pity and let me go, so that I can be reunited with my loved ones."

"Xu Gongmei, you can just forget about that!" the woman said coldly, her expression growing stern. "You can come to this place, but you will never be allowed to leave it. We won't be mistreating you here."

"But my father is imprisoned. He might not survive another day," Gongmei said as he began weeping once more. "How can I just stay put here?"

The woman guffawed. "You seem to be a person with ability. You ought to act like a grown man. Why wallow in such naïveté? When your dad wanted to become an official, he also chose to bring this kind of trouble down on his own head. Even if you hurried through the night to Thistle Gate, you'd be getting there empty-handed. Without the five thousand dollars to pay the authorities, you'd never get him out of prison. We now live in a modern world, where everyone has equal rights. If your dad's done something wrong, you can always raise an army to try and rescue him. If you're not going to do that, you'd actually be doing him a favor staying here. Visiting him would bring on nothing but frustration. Leave him alone in that prison there. You can be an outlaw here. If you're not up to robbing anyone, I won't ask you to. All you have to do is keep me company in this place. Wouldn't that suit you just fine?"

Gongmei became desperate. "Why be someone's son when you won't even try to help when he's in trouble?" he said. "All my years of study have just taught me to sacrifice myself for my father. I know nothing about raising any army to rescue him."

"The phrase 'to rescue,' as applied to one's father, is an invention of you proponents of new learning. How can you be studying for so long without comprehending the new schools of thought?" The woman was chuckling again.

"In my heart, I only follow the old morality," said Gongmei seriously. "I don't recognize any 'new schools of thought.'"

This appeared to anger the woman. "How can you be such an ingrate?" she said. "You live if you follow what I say. Otherwise, you die!"

By this time, Gongmei had already made up his mind not to be concerned about his own life. Death would release his soul, to fly freely to join his imprisoned father. How much better that would be than to be detained here, to suffer the sneers of this female brigand! He therefore responded with great resolve. "If the mistress wants to release me, then please do so. Otherwise, just shoot me dead. Not on your life will I agree to remain here as your companion!"

The woman lifted her willow eyebrows. Her almond eyes were opened wide. In an instant, a gleaming blade was in her hand. Gongmei trembled but shut his eyes tight and stretched out his neck to receive the blow. Her angry words filled his ears: "Xu Gongmei! Say 'No!' three times to my face if you dare. By the third 'No!' I will be cutting you in two!"

Gongmei was indeed hoping for a quick death. So, standing before the woman with his eyes shut and his head held high, he shouted out "No! No! No!" After the third "No!" he crumpled to the floor. But even though he was down, he was not cut.

THE POWERFUL GENERAL Zang Jing had slept well. He was just about to rouse himself when he saw the cold gleam of a dagger stuck into his pillow. The shock he suffered could not be exaggerated. "Oh no! Oh no!" he blurted out as he pushed at the concubine lying by his side. "Someone's been here to assassinate me!"

Still sleepy, the concubine rubbed her eyes, then also caught sight of the half-buried blade. Her hand went quickly to her powdered neck but felt no puncture hole. Only then did she cry out in tearful hysteria: "Somebody come catch the assassin!"

The general managed to take some control of the situation and ordered the concubine to quiet down. Then the maidservants, hearing the weepy commotion, came together to rap on the door and ask what the matter was. "Nothing," General Zang told them. "Your mistress had a nightmare, nothing more. Everything's fine now." Thus assured, the servants returned to their quarters.

Inside the room, the general and his concubine scrambled out of bed and looked everywhere. They found nary a trace of forced entry;

nothing was missing. The windows remained bolted up, with the exception of two shutters on the one facing west, the bronze lock to which was left open. The intruder must have entered and exited from there. The ability of the person to travel on rooftops and over walls was indeed frightening. They then removed the dagger from where it was stuck three inches deep into the lacquered wooden pillow. What if it had been into someone's head or neck, instead? The act was clearly a warning, but about what? As General Zang was putting the dagger down, the concubine's eyes fell on something red sticking out from beneath the pillow. She pulled it out and saw that it was a visitor's card. Not knowing how to read, she handed it to the general. As he looked it over, Zang Jing's tongue stuck out an inch and a half from his mouth and remained that way for a full half-minute. What could have been on the card? Merely a little jingle in four-syllable lines:

Zang, be not slow:
Let the man go.
My cold blade but
Your pillow cut.
Unless you heed,
Your neck will bleed.
My crystal sight,
You ought not slight.

Strange as it seemed, General Zang the almighty—a man who could say no to the president himself, who would dismiss an order from the commander-in-chief with a wave of his hand—was utterly overcome by a tiny card with those thirty-two syllables. Straightaway, he issued an order to set the prisoner Xu Jinglian free. He even took the time to proffer his personal good wishes, along with copious words of apology.

Having thus escaped death, Jinglian returned home to his wife. The couple hugged each other and wept with joy. Both had been certain that Zang Jing was a monster who would send anyone to his death without batting an eye. How in the world could Jinglian have emerged unscathed after falling into his clutches? "Is it possible that Commander Mo did not agree with him, thinking that he acted too harshly?" said his wife.

"Not a chance," said Jinglian. "The commander's a man of limited ability. The general wouldn't give him the time of day."

"Then perhaps the governor did not approve of what he did, taking it as an abuse of power."

"That's even less likely," said Jinglian. "The governor's the general's lackey. Anything the general wants, the governor would never dare object to."

As they were thus deliberating, a red card suddenly fluttered down into the garden. Greatly startled, Jinglian hurried over to retrieve it. The two of them read it together, shoulder to shoulder. The ink on it was hardly dry. This is what it said:

The one who has rescued you is none other than your son. Since the vicissitudes of officialdom are so unpredictable, you need to make plans to return home. Tomorrow, father and son can rendezvous at the Prosperity Hotel ten miles from Thistle Gate. Everything will be made clear to you at that time.

The extraordinary missive seemed really to have come down from heaven. No one was in the garden at the time; they heard no sound from the rooftop. How could the couple have any idea who the sender might have been? After his recent sufferings, Jinglian had quietly lost all taste for officialdom. Fortunately, his possessions were few. So were his servants. He could therefore pack up quickly for his journey home. The very next morning, he rented several mule wagons. Amid the clopping of hooves and the rumbling of wheels, they, too, became travelers on the road out of Thistle Gate.

A dozen miles beyond the city, they stopped for the evening at the Prosperity Hotel. Even before Jinglian and his wife alighted from their mule wagon, they saw their son Gongmei waiting for them at the entrance. The reunion was all the more joyous because it had seemed so impossible. They entered their room to talk privately, filling each other in on the details of their separation. They laughed and they cried, as their encounter was filled with the joy and sorrow which trigger both laughter and tears. They talked together for perhaps two hours.

Your author, however, will not expend the ink to repeat what has already been elaborated on. He'll simply proceed to tell about Gongmei, who had fallen to the floor and who had not known the length of time he had remained in his comatose state. When he came to and opened his eyes, he found himself in a room that was furnished with great care, with no hint of dust anywhere. Next to his bed sat a maidservant with dangling curls. As she stared at him, she could not stop from chuckling. Noticing that the morning sun was filling half the window as he scrambled quickly to his feet, Gongmei muttered in great surprise, "How strange! How very strange! Haven't I been killed?"

The maidservant could not suppress a guffaw. "Our mistress would never be willing to let you die. She even had the idea of rescuing your whole family. Having gotten your father out of prison, she's now making it possible for all of you to have a reunion."

"If she meant to do all that," asked Gongmei, "why did she brandish her sword and threaten to kill me?"

"She was just toying with you. She never had any intention of taking your life," said the maid. "While you were keeping your eyes shut, waiting to die, she waved a drug-soaked cloth under your nose. That's what knocked you out and made you fall to the floor. She then had someone help you into this room. While you were still unconscious, she changed into a peasant costume and did everything to free your father from prison."

"Why did she knock me out beforehand, if she'd intended to do the right thing for my father?" Gongmei wanted to know.

"That was also part of the plan," said the maid. "She wanted you to be surprised when you came to, so as to recognize her true feelings for you. The entire conversation with you last night was a test, to see whether you were truly intent on saving your father. After watching you fall down, she sighed again and again. 'Only a man like this is worth caring about,' she was saying. 'If I don't help him out, who will?' "

Gongmei was still befuddled, when suddenly a shadow flitted across the whitewashed wall. The beautiful woman from last night landed on the floor from the roof, much like a leaf floating to the ground from a tree in the garden, making only the slightest of sounds. Indeed she had a different appearance. Her hair was disheveled, her clothing homespun. She had the look of a woman from a country village. She entered the room and smiled at Gongmei. "Don't you look down your nose at us outlaws," she said to him. "How many cold-blooded animals are out there in the world? Compared to them, we have the warmest of hearts. So fine, fine. Tomorrow afternoon, you and your loved ones will be reunited." Gongmei couldn't wait to ask how this was to come about. The woman took the time to rest and eat before slowly telling him all that had transpired.

She had prepared her two messages even before setting out. Shielded by the descending darkness, she deliberately took the byways and footpaths. When she got to Thistle Town, the gates to the city wall were still open, and she was able to slip inside. As the night went on and things quieted down, she utilized her ability to scramble on rooftops to get quickly to General Zang's house. There she stuck her dagger into the mandarin-duck pillow while slipping her prepared message under it. The couple in bed remained fast asleep, totally unaware of anything happening. After that, she jumped out of the window and onto the roof, remembering to pull the shutters to, so that there would be no trace of disturbance. The following morning, she remained near the prison house to make sure that Xu Jinglian had indeed been released before hurrying to where his family was. Still undetected, she sprung to the roof, crouching down along the ridge to await his homecoming. It was soon afterward that she sent the second message fluttering down. With her tasks accomplished, she leaped down before she could be noticed and hurried back to her own place. When she arrived, she had enough energy left to get up quietly onto her own roof and make her grand entrance.

Gongmei was overwhelmed by the account. He was on his knees in an instant, kowtowing in gratitude for all she had done. She personally helped him to his feet, then ordered a banquet set in his honor. Their conversation flowed from ancient history to contemporary concerns as they ate and drank. He realized that the woman was a rare individual, as accomplished in book learning as she was in martial arts. He wanted to know her name and how she came to be an outlaw. But to all his inquiries, she responded only with a smile. "Why do you persist with your questions?" she asked as he continued to press for answers.

"I want to see how I can repay you in the future," was Gongmei's answer.

"I came to my present state because I was forced to by circumstances," she said with a trace of pain. "I can only tell you that it's still too early to reveal my name and background. If, indeed, you appreciate what I have done for you, then wait quietly for me in your hometown. I should be able to settle scores with a great enemy within a year. After that, I will go to Shanyin to look for you, to share my life with you ever after. Are you willing for me to do that?"

"If all that can come to pass," said Gongmei, "it will be so fortuitous for me. How can I not be willing?"

Later, when they'd finished their meal, the woman ordered a couple of manservants to blindfold Gongmei once more before taking him outside; then he was put back on his horse. The blindfold was not removed until they were on the Guantang Highway. When they reached the Prosperity Hotel, everyone dismounted. His escorts returned his luggage and told him to spend the night there so that he could join his parents in the morning. They also guaranteed the fam-

ily's safety for the long journey home before galloping away. Gongmei stayed the night at the hotel. And at noon the following day, just
as he had been told, he met his parents there.

After all they had been through, the three were thus reunited. Gongmei helped his parents onto the mule wagon, which now left Thistle
Gate by the same road. How laden with grief their coming had been,
how joyful their departure!

—*1924*

The Windmaster

. . . .

Zhang Mingfei

When Liang Mengxian of Pu City was about twenty, he accompanied a tea merchant to Xinjiang on business. He was gone for three years before the merchant notified Mengxian's family by letter that he had run into a windstorm in the desert and disappeared. Inevitably, his mother and wife wept bitterly at the news, certain that he had died.

Now the desert was nothing but dust and sand for who knows how many hundreds of miles. Not only was there no sign of human life, there was not even water or greenery. The road the merchants usually took traversed its narrowest part, which was still over thirty or forty miles wide. To get across took at least a day. As the sand was soft and deep, footing was difficult. Any heavily loaded horse or mule cart would roll halfway back for each advance. Whenever the wind whipped up, the vehicles had to be linked together and drawn into a large circle, while the people and livestock had to hug the ground in order not to be swept away. When a windstorm was about to start up, those familiar with the area all seemed able to predict what would happen. Methods of forecasting were many. The simplest was to feel the temperature of the sand beneath your feet. Should that be going up, then the storm would be there within a half hour. Or if you encountered an unusual gust and saw the sand at a distance rise up to form a hill, then a gale would be upon you in a matter of seconds. For this reason many travelers, helpless after noticing the phenomenon, were hurled halfway up the sky, where they either died from asphyxiation right away or from the fall back to earth soon after. Even if they somehow survived, they were likely to succumb subsequently to hunger or thirst. Liang Mengxian's family concluded therefore that he had to be dead, even as they continued to hope against hope that he had somehow survived. This kind of immediate psychological reaction was natural. But then one day turned into two, two days into three. Before anyone knew it, nearly eighteen years had gone by.

Mengxian's mother, Madame Sheng, was then turning sixty and took the occasion of her birthday to arrange a wedding for Mengxian's son Jingcheng. Their house was packed with well-wishers and guests; almost everyone in the district was present. While they were drinking and feasting, a stranger suddenly came through the door asking where the old lady was. Everybody assumed he was there to tender birthday greetings. The person in charge of hosting the guests left his seat to thank him and invite him to join them at the head table. The man merely nodded, mumbled an inaudible response, and headed for the inner rooms. His host had no choice but to follow. Madame Sheng was exchanging toasts with several elderly women neighbors when the host burst in and announced in a loud voice, "A gentleman's here to give birthday greetings!" Madame Sheng could barely turn around before the man rushed over to her, got down on his knees to hug her around the legs, and called out "Mama!" Then he burst into tears. Everyone was startled. Recoiling from the shock, Madame Sheng managed to tell him in a trembling voice to stop crying. "Could you really be my boy Mengxian?"

"I am none other," sobbed the man as he looked up at her. "You probably don't recognize me anymore. I've been gone for all of eighteen years."

Madame Sheng brushed away her tears to scrutinize the man's face. She saw that it was worn out with age, its emaciation giving much greater prominence to the bones. The bloom of youth had long since departed. Still, the features were identical to those of a younger face she had known. Not daring to make up her mind right then, she told the man to get up. Then she asked her daughter-in-law, Madame He, to come forward, along with a few of the older neighbors.

By that time, the news had spread to all the guests, who now crowded into the room to gape. The man greeted the older neighbors one by one, recalling with them shared conversations and events of long ago. To a person, they believed he was Mengxian. Madame He kept silent for a long time, uncomfortable with the situation. Then she whispered into Madame Sheng's ear: "Don't you remember? There was a dark mole on Mengxian's chest, with hair growing out of it."

Thus reminded, Madame Sheng turned again to the man. "Your bearing and looks are indeed those of my son Mengxian," she said to him. "It's just that Mengxian has been gone for so long without any communication. For me to take you as my son even if you are not is a small matter. For my grandson to consider you his father by mistake would make us a laughingstock. I remember that my boy Mengxian had a mark on his person. So remove your upper garments and let me have a look."

The man then bared his chest. "You probably want to see the mole," he said as he pointed to it.

Tears flooded Madame Sheng's face. "My son," she wept. "Why haven't we seen you or had any letters from you for so long? Did you forget you still have a mother in the world?"

"How could your son ever forget his mother?" said Mengxian. "But for going on twenty years, I passed my days in the uninhabited valley of a desolate mountain. For as long as a year sometimes, I did not encounter another human being. So how could I have gotten any news to you?"

"Where on earth have you been?" Madame Sheng wanted to know.

"It's a very long story," said Mengxian.

"THE YEAR I WENT OFF, I took a shipment of tea over the desert in a caravan of fourteen mule carts. As we went along, I saw a hill of sand growing ever taller off in the northwest and knew that a windstorm was coming. So I linked up the carts and formed a circle with them as everyone threw themselves on the ground. Before we could blink, a whirlwind was upon us, showering down sand and rocks until we were half-buried. After the initial gust, everything appeared dark and gloomy as we began to scramble to our feet. The shadowy storm, now a mile or so away, looked much like a mushroom, broad at the top and thin at the base. We thought the danger was past and began to pitch our tents for the night, intending to set off at first light. The swirling sand continued to rain down on us, making rattling noises against our tents. We ate some of our provisions, drank some water, and were making relaxed conversation with each other when we heard what sounded like a thousand hoofbeats thundering toward us. We went outside to look and saw that half the sky to the southeast had turned black: The windstorm was coming back at us, hurtling sand and pebbles like arrows shot from bows. There was nothing we could do but cower in our tents, covering our heads with our sleeves as we lay there. In a split second, everything before my eyes turned black. Then I felt myself flying through the air. The swirling sand prevented me from opening my eyes. I took breaths only with the greatest effort because my nose was so plugged up. Each time I inhaled, my nostrils would fill up with sand. My skin was blasted raw, and I felt extremely cold.

"I had been flipping about in the air for quite some time when I felt someone grab hold of me. By then the sand had so battered my eyes I couldn't get them to open. My senses were completely disoriented. But I could still feel the person carrying me to another location, and my nasal passages gradually cleared up. The person also brought water to wash out my face and eyes. The splash of coldness cleared my head. I realized I was lying on a mountain slope with tall, precipitous peaks in every direction, but without a single bit of vegetation. There was only the brown earth with boulders strewn about. The sky was a dull yellow, the setting sun a lifeless white spot in the darkening gloom. I wanted to get to my feet, but my limbs were so numb I was unable to do so. I just lay there on the ground, resting. How could anyone have rescued me from such a fierce windstorm, I was thinking. What kind of place was this? Was I dreaming? In touching my head and face, I realized I was still wet from the cold water the man had sprayed on me with his mouth, trying to wake me up. What kind of person could he be?

"I was wallowing in my depression when I caught a glimpse of a shadow fleeting past. A man was then standing beside me. He was perhaps thirty, with a youthful build. His features were delicate and sharp. 'How are you feeling now?' he asked, smiling slightly.

"'Not bad,' I said, 'except that my strength is sapped. I can't get myself to stand up.'

"'That's fine,' he said. 'So all the trouble I went through today was not for nothing. I'll take you to a place where you can rest up before worrying about anything else.' As he spoke, he extended his arm and tucked me under it. He seemed to be flying as he sped with me from one mountaintop to another before coming to a small thatched hut in the middle of a clump of trees. He pushed open the door and set me down inside. 'Sleep here for a while,' he said. 'When you get thirsty, there's water in the crock. Help yourself to the steamed bread in the jar when you're hungry. Your basic needs will be easily met. But there are tigers and leopards and strange wild beasts roaming these parts. Never set foot outside by yourself.' Even as I was acknowledging these instructions, the man was already out the door. When I lay down, the ground felt soft as a quilt. I probed at it with my hand and realized that it was covered with four or five inches of fine grass. I also found the water crock and drank a large gulp. I shut my eyes to relax, and fell asleep before I knew it. The nap revived my whole body, even though my skin still stung. I ate some of the bread, then felt the urge to defecate. But, remembering what the man had said about going outdoors, I held myself back.

"After what seemed to be a long while, morning finally came. I got up, opened the door, and picked out an empty spot behind the hut, where I could relieve myself. From the gurgling sound of water, I found the creek and washed my hands. My spirit thus lifted, I slowly walked back toward the hut, studying the lay of the land as I went along. All around, the mountain peaks were jutting into the clouds. Numerous ancient pines grew up to the timberline, forming dense layers of lovely verdure. Squirrels leaped from one branch to another among the pines as I watched, standing very still. When I heard the sudden howling of the wind, however, I hurried to the hut, afraid that a tiger was about to appear. That was when I saw a figure seemingly descend from the sky, landing in front of me. It was none other than that thirtyish man. 'So you've recovered your spirits,' he concluded. 'Excellent, excellent.' I bowed down to him in thanks for saving my life. He took my hand to help me up, and we sat together on a large, flat piece of rock. He took out wine and dried venison for me to eat and asked me my name, place of origin, and occupation. I told him everything in detail before asking the same from him. He merely smiled, giving no answer. 'I now have a favor to ask of you,' he said as I finished the meal. 'I don't know whether you'd be willing to help me.'

"'I owe you my life,' I said. 'Just tell me what you want. I will spare nothing to carry it out.'

"'The job's not difficult to do,' he said. 'Only, it might be hard on you to have to remain here day after day. Tell me, can you see yourself living here for ten or twenty years? Please think it through before giving me your answer.'

"I did ponder the matter for a while. 'As long as it helps you out,'

I told him resolutely, 'there is no reason I couldn't be here for the rest of my life.'

"The man was delighted. 'I am most grateful to you,' he said. 'Now come with me to my place.' He stood up and, taking me by the upper arms, began to fly through the air straight toward a mountain with many pines. All I heard was the wind whistling past my ears. Before I realized it, we were standing on a crag. He released me and asked me to follow him. We went around to the other side of a huge pine, where I saw the entrance to a tunnel. It was only three feet high, and appeared pitch-dark inside. Ducking his head, the man went in as I tagged behind. The path was very uneven. I stumbled along for perhaps a half-mile, bracing myself against the walls. Then we saw a shaft of light off to one side. We turned toward it to find ourselves before a small, round opening, perhaps a foot across. The man leaned over and squeezed himself through. I did the same and found that we were now ringed by mountains that reached up to the sky. In the middle was a flat piece of ground perhaps sixty or seventy acres in size. The area was overgrown with trees; lush greenery sprouted everywhere. A patch of sunlight was visible in the middle of the forest. The man headed down a slope toward it as I followed.

"Going through the trees, we came upon a very large pond. On one side of it was a house surrounded by a six- or seven-foot hedge of vines. The roof consisted of large pieces of bark, upon which grew moss and shrubs. He led me through the hedge and into the house, where he indicated that the room to the left was the sleeping quarters. Behind that was a pantry area where food and utensils were stored. A library was off to the right, with the kitchen in back. There was a small shed behind the kitchen with a door but no windows; the door was sealed with multiple locks. 'What I am asking you to do for me is to guard this shed,' he said as he pointed to it. 'If I don't let you see it, though, you'll surely become curious after a while and maybe think of a way to get into it. Should you do that, you'll come to harm, and what good would that do me?'

"He opened up the locks one by one, then pushed open the door to reveal an utterly empty place. Nothing whatsoever was inside. 'I have my own use for this shed, which you cannot know about,' he said. 'After I leave you, do not under any circumstances come in here. If you do, it will cost you your life.' He refastened each of the locks even as he was speaking.

"Turning left as we emerged from the kitchen, we came upon a vegetable plot that extended all the way to the edge of the pond. Half of the plot was planted with vegetables, the other half with wheat. 'The land here is extremely fertile,' the man told me. 'There's also a water source nearby. The weather's neither too hot nor too cold. You'll be able to grow what you need easily, so food won't be a problem. As for what to wear, the trunk there contains clothing for all seasons, sufficient for eight to ten years. I will definitely come back every five or six years and resupply you.' We then walked back to the library and seated ourselves. 'You think about it yourself,' he said. 'What else might you be needing?'

" 'It seems everything's supplied,' I told him after giving the matter some thought. 'Let me live here a few days to see if there's anything I may be running short of.' The man nodded his agreement.

"The two of us remained together there for ten days. Each day, I chopped firewood, cooked, ground wheat, fished, and tended the vegetable plot, becoming thoroughly familiar with all the chores. I needed nothing else. 'I'll have to be going today,' the man then told me. 'I can't reveal my name to you, but you have to call me by something. From now on, just refer to me as "Windmaster." Now you'll have to excuse me.' He had hardly stopped speaking when he pushed off with his feet and rose into the air. Like a gust of wind, he was quickly gone.

"Every day after that, I went on cutting firewood, making meals, grinding wheat, fishing, and gardening. In my leisure time, I'd walk about outdoors until I became tired. Then I'd go back to the library to sit and rest. The Windmaster had quite a collection of books, which I read for enjoyment. I was careful about keeping the lamp lit for too long, aware that once I used up the oil, I would be in trouble should I need to do anything after nightfall.

"A good number of years went by this way, until I noticed with concern that the salt was almost used up. As I was fishing in the pond one day, I heard a low whistling of the wind blowing by. Before I could look up, the Windmaster was standing at my side clutching a large bag. I stood up quickly as the man patted me on the shoulder. 'It's been six years since I left you here, and you seem to be well,' he said with a smile. 'I calculated that you are about to have bland meals, so I've brought you some salt.'

" 'Are you leaving again right away?' I asked.

" 'I want to stay around for ten days or so before I go,' said the Windmaster. 'I very much respect you for your dependability and loyalty. These last six years, I was able to carry out just one of a number of tasks. For this reason, I've been feeling uneasy day and night and don't want to waste time dallying here. Even though my actions have been bizarre, just don't take me for some kind of weird demon. Understand that someone has owed me a blood-debt for over two decades —ever since I was twelve years old—and I have only recently been able to finish him off. I can give you an account of the whole story, but it'll be a long one. Let's have our talk in the library.'

"So I put away the salt and brewed a pot of tea; then we went to the library to sit down. 'I may look to you like a formidable person with extraordinary abilities,' the Windmaster told me with a painful sigh. 'But actually I've been through more suffering than anybody. You should know that I've become lonely and alienated in the world. Who brought me to my present state? It was that dastardly man!

" 'My father operated a ranch in Yutian in Xinjiang province. The property was worth several hundred thousand silver dollars. The family owned a piece of pink hibiscus jade with a rich, smooth translucence and weighing more than twenty catties. It was indeed a priceless possession. Now, my father was a friendly sort. He never failed to offer hospitality or to render aid to any visitor to the area, be he an official or a hireling—or even a political exile. That particular year, a dismissed official was sent there from Shandong; it was said that he received his sentence for having embezzled funds from a conservancy project on the Yellow River. The man was a Manchurian called Jide. Because he came to us for protection, my father gave him the usual assistance. From then on, Jide came often to our house. Those Manchus were always clever with words, and my father took everyone at face value. Finding that the man could talk up a storm on any topic, my father developed a strong admiration for him as someone with an unlimited store of knowledge. After some time, they became the best of friends. In a discussion on objets d'art one day, the man was shown the hibiscus jade. That was what triggered his evil intentions.

"'At the time, the regional official of Xinjiang was also a Manchu. His name was Hengchang, and he was the brother of some imperial concubine or other. Because it was the empress' fiftieth birthday, he was gathering gifts together, looking around for rare treasures to send to the court. Jide went bragging to Hengchang about that piece of jade in my family, telling him that it would make enough of a pleasing tribute to the empress to assure him of a promotion. Hengchang then asked Jide to broach the subject with my father, offering to buy the jade for ten thousand dollars. My father was unwilling, explaining that the jade had been in the family for two generations, that it could not be sold under any circumstances. Hengchang was willing to let the matter rest, but Jide was not. He cooked up an evil scheme, bribing a man to accuse my father of the high crime of treason for having offered horses to Muslim rebels. With no warning they came, confiscated our property, and threw the whole family into prison. The hibiscus jade naturally fell into Hengchang's hands, from where it was sent off to Beijing as tribute. Many in official circles knew the injustice of the case against my father. But because Hengchang was related to royalty, they just dragged the case out. Hengchang did win the empress' favor for the gift, though, and was promoted to provincial governor. With his new status, Hengchang was able first to obtain a pardon for Jide, then to make him principal prefect of the provincial capital. My family all rotted in prison for over three years without any hearing.

"'Then Jide went to Hengchang to urge him to finish the job they had started, so that there wouldn't be any future problems with survivors. Hengcheng then ordered Jide to interrogate my father. Knowing my father would never confess to anything, Jide resorted to devious means. Without ever questioning my father in open court, he readied the written confession he wanted, while plying my father with food and drink for days on end. Whenever the case was brought up, he would slap his chest and swear that he'd take care of everything; then he would change the subject. This went on for months as he complained daily about the difficulty of settling legal matters, or what a person needed to go through to obtain a pardon for a crime. Anxious to get out of prison, my father had no choice but to discuss his options with him. It was then that he took out the prepared confession, reading each sentence out loud to my father, making up changes as he went along and suggesting different ways to make the legal problems disappear. My father was illiterate. How was he to know that what the man was reciting and what was on paper did not mesh? He was thus tricked into signing the confession, whereupon everyone in the family was quickly saddled with the label of "traitor" and sentenced to die.

"'Fortunately, the sitting provincial judge, a Guangxi native named Cheng Liang, was an honest man. He knew from the first that my family was falsely accused, and spoke out several times on our behalf. But since my father was never tortured and had already signed the confession, there was nothing he could do aside from commuting the death sentence for my mother and me. We were sent to the Amur region in the northeastern frontier, to be camp slaves for soldiers there. I had had two elder brothers, sisters-in-law, and nephews and nieces, all of whom became ill and died in prison. At the time, I was just twelve.

Along with my mother, we made our way with great difficulty to the Amur. Under the weight of her trials and tribulations, my mother then passed away. Still a child, I was all alone. Under those forbiddingly frigid conditions, I had to feed horses and run errands for Manchurian soldiers. When I became deathly ill from the cold, the hunger, and the fatigue, the soldiers merely left me in the stables to fend for myself.

" 'I guess my life was not fated to end there. A Mongolian Lama, who subsequently became my teacher, suddenly showed up and spoke with the vice-commander about me. He helped me recover, then took me to some mountains by the steppes of Inner Mongolia, where he taught me many skills. I waited until my teacher passed away before moving the remains of my parents and family here to be buried. Because my teacher had charged me to finish a task for him, I lived here for over ten years. It wasn't until you came to watch the place that I was freed to seek my own vengeance. When I left you, I went looking for Hengchang and Jide. I learned that Hengchang had died some time ago. Jide, on the other hand, had become the commander at Zhapu in Zhejiang and had then retired; I couldn't find his latest whereabouts. It was after almost five years of looking that I learned he'd become a monk on Mount Wutai in Shanxi, to do penance for the transgressions of his life. He was keeping the strictest of monastic vows. Since I, too, am a disciple of the Buddha, I would not venture to kill anyone who had really dedicated himself to his truths. I watched him for more than two years without seeing him violate any of the precepts, so there was no way I could act against him. Then, the day before yesterday, he became tempted by the sight of a couple of young nuns on pilgrimage. Presuming on his seniority, he took advantage of the time set aside for meditation to flirt with them. Only then did I recount his past sins to him and take his life in revenge. As I was coming back here to visit the graves, it occurred to me that it's probably time for you to be running out of salt. That's why I brought some along for you. The next thing I have to do is look up our benefactor Cheng Liang. As soon as I've repaid his good deed, you can go home, since I'll then be able to handle my affairs on my own.'

"His story startled and touched me. I looked around the place and wrote out for him a list of everything I needed. One after the other, he brought me everything; then in about a fortnight he went off again. This time, it was eight years before he reappeared, seemingly blown back by the howling wind. 'I can now take you back,' he told me. 'Only, you shouldn't be leaving empty-handed. Recently I acquired a load of tea from a tea merchant I encountered on the steppes. It's worth tens of thousands. I'll just hand it over to you.'

"I WAS OVERJOYED AT THIS, but then became saddened by the thought of home. After such a long absence, I didn't know what had become of you all. The Windmaster knew what was troubling me. He told me he had visited you a number of times, each time leaving cash by mother's pillow. Did that really happen?"

"It did happen—four times altogether," said Madame Sheng. "Each time, the amount was between three and five hundred dollars. I was uncertain at first, so I put the money away, not daring to spend it. I started using it only after a long time, when I saw that all was well. Most people thought it was money I'd saved from before."

"The Windmaster comforted me," Mengxian then continued, "talking with me through the night. As it happened, his former bene- factor Cheng Liang incurred the ire of Hengchang for commuting their sentence. The latter soon trumped up a charge to dismiss him from office. Cheng had never been wealthy and had many mouths to feed. Before he could get all the way back to Guangxi, he got stuck in Jiujiang, where his situation was becoming desperate. The Wind- master found him there. He joined his household disguised as a ser- vant, then concocted different schemes to quietly provide him with cash to meet the family's needs. He also found the means of setting up an estate for the man during the seven years in his service. Only at Cheng Liang's deathbed did the Windmaster reveal his identity and purpose. He did not leave Jiujiang until after Cheng Liang's funeral. Then when he was on the Henan Circuit, he ran into a tea merchant from Hubei who was surrounded by robbers and about to be killed. The Windmaster rescued him, then escorted him all the way to the steppes. The merchant gave him half his cargo, which he accepted to give to me as severance. When I traveled by the steppes on my way here with the Windmaster, the merchants there had already sold the tea for him to a Russian for a hundred thousand rubles, which amounted to over sixty-seven thousand silver dollars. The Windmaster then told me to get on home, that he would bring the money along after me."

"If, as you say, the Windmaster is so powerful, why would he have needed you to guard his house?" Madame Sheng asked.

"I've asked him that myself," said Mengxian. "Since we were about to leave each other, he told me the reason. He's someone who's practicing to achieve Diamond Impermeability. His teacher, who died before achieving it himself, had charged him to continue the attempt. It is said that this state is reached by someone only once every sixty years. That empty, consecrated shed about which he was so secretive had to be perfectly spotless and hermetically sealed. He'd had to recite a purgative chant in it eighteen thousand times. Even though the Windmaster had already attained the proper level of training, he still needed more seasoning. Meanwhile, he was concerned that some evil spirit or wild animal would defile the place, and so entrusted me with the job of watching over it. It was all in accordance with his teacher's instructions. His teacher had also told him that he would succeed only if the person helping him had lived through a life-threatening calamity. Accordingly, he had previously rescued a hundred and ten persons out of windstorms in the desert, all of whom had died almost as soon as they were taken out. I was the only one who managed to survive. That was why he entrusted me with everything."

"How could he possibly have gone into the swirling sand and

rocks of a windstorm to save someone?" said Madame Sheng. "It's hard for me to believe it."

"The uncanny powers of Diamond Impermeability are even more incredible," said Mengxian. "Consider when the Windmaster brought you cash. How was it that you never detected so much as a trace of his comings and goings?" Madame Sheng had no answer for this. Many of their friends and relatives also marveled at all the events, unable to fathom how they could have occurred.

THAT EVENING EVERYONE took the occasion of the birthday feast to celebrate Mengxian's return. The boisterous merrymaking lasted till dawn, when a sudden breeze blew past. When the people opened their sleepy, bloodshot eyes, they saw in the hall sixty-odd barrels of silver bars lined up in neat rows, each with the paper seal of the Hundred Rivers Monetary Exchange. All this happened between the twelfth and thirteenth year in the reign of the Qing dynasty emperor Guangxu [1886–1887].

— 1924

From *Marvelous Gallants,* Chapter 40

．．．．．．．．．．．．．．．．．．．．．．．

Xiang Kairan

The Young Master Zhu Transports Silver Homeward;
A Bogus Beggar Solicits Food to Spy on the Hero

Now, let me tell you about Zhu Zhenyue, who was originally a native of Blackbird Mountain in Changde. His father was Zhu Pei—Zhu Ruolin to his friends—a county magistrate in Shaanxi for over a decade. Born in Shaanxi, Zhu Zhenyue was doted on by his parents because two of his older brothers had died in infancy. By the time he was twelve, Zhu Zhenyue had a burgeoning reputation in his hometown for literary talent, having been personally tutored by his father. In his thirteenth year, when he accompanied his mother to receive incense at Retribution Monastery in East Gate, he was seen by the abbot Snowgate. The abbot said that Zhu Zhenyue was endowed with exceptional inner vitality and insisted on taking him in as a student. Now, his parents considered him their ultimate pride and joy. How was it then that they became willing to apprentice him to a monk? Well, the credit really belonged to Snowgate, who did everything he could to persuade them and, in the end, was able to talk the couple into accepting the idea. So it came about that Zhu Zhenyue bowed down before the abbot and officially became his student.

The arrangement, however, did not include Zhu himself undergoing tonsure and becoming a monk. Snowgate, who was one of the three greatest swordsmen of the Hua School during the Xianfeng period [1851–1862], accepted Zhu as a student only to pass on to him his swordsmanship.

Now, who *were* the three greatest swordsmen? The first was Guangxi's Tian Guangsheng and the second Zhou Fating of Jiangsu. The third was of course the monk Snowgate of Retribution Monastery. And why was the Hua School so called? That's because all three of these swordsmen had studied south of Mount Hua in Liangzhou.

And so Zhu Zhenyue practiced swordsmanship for several years with the monk Snowgate. As a naturally gifted individual, he was able to succeed more quickly than an ordinary person, no matter what he attempted. So even though Zhu Zhenyue could not claim to have acquired all of Snowgate's skills, what he attained after those years of hard work was already rather extraordinary.

At the same time that Zhu Zhenyue was apprenticed to Snowgate, Zhu Ruolin was promoted to the magistracy of Xi'an. In nearly twenty years as an official in Shaanxi, he had saved up some two hundred thousand taels of silver. The Nien bandits were wreaking havoc in Gansu at the time, and Shaanxi was also reeling from the threat. Zhu Ruolin was concerned that, in any crisis, the money he'd accumulated in a career would become too burdensome to move back to his hometown. He knew that Snowgate had formidable martial skills and, among potential robbers, there were none who did not respect his reputation. He therefore wanted Snowgate to escort the silver by boat to Changde. Snowgate, on the other hand, as one who'd left worldly concerns behind, was unwilling to accept the assignment. Instead, he guaranteed that Zhu Zhenyue would be fine for the job, that, with him, nothing at all could go wrong en route. Since Snowgate was adamant, Zhu Ruolin had little choice but to follow his recommendation and leave everything to heavenly providence. Even though he was concerned that his own son be entrusted with such a weighty responsibility, as long as Snowgate declined to go himself, there was no other appropriate person for the job.

Zhu Ruolin bought gold with half the silver and hauled everything by land to Fort Dragon-Colt. There he leased a large boat, loading the precious metals onto it. At the time, Zhu Zhenyue was only twenty years old. It would be the first time for him to embark on a journey as the sole person in charge. Also, he had to take with him such a large sum of hard cash. Among those who truly knew what he was up against, there were none who were not concerned for him.

For his part, Zhu Zhenyue acted as if he were doing nothing out of the ordinary. "You all know that this boat is carrying two-hundred thousand taels worth of gold and silver," he said to the sailors soon after getting on board. "To sail this kind of boat on rivers and canals is not child's play. You should all take heed. On the other hand, I urge you all not to fret, because it is not up to you to guard against robbers. If they do show up to take things by force, what's the use of my telling you to be careful? By saying 'Take heed' to you, I am only telling you to follow my instructions closely. Wind direction is crucial on any water route. In going this time to Changde, no one can predict the number of days the voyage will take. According to established practice, whenever the wind is with us, we sail on ahead. When it is against us, we have to tie up. If by chance the wind were to blow against us for ten days or a fortnight, we'd be moored for ten days or a fortnight without moving forward. On this trip, however, we shall not be following such practice. Whichever way the wind blows, if I tell you to set sail, you must do so without hesitating, even if a veritable gale is blowing in the opposite direction. Or when I say to drop anchor at this dock for however many days, I don't care whether a favorable wind is with us all day and all night: We will not be budging. If upon passing a port it appears we could stop, do not do so should I say not to. Or if we be among the reeds far from human habitation and at a highly unlikely place for stopping, you must nevertheless stop if I tell you to stop. In other words, you must obey my commands—*respect* my commands—on all occasions. Anything that may happen then, even if it be a huge catastrophe, will not be on your heads."

Upon receiving these instructions, the sailors voiced their unanimous agreement. Once underway, they followed all orders to the letter. When they docked anywhere, Zhu Zhenyue invariably went ashore to pay his respects to one or another person of reputation in the area. As they went on, even though there were both veiled and open threats, no one would contend with him. As young in years as he was, he never set out with the intention of hurting anyone. Each time, he'd merely put on a show of his impressive martial skills, and potential robbers would stay away. Because of this, there were none among the provincial outlaws who had not heard of Zhu, and none who did not hold him in high regard. None, moreover, bore him enough of a grudge to want to seek vengeance.

The boat sailed on for quite a few days. Now nearing the boundary of Hunan province, it docked at Whitefish Cliff. Knowing of no threat in the area, Zhu Zhenyue did not make his usual courtesy call ashore. It was harvest time. In the evening, the moon shone bright and clear as a mirror. Zhu sat by himself near the bow of the boat, reflecting on the journey thus far. As the only person in charge, he had escorted this boatload of gold and silver all these months and had encountered his share of potential robbers. Now he had actually gotten to Hunan without incident. A few more days of good winds and he'd easily reach his ancestral home. Just twenty years old, and he'd been able to venture into territory rife with outlaws to complete such a daunting task. Indeed, among heroes past and present, have there been many who could have done any better? As his thoughts reached this point, his spirits soared. He called out to a servant to bring him a jug of wine, which he savored slowly by himself in the moonlight. Before he knew it, the time was approaching midnight. Feeling the chill of the evening damp, he was on the verge of retiring to the hold for the night.

All of a sudden, just as he was rising to his feet, he felt the boat dip slightly into the water. Ever alert, Zhu knew at once that someone of great prowess had just jumped on board. Looking up in the moonlight, he saw an extremely imposing figure standing on one leg at the top of the mast, with the other leg raised up to the sky. The man moved with great agility, dropping down to the bow in a flash before Zhu Zhenyue could finish asking, "Who's there?" He landed like an autumn leaf fluttering down to earth, with no perceptible sound. Zhu was thoroughly taken aback by this display but nevertheless wanted to learn the man's name before engaging him. But the other fellow flashed his sword before Zhu could get another word out, thrusting it at Zhu's face. Zhu Zhenyue could not restrain his anger at such lack of decorum and counterattacked with his own sword. The two fought for some time before the man, ultimately no match for Zhu, ran off like a thoroughly frightened animal, wounded in a number of places. His victory notwithstanding, Zhu was most perturbed. "I've never heard of anyone with his kind of ability at Whitefish Cliff," he thought to himself. "Besides, the style of the man's swordplay is exactly like mine. He came so suddenly and refused to respond to my query. Did he come here to rob me, or just to see how I fight? Having gotten this far with his swordsmanship, he shouldn't be bugging out his eyes at this little bit of cash. But if he came to test my skills, why then was he unwilling to talk to me? My teacher once told me that, counting himself, there are only three persons who practice the Hua style of swordplay, one in Guangxi, another in Jiangsu. No one among them lives in the Hunan area. If the man belongs to my school, it would be simple indeed for him to come openly to find out what I can do. Why, then, did he come on like this? Had I been a bit less scrupulous, I could have made the mistake of taking his life. Wouldn't it be too late for regrets then? He may have been beaten this time, but he never let up at all in the fight, as if he wanted to put both our lives on the line. If his purpose in coming was to test my swordsmanship, he shouldn't have attacked with such fury." In thus turning the questions over in his head, Zhu Zhenyue could not come up with a single answer. There was nothing for him to do but set the matter aside and wait for some future opportunity to learn the whys and wherefores of the man who had come.

The boat sailed on for several more days and now reached White Horse Pass, only about twenty-five miles by water from Changde. With favorable winds tomorrow, their journey would end in another day. Because his momentary relaxation at Whitefish Cliff had brought on the formidable intruder, Zhu Zhenyue no longer dared let down his guard. It did not matter that they were just mooring at a quay outside a little country town; he had to go ashore to look around. He was afraid that, on the eve of great success, something untoward would happen to undo all his previous efforts.

Day was just dawning as the boat reached White Horse Pass. Zhu Zhenyue gave the usual instructions to the boatmen as he was about to go ashore. "After I'm gone, all of you keep an eye on the boat from prow to stern. Do not under any circumstances allow any stranger to come aboard." From the time they left Fort Dragon-Colt, these were the identical words Zhu Zhenyue had spoken to his charges prior to venturing on shore after each docking; the boatmen were tired of hearing them. All along the way, no outsider had ever asked to come onto the boat. So other than chorusing a perfunctory "Yes, sir," the sailors paid little attention to the instructions.

Only a moment after Zhu left, a disheveled beggar, all bent over, with a dirty, greasy face, trudged slowly to the side of the boat, extending his hand to ask for something to eat. "Go do your begging somewhere else!" a boatman shouted at him, trying to shoo him away with a wave of his hand. "We haven't got anything here for you."

The beggar appeared stunned. "Where in the world do you want me to do my begging?" he asked tearfully in a supplicatory whine. "I've begged and begged around here for the larger part of a day, and not so much as a single grain of rice has reached my lips. Take pity on me, please. I'm so hungry I can't move anymore. I don't care what little bit you can spare. Just let me have some of your leftovers!"

The boatman detected traces of Shaanxi accent as the beggar spoke, and could not help but be touched by someone from home. "Where are you from?" he asked as he looked the man over several times. "You look like you're very young, probably no more than sixteen or seventeen. Your face is not that of an ordinary vagabond. How did you come to be a beggar in these parts?"

At this, the beggar's tears flowed more copiously. "I was originally from Shaanxi," he replied. "From the time I was six or seven, I've been following my father to Changde, where he does business. My family owned quite a bit of property. It's just that I've been a no-good. I never wanted to study seriously or to work properly as a tradesman. Last year, when I came to White Horse Pass with my father to collect payments, I became infatuated with a woman and could not bear to be parted from her. After we got back to Changde, I stole two hundred taels of silver from my father to return here secretly to live with her. The two hundred taels didn't last long. Once the money was gone, the woman didn't want me anymore and kicked me out. I was too ashamed to go back to Changde, so I just hung around here. My poor father. I'm his only son. Losing track of me unexpectedly like this—you can't imagine the anxiety he must be feeling. I can no longer go on like this. I want with all my heart to get back to Changde. It's only twenty-five miles by boat, but I've got no money for the passage. As decrepit as I've become, no one would want to take me on board. By land the distance would be over fifty miles. Sick as I now am, how in the world can I go anywhere on foot? Looks like I'll die here in White Horse Pass soon enough. Forget about burying my remains in my ancestral home. Even getting them back to my father in Changde will be beyond the realm of possibility." At this point he covered his face, sobbing ever louder.

Now the boatman was very much a tenderhearted sort. Hearing this woeful tale and seeing the man's pitiful state, he could not but hesitate. "I, too, am from Shaanxi," he said, "and it's remarkable to meet someone from home in this place. As it happens, this boat is headed to Changde. If the wind is with us, we'll be there by tomorrow. To take you along would not ordinarily be a problem. Only, this is no ordinary boat, but one chartered by Master Zhu of Xi'an. Master Zhu has directed us to never let any riffraff on board. The consequences would be extremely serious, and I don't dare take on the responsibility. As for getting you some victuals, that's not a problem at all. I can see to it that you'll be fed. I can also get you a couple of sets of clothing that, while they may not be a perfect fit, will be good enough to improve your present appearance. Then you'll find it easier to get water transport to Changde." The boatman then went belowdecks, emerging again with a large bowl of rice and vegetables. He told the beggar to eat on shore while he himself remained on the boat. Then he found and brought out several sets of used clothing.

After eating just a little, the beggar returned the rest of the food to the boatman. "When you're past a certain point in your hunger, it's hard to consume all this food at once," he said. "It'll be best to divide what's left into several portions and eat each one very slowly. I'm overwhelmed with gratitude to you, doing all this for me just because I'm from your home province. I've begged for food along this river for months now. Sometimes people would pass bits of leftovers to me. But to talk to me in such a kindly way as you have, well, I've never met anyone quite willing to do that. This has truly been a rare day. I've been able to meet someone from home, someone who feeds me and tries to clothe me as well. So I have even less reason to be ungrateful or complaining. It's just that even with the clothes from you, I still think it would not be possible for me to hitch a ride to Changde. I'm physically weak, worn down with illness. If I put these clothes on, I'll surely be robbed of them by the other beggars in a matter of hours. I might even get beaten up in the process. So I don't think I'll be wearing the clothes. It would have been better for you not to have gotten them for me. If you're really taking pity on me, though, you might want to give me just a square foot of space inside your ship's bow to hunker down in for a few hours. Should I then get to Changde, I would be as beholden to you as I am to my parents, since you would have given me new life. My gratitude to you then would remain till I'm in my grave. Once we get to Changde, I'll invite you to my home to honor you with hospitality. As the old saying puts it so well, 'If you're going to help somebody, then help him to the very end.' Are you, sir, willing to carry your compassion to the last mile?" He choked up again as he spoke, his eyes welling up with tears.

Hearing all this, and in view of the situation, the boatman's heart could not but soften even further. "All right!" he answered with sudden resolution. "Let this be on my head! Go squat yourself down inside the bow, and don't make any noise. Once we just get to Changde, even if Master Zhu finds out, it won't matter." The beggar repeated his thanks as the boatman led him to the bow of the boat. Lifting up a couple of boards, he indicated to him to get below. "Each time Master Zhu returns from his trips ashore, he never fails to inspect the entire vessel. So don't make a sound under those boards. Wait until the Master comes back and completes his inspection. Then I will let you out and find you some place to sit down."

The beggar bowed deeply. "I'd never dare get you in trouble by making the slightest noise," he promised. He then squeezed himself into the space, curling up into a ball. The boatman replaced the boards, assuring himself that Master Zhu would never know the difference.

Around dusk Zhu Zhenyue returned and went through his usual inspection fore to aft. He then summoned the boatman to his cabin. "You surely have a lot of nerve!" he shouted out. "How dare you disobey my orders by stowing someone away in the bow?" The boatman, his face ashen at these words, was too shaken momentarily to utter anything in reply. Zhu pressed him unremittingly for an answer. "Go on. Speak up. Who's the person you've taken on board?"

Convinced that the Master already knew everything so that further denial was futile, the boatman could only own up. "Cease your anger, please," he said. "I would never take any evil person on board. This is a young beggar whose family also lives in Changde. He has been stranded here without any means of getting home. He came to the boat to beg for food and then implored me to find him transportation back to Changde. I shouldn't have been so muddleheaded, but I felt pity for him and concealed him in the bow. I thought it would only be for a day or so, until we get to Changde. So I never reported the matter to you."

Zhu pondered for a second. "Take me there for a look," he said as he got up. "Let me see what kind of individual this little beggarman is."

The boatman then brought Zhu Zhenyue to the bow and lifted up the boards. "Hurry out here and pay your respects to the Master," he said to the beggar. "The Master already knows that you're here, and I dare not cover for you any longer. Don't blame me if I can't save you now."

The beggar got up gingerly. He stood there with a downcast face, as if in great fear. Zhu Zhenyue looked him over carefully, then swung his hand around to slap the boatman across the mouth. "You stupid fool!" he rebuked him. "How can you be so ignorant of proper manners? To make him hunker down in there like that—that's no way to treat an honored guest!" Then he turned and put his hands together in greeting to the beggar. "Kind sir, please forgive the boatman, a simple country bumpkin whose pedestrian eyes could never recognize an exalted person such as yourself. Because I was not here, we have greatly mistreated you. Please go ahead to the forward cabin so that we can sit down and talk over everything!"

Strange as it may seem, the beggar, who appeared to be frightened out of his wits on first seeing Zhu, changed his expression instantly at these words. A smile spread across his face as he, too, folded his hands to return the greeting. "How dare I accept such kindness?" he responded. "Everyone in the trade has been saying that you are an exceptional person. Now I'm deeply impressed to learn that there's substance to your reputation. Right at this moment, though, I have something to take care of. Let me return on another day to seek instruction from you."

He started to leave, but Zhu Zhenyue would not even think of letting him go. "If you're not going to do me the honor of staying, then you shouldn't have bothered to come here," he said as he blocked the way. "Our accommodations cannot match those of home, and we have been remiss in our treatment of you. I'm only inviting you to share a cup of simple wine and to allow us to learn your name. Do let me show you a little respect."

The beggar hesitated for a moment. "All right!" he finally nodded. "This encounter with you is a special occasion."

Straightaway Zhu Zhenyue ordered the cook to prepare food and drink before leading the beggarman into his cabin. Taking out some of his own clothes, he presented them with both hands to the man. "Please change into these for now, so that we can drink and talk." The man did not hesitate. A servant brought water for him to wash the grime from his face. He put on the clothes, which instantly brightened his appearance. His features sparkled like imperial jade. The sailors sneaking peeks at him were all astonished.

A feast was soon laid out. Zhu Zhenyue insisted that the beggarman take the seat of honor, with himself as principal host. Only after three rounds of drinking did Zhu raise his cup. "Under the directive of my parents and my teacher, I've made bold at present to escort two-hundred thousand taels of gold and silver back to Changde," he announced. "This money represents the savings of a career in officialdom for my father, and not a cent of it is ill-gotten. Any number of gallant individuals along the way have taken this fact into account and decided to let me pass without incident, so that I have peacefully gotten this far. Since you have now come, I expect you must have some pressing cause. If you would care to indicate a specific sum, whatever your needs, I will present it to you with no regrets whatsoever. Only, I must request that you leave your name." He then filled a cup with wine to pass to his guest.

The beggar broke into loud laughter. "The young Master's power of discernment is indeed superior," he said. "But your conclusion that I have come here for monetary reasons, to relieve some pressing financial need, can only be regarded as misguided. My family may not be wealthy, but I have never wanted for money. So I will not be able to accept your kind offer."

At this, Zhu Zhenyue could not prevent embarrassment from showing on his face. "I deserve to die for taking a gentleman for a petty thief," he quickly apologized. "I can only hope that you will forgive my foolishness and instruct me as to the reason for your presence here."

"Does the young Master still remember the robber he encountered at Whitefish Cliff?" the beggar asked quite unexpectedly.

"How can I forget?" said Zhu Zhenyue, startled. "But I did not take the man to be a robber at all. What kind of person is he, anyway?"

The guest stared intently at Zhu. "How did the young Master know that the person was not a robber?"

"That was not at all difficult to figure out," said Zhu Zhenyue with a smile. "A man with that kind of ability, how could he have been a robber? Or if he were, there are many other places for him to steal from without having to go against someone from the same school. For such reasons, I decided he was no robber."

"Perhaps he didn't know it was you. How can you be sure?" The beggar continued to press him.

Zhu Zhenyue shook his head. "If he didn't know it was me, he wouldn't have come at me the way he did. Even now I have to ask you to tell me what that person came for. I never got his name at the time or learned who he was. I am simply concerned that I have no way of finding out."

"Just as you have said, the man's no robber," said the beggar with a smile. "But since he was unwilling to reveal his name to you, I won't dare take the liberty of doing so. Because you seriously wounded him, he's still receiving treatment at his home. He has a friend, however, who's rather upset with what transpired; he wants to come and see what he can do against you, and he's sent me ahead to scout out the situation. You'll be all right if you just exercise a bit of care tonight. I thank you, young Master, for your hospitality. I know we'll have occasion to meet again!" He then stood up to take his leave.

Zhu Zhenyue did his best to detain him. "It's not yet dark," he said. "There's still a lot of time. Why not stay a while longer? I am in need of more of your instruction."

The beggar sat down once more. "It may still seem early to us," he said, "but in coming here I had agreed to meet with the man who sent me by the beginning of the second watch, to report what I found. He is waiting to hear from me before venturing here. If I fail to appear by the appointed time, he'll conclude that you've found me out and killed me. Then he'll come to avenge my life. With vengeance in his heart, he would inevitably be most unforgiving when he met and engaged in any fight with you. In my humble opinion, it would be to your advantage to let me go back earlier, to prevent the life-and-death situation that occurs when mortal enemies come face-to-face. In the event of such a conflict, it would be too late for regrets. Even I would then be concerned about how I could repay you for your magnanimous hospitality."

In spite of his efforts to control it, the anger these words stirred in Zhu Zhenyue showed on his face. "You may have spoken with the best of intentions out of concern for my welfare," he said. "But you also cannot deny that you hold no proper respect for my capabilities. I therefore will not accept your kind offer. As the old saying puts it so well, 'Those who intrude are not kindly; those who are kindly do not intrude.' Even if he's not seeking revenge, I may still not be his match. But even if he were seeking revenge, I would still not be afraid of him. I never intended to detain you. But since you put things the way you have, I cannot do otherwise but keep you here, if only to see how he'll go about avenging you. Don't you go back there to give your report. Just remain here and help yourself to more wine."

The beggarman had noted Zhu Zhenyue's reaction to his earlier statements. Seeing Zhu get angry, he wreathed his face in smiles and stuck out his thumb to show approval. "From this kind of spirit alone, you show yourself to be a worthy man," he said. "I'll just sit down right here, as you wish."

"Don't take offense at this question. But, in a while, when the man comes to avenge you, and I cannot avoid fighting him, what will you be doing then?" Zhu suddenly wanted to know.

"I'll just be sitting right here, not moving a muscle," said the beggarman with a grin. "The young Master is a world-beating hero who obviously does not need my help. And if that person needed me, he wouldn't be coming to meet you. I'll just watch you two from afar. No matter who wins or loses, I will not get myself involved."

"That's fine," Zhu Zhenyue nodded. "A man's word once spoken, like an arrow shot in battle, can never be taken back. You also need not concern yourself with whatever preparations I make." The beggar repeated his agreement.

Zhu Zhenyue then summoned all the boat hands to come before him. "Move your drums and gongs under the main mast. Around midnight, as soon as you feel the boat bob up and down ferociously as if in a storm, then all of you begin to beat on them. Shout out at the same time. No matter how loud the ruckus you make, do not stop until the boat is still again." They gave their affirmation with one voice before going off in different directions to make ready. No one dared ask what this was all about.

After sending the boatmen off, Zhu Zhenyue went back to resume drinking with the beggarman. He refrained from inquiring about the latter's background as well as the background of the man at Whitefish Cliff, certain that he would not be told. The two drank until about the second watch, when Zhu took out a suit of light armor from a chest. "Please sit here by yourself for a while." He smiled at his guest as he strapped it on. "I'll be right back to keep you company."

The beggar quickly stood up and filled a cup to present to his host. "Please down this wine as my wish for your success over your challenger," he said.

Zhu Zhenyue accepted the cup, then put it down. "Let's hope I can benefit from your good karma," he said. "It won't be too late for me to down this when I return." He then stepped outside the cabin, reminding himself that since the man at Whitefish Cliff had taken to the mast, perhaps his friend would do likewise. Why not wait for him up there? So he leaped to the top of the mast.

Only a few days had passed since the time of his encounter at Whitefish Cliff. The evening moonlight was still sparkling. Zhu had waited up there for nearly an hour when his attention was jolted by a shadowy figure streaking more swiftly than an arrow across the white-sand beach, straight toward where he was. Without waiting for the man to get close, Zhu shouted out "Welcome!" in a loud voice. The dark figure seemed startled. Then, in a snap, he arrived beneath where Zhu was standing. Trailing a stream of white light, he swiped his sword at Zhu's feet. It goes without saying that Zhu dared not relax his concentration, flashing his own sword to engage the attacker. The two fought ferociously, now leaping up to the top, now tumbling down again, neither willing to leave the mast as they went around and around its base. In the moonlight, Zhu Zhenyue could make out the man's face, which appeared extremely sinister. He had a full head of disheveled hair that hung down all over his back and shoulders. His face and cheeks were covered with whiskers, more than two inches thick and spread out to look like a bamboo cage. His age was difficult to assess, but judging from his appearance, he would have been between forty and fifty. His body was not particularly imposing, though he was extremely agile in his movements. His skills were far and away superior to those of the man at Whitefish Cliff.

Battling him for more than ten rounds, Zhu Zhenyue saw that the man's fighting style was exactly the same as his own and could not let the uneasy feeling about this pass. "Isn't the intruder a member of the Hua School?" he shouted out while parrying another blow. "Why not reveal your identity before we fight on?" His opponent went on as if he heard nothing, but his attack became even more vicious. Zhu's anger rose as he silently cussed at the man's lack of decorum; meanwhile, he called up all the skill he could muster to ward him off. They were about to separate again when the drums and gongs below the mast suddenly erupted. Together with the shouts, they produced an earth-shaking din. The intruder appeared disconcerted, then suddenly changed the direction of his attack to Zhu Zhenyue's lower body. Zhu recognized that this kind of swordplay was the most lethal of the Hua School's repertoire, its ultimate level of attack. It is not usually deployed in a fight, because any opponent unfamiliar with the moves, no matter how skilled, could not possibly avoid losing either life or limb. Even swordsmen of the Hua School who have themselves practiced the moves would be injured unless they were superior to the attacker. Now, the level of their swordsmanship was just about even, but when his opponent struck at him with this ultimate attack, he cried out, "Uh-oh!" and leaped some ten feet above the mast. As he did so, he felt the other's sword slash slightly into his right heel. He reacted with his own ultimate move, thrusting at the man's face, and heard the sound of the blade—*cha!*—as it struck home. Then he saw the man wipe his head with his hand and dash away to the shore. Zhu Zhenyue jumped down from the mast but did not pursue him. The noise from the drums, gongs, and shouting quickly ceased as the boat steadied itself.

The beggar was quick to welcome Zhu as he strode into the cabin. "Congratulations! Congratulations!" he repeated. "What a fight!"

"The son of a bitch was truly awesome," Zhu Zhenyue said, managing a smile. "I very nearly couldn't get back here with my life." As he spoke he removed the light armor and applied medicine to the cut on his heel. "For certain, I am impressed with the man's skill," he said to his guest. "Still, one cannot say he is without peer. His hideous looks, on the other hand—I'm afraid we'd never find their like in the whole human world. Now that he's crossed swords with me, can you reveal to me his name and background?"

The beggarman continued to demur. "There'll come a day when you'll learn everything. This is not the time for me to tell you," he said, smiling. "Take care of yourself, young Master. I will now take my leave." In a blink, he was on the shore, letting out a long whistle and then disappearing from sight.

Zhu Zhenyue sighed repeatedly. "This person's actions are truly unfathomable," he thought. "This is only my first venture, and I've never given anyone cause to take me as an enemy. Both my opponents, moreover, are members of the Hua School. This bogus beggar is more than likely a member as well. Since we are all alumni, and since we'd never had occasion to cause trouble for each other, what made them come on twice like that? Good thing I set up the drums and gongs, which startled the man sufficiently for me to return that blow to his face. Otherwise I would've lost. I don't know what kind of exercise he's been doing to make his facial skin so tough. My blade seemed to just slide off with a *cha* when I struck him."

As he was pondered one thing and another by himself, Zhu Zhenyue became aware of the boatman entering the cabin. "I didn't follow your instructions today, and it almost brought disaster," he said, knocking his head on the floor in apology. "Who was to know that the little beggar actually intended to spy on us? If not for your foresight in recognizing that someone had come on board, I would not have been able to shoulder the huge consequences even if I were to grind my bones to powder."

"I didn't really have any foresight," said Zhu Zhenyue as he helped the man up. "That bogus beggar did not do his act badly at all. But he was careless about one thing, which left me an easily detectable clue. The deck of this boat has always been kept shiny and spotless. Ordinarily, even when you fellows return from shore, those with shoes on remove them on the gangplank. Even if you went barefoot, you'd wash off the dirt before touching the deck. People from this boat never stomp around with sandy or muddy feet. The man was evidently afraid of bumping into me returning to the boat and thus messing up his scheme. So as long as he was able to talk you into letting him come on board, he did so hurriedly, without considering the various footprints his dirty feet would leave on the otherwise spotless deck. Since the time was near dusk, you never paid attention to the footprints. When I returned soon afterward, I saw them. I noticed that they were all pointed toward the bow, with no evidence of the person getting off. It would be obvious to anyone, then, that whoever had come on board had yet to leave." Only after this explanation did everything that had transpired become suddenly clear to the boatman.

—*ca. 1923*

IV. Críme

. . . .

IN THE CHINESE TRADITION, stories of crime and detection are closely connected with those dealing with martial gallantry. Evidence of this is usually traced to the oral storyteller Shi Yukun (fl. 1851–1875) of Tianjin, who began by performing tales of the crime cases solved by the righteous Judge Bao referred to in "The Black Cat." In 1594, such stories, which often venture into the supernatural, were written down and published in the popular collection *Bao Gong An* (The cases of Judge Bao),[1] referred to in the same story. But in telling his stories, Shi Yukun reportedly shifted focus from the judge to his gallant aides, the ones who investigated the crimes for him. Even though the martial prowess of these *wuxia* aides eventually superceded both the supernaturalism and the rational wisdom of the judges in meting out justice, the popularity of old crime-case stories has continued up to the present, with Western readers getting a taste of them through the adaptive renderings of the Judge Dee stories by the Dutch sinologist Robert Van Gulik.

Unquestionably the most traditional of the three stories in this section, "The Black Cat" runs into the same basic problem as the stories featuring the all but supernatural feats of the *wuxia*: How does it satisfy the reader's desire to fantasize, while retaining some semblance of credulity? One way is to appeal to the reader's visceral desire for justice, something the author Xiang Kairan, better known for his accounts of righteous vengeance in *wuxia* stories, does only too well. Many Chinese readers, even in the 1920s, were evidently convinced of the existence of some kind of karmic reparation that works —through an animal in this case—to right wrongs. More interesting, though, is Xiang's attempt, in the traditional guise of a narrator-commentator, to champion the idea that "some accounts of the supernatural are not at all wild fantasies, certainly not the unfounded fabrications of those who set them down in writing." The statement echoes that of Gan Bao, who insists in the preface to his famous fourth-century collection *Soushenji* (Records of an inquest into the spirit-realm) that "the way of the spirits is not a fabrication."[2]

The interplay between fantasy and believability clearly continues in the other two stories, which are unabashed derivatives of tales of crime detection popular in contemporary Europe. Sun Liaohong's master thief Lu Ping is a direct adaptation of Maurice Leblanc's Arsène Lupin, while Cheng Xiaoqing's super-sleuth Huo Sang is his version of Arthur Conan Doyle's Sherlock Holmes, complete with side-kick and chronicler-narrator Bao Lang, the equivalent of Dr. Watson.[3] Both "The Sunglasses Society" and "The Ghost in the Villa" seemingly shift their appeal from the traditional supernaturalism to the "scientific" rationalism that considers all ghosts and spirits superstitious fabrications. In so doing, they meet the need for fantasy with the rational deeds of the master detective or the master thief, rather than with descriptions of the supernatural, the credibility of which reasoning undermines. By explaining away the supernatural or the incredible through the use of reason, it argues against the traditionalism that informs Xiang Kairan's story as well as so many other traditional stories. As Bao Lang puts it, "Everything seems to be rather simple once you've explained it. But before the truth is revealed, one could easily have suspected the phenomena to be the work of ghosts or spirits."

Closer consideration of either Cheng's hero or Sun's hero, however, will reveal that the old appeal to wishful fantasy very much remains. Quite like a *wuxia,* Huo Sang is himself able to go to the quarters of a gang of criminals and learn their secret plans simply by "eavesdropping on them." Even more incredibly, he prevents them from carrying out their plans by warning them "in a polite way" of possible consequences and by telling them who he is. Lu Ping, whose reputation alone makes everyone tremble, is even more obviously a fantastic hero. His ability to disguise himself is nothing short of magical, as are his anticipations of the actions and decisions of the jewelers he robs. How can he know that Mutao the host will be entering the sitting room by himself? How does he get his henchman into the party? Sunglasses and alcohol consumption do not really explain why the false Mutao can remain undetected. Sun does an adequate job in explaining away all the puzzles. But the feeling that the explanations are much closer to rationalizations than to credible reasoning is not thoroughly dispelled—or exorcized.

Notes

1. See James J. Y. Liu, *The Chinese Knight Errant,* pp. 117–120.
2. See Robert Ford Campany, *Strange Writing: Anomaly Accounts in Early Medieval China* (Albany: State University of New York Press, 1996), pp. 55–61, 147–149.
3. For a study of the Huo Sang/Bao Lang and the Lu Ping stories and their authors, see Jeffrey C. Kinkley, *Chinese Justice, the Fiction* (Stanford: Stanford University Press, 2000), pp. 170–240.

The Black Cat

· ·

Xiang Kairan

N
o one who has read the crime-case stories of Judge Bao and Judge Shi will forget that the two collections contain an account of a sparrow playing plaintiff and another of a brown dog taking revenge.* Among the readers of such hogwash would be uneducated women and children intellectually incapable of discerning truth from falsehood. There would also be traditionalists who cling to their belief in karmic retribution and who, their doubts notwithstanding, lack the courage to question the veracity of what they read. All others would object to the stories as preposterous in the extreme. They might very well ridicule the authors as deficient in knowledge concerning crime detection. Unable to portray their heroes properly, these writers could only resort to accounts of the supernatural to hoodwink the gullible. Upon reading those kinds of stories, I myself could hardly refrain from feeling the same way. Today, however, I unexpectedly encountered someone from Hofei in Anhui who had just come to Shanghai. Quite by chance, he told me

---

*The reference here is to two dispensers of legal justice in popular lore, immortalized in tales of their exploits in two collections published in the nineteenth century. *Trans.*

about an extraordinary case that took place in his native town toward the end of last year. The case actually demonstrates that some accounts involving the supernatural are not at all wild fantasies, certainly not the unfounded fabrications of those who set them down in writing. My intention here is not to advocate superstition. But during these times of loss of personal trust and decline in social mores, if I can discover and present a few of these deeply touching stories, they can perhaps be regarded as helpful in areas where laws are ineffectual, and where the detective's ability to reason falls short. The ancient sages and worthies had this very idea when they set up their teachings based on the existence of ghosts and spirits.

Last year Liu Dacun, a shopkeeper in the city of Hofei, went alone on the twelfth day of the twelfth month to a western district some twenty miles away to collect debts. In all, he collected five silver dollars, four twenty-cent silver pieces, and fifteen coppers. He had wrapped everything in a large handkerchief and was on his way back to the city when he felt the urgent need to relieve himself. Because it was unseemly to defecate by the roadside, he went over by the foot of a nearby hillock. As he squatted down to do his business, he shoved the parcel between his lips, holding on to it with his teeth. Just as he was finishing up and before he could get to his feet, a large black cat bounded over. Leaping up to Liu Dacun's face, the animal snatched the parcel from his mouth and ran off. Greatly startled, Liu hitched up his pants as fast as he could to give chase, hissing the usual summons all the while. But even though the confounded cat was not going very fast, it ignored him as it headed directly toward the hillock.

Since Liu Dacun needed every bit of his capital to carry on his small business, he would never have been willing to just let the animal go. That a cat could snatch a parcel of cash from a man's mouth was, moreover, too improbable an occurrence. Liu Dacun just had to get to the bottom of the matter. After going a short way, Liu saw ahead of him a sarcophagus within a grove of trees. It was built of earthen bricks on four sides, with a tile roof on top. The bricks and tiles still looked new. The cat, still carrying the cloth-wrapped parcel in his mouth, ran to the front of the sarcophagus before turning to look again at Liu Dacun. Then it squeezed itself through a gap between two of the bricks. Liu Dacun hurried over and saw that the gap was less than two inches wide. What terrible luck, he was thinking. Such a large cat, but it managed to crawl through this little bit of space. Had the cursed animal gone anywhere else, there would be a way to get at it. But it had to get in right here. Liu could not know who was entombed inside. Since he couldn't contact the person's family, moreover, he could not very well disturb the bricks and tiles on his own. That would be against the law. Well, it would soon be New Year's, so he might as well give up trying to retrieve the money. Better not stir up anything he might later regret. A typical tradesman, he wasn't at all daring. Having thus mulled the situation over, he decided that he'd rather concede those few dollars. So he went down the hillock and started down the road going home.

He had walked no more than a mile or two before it was lunchtime. He was still a good distance from the city and his stomach was growling with hunger, so he thought he would eat at a local diner before going on. He entered a place and ordered some dishes and rice. But as he was lifting his chopsticks to shovel in the first mouthful, he suddenly caught sight of that big black cat again. At first he thought it might have been a cat from the diner, similar in color and size to the earlier one. But then the cat sprang onto the table and snatched the salted duck, plate and all, in its mouth, jumped back down, and ran toward the door. No way could Liu Dacun contain himself this time. He scooted after the animal, the bowl of rice still in his hand. Outside he saw that the cat was not all that far ahead. In his agitation, he raised his hand and hurled the bowl at it. He would have been glad to see the animal smashed to death. But, strangely enough, the hurtling bowl never made contact with the cat. It landed instead on the head of an army sergeant who was there to enforce the winter curfew. The poor man was knocked to the ground unconscious, blood gushing forth from his wound. The soldiers who were with him took Liu Dacun to be an assassin and rushed ahead to tie him up before he could explain himself. The wounded sergeant was sent to a nearby branch of the Red Cross for medical attention as Liu Dacun was brought under guard into Hofei.

When the county magistrate was told that an assassin had been arrested for making an attempt on the life of an army sergeant, he naturally wanted to hear the case without delay. Now, this magistrate was an astute and energetic individual. Since taking office, he had proved to be highly concerned for the welfare of those in his charge. As soon as he noted Liu Dacun's appearance and bearing in court, he knew in his heart that there had to be some mistake. The man was, from all indications, an honest tradesman. How could he possibly have tried to assassinate a soldier? As the interrogation commenced, Liu Dacun recounted the details of his two encounters with the cat; he also submitted his business ledger as evidence. The magistrate was even more surprised by the testimony and questioned Liu in detail several times over. But Liu's testimony remained consistent. There was no indication that he'd made up anything to avoid punishment. The magistrate had no recourse therefore but to detain him, while secretly sending trusted aides to the countryside to find out about the person inside that sarcophagus. How long had he been dead? What did he die of? Who in his family survived him?

The clandestine investigation was quickly completed. The dead man was surnamed Chen and was over thirty years of age. Like Liu, he had been a tradesman. He and his wife had accumulated little wealth, but they did manage to eke out a living. His wife had been five or six years his junior, and the couple had normally gotten along very well. Chen passed away only the month before, though no one outside of the family knew from what sort of illness. Neither did anyone know of any scandalous rumors concerning the behavior of the wife. Certain crass individuals, eager to earn a bit of money as go-betweens, did approach her about arranging a remarriage. But invariably, each one was driven away with merciless insults and curses.

In pondering this report, the county magistrate thought that the occurrences seemingly precipitated by Chen's death were surely curious. It was odd enough that a black cat would carry off the man's kerchief-wrapped parcel, not to mention snatch it from his very mouth. And then, in getting away, it had gone into the space between bricks, a space no more than a couple of inches wide. Wasn't that even more unbelievable? According to practice, a sarcophagus was made up of bricks laid against a coffin inside; all gaps were supposed to have been filled in with mortar. How could there be room within it then for a large cat to roam about? And how could that cat have trailed Liu Dacun after he had walked nearly two miles to have his lunch? Never had he heard of a cat so bold as to leap onto a table to snatch food while someone was still eating, not to mention run off with it, plate and all, in its mouth. The facts were becoming more incredible as he sorted them out in his mind. Liu Dacun, moreover, was not at all near-sighted. How could he have been so unaware of a sergeant going past with a squad of soldiers that he'd throw a bowl at the man's head? Even the world's biggest fool wouldn't attempt to assassinate someone using a bowl as a weapon! Had the sarcophagus contained an unmarried person, or one who was already fifty or sixty, then the strange happenings might be considered purely coincidental, perhaps attributable to mental imbalance on Liu Dacun's part. But they had occurred in such a puzzling situation. How could he rest until he got to the bottom of this case? To do that, however, would require opening up the sarcophagus for inspection when no one had yet come forward with a complaint. To disturb a final resting place on the basis of a wild, intuitive hunch would surely be seen as reckless disregard for the dead.

The magistrate pondered these matters alone for a long time. He then summoned Liu Dacun back to the arraignment room and told him his idea of opening the sarcophagus for a look, in order to right any possible wrong the deceased man might have suffered. Once more he asked Liu whether everything had happened as Liu said. Having been through both bizarre incidents, Liu Dacun agreed that the dead man must have been the victim of some sort of injustice. He had been thinking of asking the magistrate to examine the corpse but had found it difficult to make the suggestion. After all, he was an insignificant shopkeeper who knew neither the law nor the ultimate propriety of voicing such an opinion. He was, moreover, a timid sort who worried about his own liability if his request were followed and nothing was found. For these reasons, he had never dared to broach the subject. But after hearing the magistrate and learning that their thinking was similar he made bold to voice his opinion. "What I personally encountered in those two incidents was indeed bizarre," he said. "I am willing to conclude that the dead man must have been wronged. If you find nothing inside the sarcophagus, then deal with me according to the law and I shall have no regrets. The dead man either wanted me to set things aright for him or he could be wreaking vengeance on me. If it's to set things aright, I ought to do what I can. If I have wronged him in a former existence, then I won't be able to escape his vengeance in any case. So I beg you not to hesitate. Do go ahead and open up the sarcophagus."

Hearing these words, the magistrate made up his mind immediately to do just that. In accordance with regulations, he asked Liu Dacun to sign an affidavit; then he offered him words of sympathy and encouragement. That same day, with a coroner and various orderlies as well as Liu himself, he set out for the countryside. Arriving at the site, he promptly set up an autopsy tent and sent a man to bring in Chen's wife. The magistrate acted so swiftly for a purpose: He wanted to allow her little opportunity to carry out any sort of cover-up.

In short order Chen's wife was brought before him. He saw that her face was ashen from fear; her whole body trembled unceasingly.

The orderlies shouted for her to get down on her knees even as the magistrate told them to step back. "Are you surnamed Chen?" he asked her gently, a look of kindness on his face. "Yes," the wife managed to force out from within her throat.

"Is your husband in there?" asked the magistrate, pointing to the sarcophagus. At this question, the wife trembled, each of her thirty-six teeth chattering one against another. Then, with great effort, she managed to steady herself.

"The one in there is my husband," she affirmed with sudden resolution after a pause.

The magistrate noted that her two replies differed greatly in spirit and tone. He deduced that she must have done something unconscionable, that she was just then realizing she had been found out. Because the matter now threatened her life, she could not stave off the fear in her heart. Under the current situation, she realized that the greater her fear, the more clearly her guilt would show on her face. So she steeled her nerves, drove out her panic, and was thus able to give a resolute reply.

The magistrate pressed on. "How long has your husband been dead?"

"He passed away on the seventh day of the eleventh lunar month, just a month and seven days ago," said the wife.

"What illness did he have?" asked the magistrate. "Did he take any medicine for it?"

"My husband was consumptive," said the wife, "and had been for three or four years. He didn't take medicine for it during the latter stages."

"When *did* he take medicine, then? Which physician wrote out the prescriptions? Do you still have them?"

There was a slight pause. "During those years, he took medicine many times," she replied. "He wrote out the prescriptions himself each time, since he had some medical knowledge. We didn't keep the prescriptions, though. My husband mostly tore them up."

"If he had taken medicine many times during the years of his illness, why was it that he stopped doing so later?"

"My husband said that consumption could only be cured early on," said the wife. "As time passes, there is nothing that can be done about it, so trying to cure it would be a waste of money. That was why he stopped writing the prescriptions."

"Are you telling me that after a certain time, you were willing to sit there and watch him die without looking for a physician?" asked the magistrate.

"My husband never had any faith in physicians. Also, I didn't know of anyone suitable. Since he was adamant about it, even if I'd gotten somebody to come by, my husband would never have taken anything anyone prescribed. I never thought he would just die like that and leave me all to myself. It's really been painful for me." She covered her face and began to sob.

What a formidable person this adulteress was, thought the magistrate upon hearing this testimony. Nevertheless, no matter how well she explained herself, he was still determined to open up the sarcophagus. "So your husband did die of consumption?" he asked her once more.

Brushing aside tears, the wife answered him with evident exasperation. "If he hadn't died of consumption, would I tell you that he had? What good would that do?"

At that the orderlies shouted at her for being confrontational. But the magistrate did not appear to be upset. "To claim consumption as the cause of death *would* do you some good, wouldn't it?" he challenged her with great composure. "You should know that someone in this county has accused you of murdering your husband."

The wife could not refrain from looking a bit stunned. "What evidence is there to support such an accusation?" she was quick to ask.

The magistrate smiled. "I would of course have required unshakeable evidence in order to accept his written accusation. So tell me the truth: How did you carry out the murder?"

"The unshakeable evidence you have, sir, please bring it out for me to see," the wife requested without hesitation.

"So you won't confess until you see the evidence?" countered the magistrate. "I suggest you do so now, and save your dead husband's remains from being turned inside out. You know very well what you've done. No one who commits this kind of crime has ever been able to escape the long arm of the law. Just think about it. Your deed was carried out in complete secrecy. How then did it come about that a mere month and seven days later, I already know about it? Would I have come all the way out here to question you if I did not have solid proof? Look for yourself. I've brought along workers and a coroner. Even if you're determined to keep your mouth firmly shut, do you think you can somehow get away with what you've done?"

At that the wife's composure changed again; her body began to tremble anew. It was then that the magistrate's countenance took on an iron ferocity. He slapped the bench, shouting repeatedly for her to confess. The orderlies on either side chorused the demand. The wife managed to steady herself and to resume her earlier demeanor of resolution. "There's no question my husband died of consumption," she said. "But the magistrate has insisted that I murdered him. What wrong has my dead husband done that the magistrate would have to disturb his remains? Can he just order this kind of action at will?"

The magistrate laughed. "You've murdered your husband, so I would say that you can't get off as easily as all that! I've already concurred with your accuser about the necessity of examining the corpse. If we find no evidence of foul play, the accuser will of course be punished according to the law, and I will expect a reprimand from my superiors as well. But did you think you could cow me by pointing this out, so that I would not proceed?" With that, he gave the go-ahead to open the sarcophagus. The workers responded with an enthusiastic shout, as if called to do battle. Then they began to remove the tiles and bricks.

The task was swiftly accomplished. In less than half a minute, the interior coffin lay exposed. The magistrate turned once more to the wife. "By now anyone can see that you have no hope of further concealment. If you have any conscience, you should confess the true details of your crime now to avoid letting your murdered husband suffer the wholesale disturbance of his remains."

The wife let out a wail. "Heaven be my judge!" she sobbed. "My husband *did* die of consumption, but the magistrate insists that I murdered him. What evil karma had my husband accumulated to have to be put through all this after death? Even though I, his wife, have suffered an unrightable wrong, nothing I can do will stop the magistrate from opening the coffin!"

The magistrate knew then that even at this point, the wife was set on withholding her confession. So he sounded the order to unseal the coffin. The coroner responded with a shout as the axes fell together on the cover. With a *crack,* it was split apart and cast aside. The coroner saw that under the corpse's right armpit was a handkerchief-wrapped parcel, which did not look like anything normally belonging with the dead. He took it out for the magistrate to examine. Sure enough, when the magistrate opened it up, it contained the cash Liu Dacun said the black cat had taken from him: five silver dollars, four twenty-cent silver coins, and fifteen coppers. At this, Liu Dacun quickly stepped forward to reclaim his property.

Now that the parcel had been found within the coffin, the magistrate was reassured. Soon enough, the coroner came up to report that he had pulled out a steel rod seven inches long from the top of the dead man's skull. It was the kind of rod used in opium smoking. The wound was the only one on the body, and it was fatal. The discovery was officially recorded by the clerk.

Seeing that the autopsy had uncovered the crime, the wife immediately wanted to kill herself by bashing in her own head. The orderlies, however, having long since expected a suicide attempt with such an eventuality, were able to stop her. They brought her back to the yamen, where she quickly confessed the truth.

As it turned out, the person who carried on the adulterous affair with the wife was none other than the sergeant whose head Liu Da-cun cracked open with the bowl of rice. With the onset of winter months, the sergeant had brought his men to the countryside to help enforce the winter curfew. It wasn't long after taking up his assignment that he started the affair with the wife. They were extremely careful to keep it secret so that no one else was aware of what went on. Then the pair became annoyed with Chen and hatched their murder plot after he fell ill. An opium smoker, the sergeant had once read in a Judge Bao story of a wife doing away with her husband by driving a nail down the top of his cranium so that the cause of death would be undetectable. They thought that by doing the same thing with the opium rod, they could conceal their crime from the coroner, even if an examination of the corpse were to take place. The person who wrote the Judge Bao stories had never read anything about legal procedure, however, so he had no knowledge of autopsies. When corpses were examined for legal reasons, every bone and sinew was taken apart, cleaned off, and scrutinized. There was no possible way a metal nail of considerable length driven through the middle of the skull could escape notice. Had the sergeant not believed the fictional story of Judge Bao, he might not have committed this extraordinary crime. That he would place his trust in the idea of using a nail as a murder weapon, but not in that of an animal acting to right a wrong, ultimately became the reason for his inability to escape the karma of a just retribution. How can we deny the remarkable irony in all this?

— 1924

The Sunglasses Society

Sun Liaohong

N ow that I think of it, the Sunglasses Society had a rather ludicrous beginning. There were several jewel merchants who set aside every Saturday evening for a dinner party to cultivate mutual friendship. The participants took turns hosting. On one such occasion, one of them started bragging to his fellows that, as soon as he got hold of any gemstone, his unerring eyes could tell with absolute accuracy whether it was genuine or fake. Even among peers, he was unflinchingly self-confident, insisting that no eyesight could match his. One participant was unable to bear the boasting and started to dispute with him. The ensuing discussion got nowhere, however, since each could only repeat his opposing opinion. Finally, the host tried to settle matters. "You are both just making empty talk," said he. "Even if you go on until the sun comes up, no listener can say who's right and who's wrong. So why don't you wait until our next gathering, when each of us can bring in a sample item. Then everyone can examine what the others have brought and determine which is genuine and which is not. In this way, we'll be able to tell who among us possesses the sharpest eyesight, and also give everyone the opportunity to increase his professional expertise and not be taken in by fakes in the future." At the time, the suggestion met with general approval, and the dispute was temporarily settled.

At the following week's party, everyone did indeed bring along real and false stones of varying value, ready to prove to everyone there who had the keenest eyesight. But when all is said and done, everyone whose profession it was to sell jewelry possessed this visual ability to a considerable degree. As it turned out, the whole exercise was pretty much child's play. No one was able to fool anyone else, and the question of the superiority or inferiority of visual discernment remained unanswered. Then someone came up with another suggestion. "The kind of test we had today was too simple, and uninteresting besides," he said. "Why doesn't everyone bring along sunglasses next time? We all can put the glasses on. If anyone can *then* tell a real gem from a fake, we'll recognize him as having the keenest eyesight." Having made the suggestion on impulse and tossed it out without forethought, the speaker never expected the enthusiastic response that greeted it. Everyone thought that the idea was novel and exciting and that they should go ahead and try it. Later they decided that the lenses in the glasses should all be of the same dark green color.

It just so happened that it was the turn of a senior jeweler in his fifties to host the next gathering. His name was Xu Mutao—a man with a dark complexion, who sported a thin goatee. This time, he was having the party in his own house. Everyone was there soon after seven o'clock in the evening, and each wore a large pair of glasses with green lenses as per the previous agreement. From a bystander's point of view, the sight was nothing short of ludicrous. For the participants, everything they looked at took on a dark green hue, as if they'd gone deep into the verdant heavens. Looking around at one another, they could not contain their amusement. Then they repaired as usual into the small parlor and saw that a full banquet was laid out on the large round table. The host had recently gone to another part of the house, however, and had not returned. Good thing the people there were too well-acquainted with each other to observe formality.

They sat down wherever they pleased and began to strike up conversations. One among them, Zhao Jiqiu by name, was a handsome young man in Western garb. He had a pale face and a high-bridged nose. Normally, he wore a pair of horn-rimmed glasses. Everyone always said his looks reminded them of Harold Lloyd, the comedian in the movies. Though he had donned the dark green sunglasses for the occasion, his debonair appearance was hardly affected. He now began to speak. "Gentlemen," he addressed them with a slight smile, "we are seated here enjoying ourselves. But do you realize we may be the cause for regret on the part of a lot of hardworking farmers?"

The gathering did not understand what he was talking about. "Here we are, minding our own business," they muttered in surprise. "What do farmers have to do with us? Why would we be bringing them regret?"

"Don't you know?" Jiqiu asked with a grin. "Think about it. With so many water buffaloes here having gotten out of their pens, how can the farmers not sigh over their losses?"

Only then did they understand he was referring to their bespectacled appearances. They couldn't help breaking into laughter.

Unexpectedly, amid the merriment, Li Ren (the very person who was boasting to everyone two weeks ago), spoke up icily. "What are you all laughing about? What's so funny about Jiqiu's crack? We are all good human beings. Why should we be comparing ourselves to buffaloes?"

They had always known Li Ren to be humorless and stuffy. Still, seeing that he was seriously taking offense, their laughter gradually petered out. But one man, Lu Bi'en, was a volatile sort who would not allow Li Ren's dampening remarks to pass without comment. "Jiqiu was just having fun. Why must Mr. Li here respond so sanctimoniously? In my humble opinion, we humans are always bustling about from dawn to dusk, always worrying and fretting, never allowing ourselves any time to relax. It's as if someone invisible were holding a whip and driving us on. From this perspective, there isn't that much difference between a water buffalo and a human being, is there? But some individuals who may be unreasonable, crass, and stupid nevertheless hold on to their inflated egos. It's really they who are dumb like buffaloes!" Lu Bi'en's words were intended half to vent his own spleen and half to ridicule Li Ren.

Now, Yang Guodong, who was sitting next to Lu Bi'en, was by nature a peacemaker. To head off any conflict arising from the clash of words, he tried to calm everyone down with his own. "The gathering tonight, with all of us wearing identical sunglasses, is indeed an occasion for great fun," he said. "Why don't we just call ourselves the Sunglasses Society? The name's less pretentious and more original than, say, the Double Rocker Society or the Single Sword Society or the Society for Nunnery Encounters." The curious names Yang Guodong dragged out brought the sound of loud laughter to the gathering once more.

In the midst of this renewed merriment, the host, Xu Mutao, came in from the nearby sitting room, hunched over apologetically and clutching a stack of thick paper. He was greeted with smiles and invited to join everyone at the table. In short order, the servants brought in food. "Each of you has brought along a number of goodies today, I would assume," Mutao said smilingly after several rounds of toasting.

"That's right," Bi'en was quick to affirm. "What I brought is a string of pearls, a hundred of them, all of nearly perfect roundness. Fifty-one are genuine; the rest are not. Since Mr. Li believes that his own powers of discernment are the best, the pearls are here for his discrimination. If he can tell the difference, I will admit to everyone here that I was wrong about him. I'm asking you, Mr. Xu, to act as referee."

"I have with me two seven-carat diamonds," Li Ren also said, "but they belong to someone else. It's possible that both are genuine, or both not—or perhaps one is genuine and the other not. Actually I myself cannot tell with certainty. So I want to ask you gentlemen to look them over. But if you are unable to tell the difference, we must state ahead of time that the punishment will be . . ."

In succession, each of the guests fished in his pocket and then talked about the items he'd brought, the authentication of any of which presented problems.

"Don't let's be so impatient, so impatient," Mutao smilingly chided them. "Just slow down and listen to me. We may feel like testing each other today. But whether a jewel is real or not depends on its luster or coloring. Since you've all put on dark glasses, please tell me how on earth you can make out the color or luster of anything. Last week, we were so caught up in our own enthusiasm the problem escaped even me." When they heard this, they suddenly realized the truth of Mutao's point. No one could say a thing in response.

After a pause Bi'en turned to Mutao to ask what he thought they should do. "I think it's simply too difficult to try to examine jewels through sunglasses," Mutao said. "We ought to change one of our requirements." Right away, all of them wanted to know which one. "Just now," Mutao responded, "when I was spending all that time in the house, I picked out quite a few watercolor paintings for you. The colors are excellent and rather complex. I was thinking we could use them in our test." How, everyone wanted to know. "I'll just hold up a painting," said Mutao. "From a distance of at least five feet, you'll have to identify exactly each of the colors on it. Do it correctly and everyone will drink a toast to you. Make a mistake and you'll have to down three tumblers as punishment. Aside from that, I'll get to pull on your ears and make you bark like a dog three times. Let's take turns and put each of you to the test. What do you say?"

Everyone clapped their hands in approval, saying that the game was innovative and amusing. Only Li Ren appeared unwilling. Already surly about being equated with a water buffalo, he was even less happy at the prospect of having to bark like a dog. Nonetheless, he had to acquiesce to the wishes of the crowd. Quite by chance, his turn came up first. "Quiet, please! Quiet!" the crowd shouted with glee. "Let's hear how the first dog barks."

Li Ren saw that there was a peony flower with several leaves on the painting in Mutao's hands. The colors were extremely light and he was quite a distance away. Through the green lenses everything was a blur. He really couldn't even distinguish red from green. Nevertheless, with the guests urging him to hurry, Li was forced to guess. "The flower is pink, and the leaves are pale green," he said.

Mutao let out a guffaw. "All right, all right, all right! How on earth could you have considered yourself sharp-eyed? You can't even recognize this famous green peony. Here, take a look for yourself. No way you can get out of barking this time!" Li Ren looked at the painting after removing his glasses. The peony was greenish and the leaves reddish—exactly opposite what he'd guessed. Only then did he realize Mutao was being crafty, and he'd fallen victim.

"You've got me this time," Li Ren said miserably. "I'm willing to drink the wine and bark. But I have a request. These damnable glasses are very hard to take. They make me dizzy and befuddle my mind. Now that I've already gone through the test, let me keep them off."

"Not a chance, not a chance," Mutao declared. "After you bark, you must put them back on. Otherwise, you're not a bespectacled dog." The remark brought a roar of laughter from the gathering.

Li Ren went through with his punishment. Then it was Lu Bi'en's turn. Now, Bi'en considered himself more shrewd. He saw that Mutao was holding a painting of a parrot, the colors of which were indecipherable through his sunglasses. Bi'en was thinking that parrots normally have green bodies and red beaks, but the colors in the painting must be opposite to his expectations. He therefore spoke up without any hesitation. "The parrot has a red body and a green beak," he said, thoroughly pleased with himself because he was certain he must be right.

Mutao's reaction caught him off guard: "Wrong again, wrong again! Prepare yourself to drink and bark! Bi'en, you've gotten caught outsmarting yourself." Sure enough, the parrot was colored as it would normally be, with a green body and red beak. Thus forced to admit defeat, Bi'en drank the wine and barked thrice as his ears were pulled. One after another, everyone took their turns. A different painting was put up each time, and very few were able to guess the colors correctly; the rate of failure was sixty to seventy percent. Toward the end, everyone was getting tipsy. With so many green sunglasses matched to crimson cheeks, the gathering became quite a spectacle. Everyone's spirits were roused to an unusual degree.

"It's your idea to do this to us, loading us up with drink and making us bark like dogs," Yang Guodong then said to Mutao. "Now what should we be doing to you?" Everyone shouted their agreement to the question. But just as Mutao was about to answer, a servant burst in with a uniformed police officer in tow. The people all fell silent; they had no idea of what was transpiring. Mutao stared straight at the officer. "What's wrong?" he asked him seriously.

The officer studied the room, taking in each of those present. His face betrayed a mixture of surprise and apprehension. "Please . . . please forgive me," he stammered. "I've got an investigation to carry out. Lu . . . Lu . . ."

"Lu who?" Mutao wanted to know.

"Lu Ping's around here," said the officer, his voice fading to a whisper at the mention of the name. Many there could not make out what he was trying to say.

"What!? Lu Ping's *here?*" Mutao was in shock.

"Yes, sir," panted the officer. "Somebody called the station just now to tip us off. He said that Lu Ping had disguised himself as one of you and has joined your party. Of the nine people around this table, one has to be that famous thief in disguise." Even as he was speaking to Mutao, he kept flashing his eyes at the people there. By now, everyone understood what was happening. They let out a few unconscious oohs and aahs before exchanging glances in shocked silence.

The atmosphere remained hushed for a while. Then something occurred to Yang Guodong. He sprang to his feet. "Do you know what Lu Ping was wearing today?" he asked the officer, who was at that moment looking closely at Zhao Jiqiu.

The officer turned his head. "The informer mentioned that Lu Ping had on a very attractive Western-style suit," he answered in a low voice. Instantly all eyes, Mutao's included, fell on three individuals— Zhao Jiqiu, Lu Bi'en, and Yang Guodong—all of whom fit the description. Of the three, Lu Bi'en drew the most attention because he appeared the most ill at ease in both speech and action. Zhao Jiqiu, on the other hand, remained unperturbed. But since he seemed a bit *too* calm, he was also under suspicion. Just that quickly, the house became filled with fear and foreboding. The feeling was that everybody was a suspect in one way or another, which made everybody tremble with dread. Except for the prime suspects Yang, Zhao, and Lu, the guests broke off into little groups and spoke in hushed tones to each other. The host, Xu Mutao, stood by himself, head down as if in a trance, unable to utter a single word.

This situation went on for some time before the police officer came up with a suggestion. "Gentlemen," he addressed them in a solemn voice, "why don't you remove your glasses and scrutinize each other's faces? Then we'll be able to pick out the face that's questionable, and that will be Lu Ping's. Even though Lu Ping's a master of disguise, he can't very well fool people who see each other every day."

The suggestion woke them all up, and they hurried to remove their sunglasses. Then they rubbed their eyes and scrutinized one another —without result. Everyone seemed to resemble Lu Ping, but, then again, no one did. Lu Bi'en, who had carefully studied each face, could no longer contain himself. "Enough!" he shouted. "We who are gathered here see each other regularly. We'd be able to recognize each other's facial features even after cremation! How in the world can Lu Ping be among us?"

Yang Guodong, who had been staring vacantly at him as he spoke, became greatly agitated. Beads of sweat appeared on his brow. Abruptly, he took several steps back and pointed his finger at Lu Bi'en. "Quick!" he shouted. "Arrest him, quick! This man is none other than Lu Ping in disguise! Don't you see a red mole on each of his ears?"

All eyes then fell on Lu Bi'en's ears, which, indeed, showed the two tiny red spots. A shriek of surprise went up from the group. Some thought about running away, others about summoning up the courage to come forward and seize him. Before a melee could commence, Li Ren was wildly flapping his hands. "Hold it, hold it!" he said. "Things have taken a really bizarre turn! So you think that anyone with red spots on his ears has to be Lu Ping? From the time I learned that Lu Ping was among us, I've paid attention to everyone's ears. Don't you see that Jiqiu and Guodong's ears also have such spots? It's not just Bi'en who's like that! Take a close look, if you don't believe me." The guests gathered themselves and did just that, and discovered that Li Ren was not talking nonsense. This befuddled them even more. Different voices muttered that the case was becoming surreal.

"No matter what transpires," the police officer then suggested to them, "one among you has to be Lu Ping in disguise. It's hard to believe you can't detect any flaw in his appearance with your collective eyesight. I think you ought to search everyone's pockets. In coming here, Lu Ping's purpose has to be robbery. He therefore has got to have some sort of weapon on his person. If we can find it, won't we have found him out as well?" Some thought the idea excellent. Others, however, said that Lu Ping invariably used only intellectual finesse in his work, never force. He couldn't possibly be carrying any weapon, so searching everybody's pockets probably wouldn't turn up anything.

"The matter of pockets," said Zhao Jiqiu, "has reminded me of something else. Our gathering today is different from previous occasions, when all of our pockets contained one sort of precious item or another. Had we encountered before what we're encountering now, the risk would be really serious. Good thing that, for this occasion, all I brought with me are fakes. I just wanted to have some fun with you all. Even if Lu Ping robs me, I wouldn't be losing much. But those of you who brought along genuine stuff need to take care."

Jiqiu's words seemed to add to their burden of dread. They now regretted having taken along items of such value just to satisfy a momentary whim. So they conferred with the officer about entrusting him with the contents in their pockets; he could take everything to the police station for safekeeping. The officer, however, frowned at the idea. "I can't do that," he said. "I can't take the chance of Lu Ping tailing me once I leave here." This seemed reasonable enough, but then they thought about their own concerns. They would have to go home before long, taking along what they brought. How could they be sure Lu Ping would not follow? What would they do then? The more they thought about that, the greater their dread. So then they went to confer with their host, imploring him to hold on to the jewelry temporarily; they would send someone to retrieve everything the following day. At the very least, that would be far preferable to taking the stuff home with them that night.

Their host, Xu Mutao, had long since been cowed into complete silence. All this time, he had kept his head bowed and was trembling in his boots. Learning that everyone wanted him to safeguard their jewelry, he now hurriedly refused. "I . . . I cannot under any circumstances accept such heavy responsibility . . . I just can't do it."

Again and again, they begged him to reconsider. "Don't you have a steel safe here?" they said. "Just put the things in it. Lu Ping won't be able to do a thing about that, clever though he is."

Mutao shook his head. "I can't. To Lu Ping, a steel safe like this is no more secure than the paper one we buy to burn to the dead. Haven't you heard about the bank robberies? Where banks keep valuables is surely more impregnable than anything in my house. But even banks can't keep Lu Ping out . . . So how . . ."

"Lu Ping was able to rob the banks because he caught them unawares," the people said. "We know now that he is here. As long as you take the proper precautions, there's little he can do."

Thus pressured by one and all, Mutao could not very well refuse. So he reluctantly agreed to do as they wished. Taking out a large kerchief, he wrapped everyone's items together in preparation for putting them in the safe. In the meantime, he spoke to the officer about bolstering security by sending over a few more policemen when he got back to the station.

While he was still arranging this, weird sounds wafted intermittently from the sitting room next door. Instantly, everyone became like birds waiting for the hunter's arrows, pale with fright, helplessly looking back and forth at each other. For Xu Mutao this was, after all, happening in his home, and he did not want anything untoward to take place. He quickly parted the crowd, pushed open the door to the sitting room, and ran in. The officer hesitated and considered staying put outside, but with everybody's eyes on him, he couldn't avoid going in. The guests followed right behind, pushing their way inside. Nothing appeared unusual as they looked around, except that the shutters of a window over the street were wide open. Then they traced the source of the sounds—which were much like the moans of a sick person—to the underside of an oversized couch. Quickly they went over to lift up the couch, then let out a collective gasp: There was none other than Xu Mutao, who had entered the room ahead of them. A large handkerchief covered his mouth. Upon untying it, they noticed that it retained the odor of an anesthetic.

"Mutao entered the room just seconds ahead of the rest of us," marveled Yang Guodong. "No matter how fast Lu Ping operates, there's no way he could have drugged a person and then escaped with the goods in so short a time."

Lu Bi'en was disconsolate. "He might have had enough time, or he might not have," he said. "All I want to know now is, what happened to our things? That is the real question." He turned to Mutao as he spoke. "Where are the things you wrapped in your handkerchief?"

Mutao had not totally recovered his senses. In response, he could only lift up a pair of utterly lifeless eyes and look numbly around at everyone. "What's that? What's that?" he mumbled.

"The things we gave you just now, what you wrapped up in the handkerchief," the guests couldn't wait to ask. "What's happened to them? Did Lu Ping get away with them?"

Mutao registered shock. He clenched his fists and leaped up. "What . . . what things? Who gave anything to me?"

All were baffled at Mutao's reaction. "How did you get under the couch?" Yang Guodong finally asked.

"I don't know myself," said Mutao. "I only remember telling the servants to set the dining table before I left to come in here. I don't even recall why I came in, and I surely didn't expect to find someone already in here. The person's dress and features were very much like my own. Just as I was about to question him, he rushed over to me before I could react and put something over my nose. I felt a strange odor in my nostrils and drifted into unconsciousness. Whatever happened after that, I cannot say at all. What 'things' are you talking about?"

At this, Zhao Jiqiu began to rave. "We're done for! We're done for!" he shouted. "You're telling us that you were drugged *before* joining us for dinner. In that case, the one who came into the parlor was none other than Lu Ping, disguised as you. By now, he's out the window and long gone."

"No wonder there were red moles on the ears of Lu, Yang, and Zhao!" Li Ren shouted out. "When this cunning thief was tugging at your ears and ordering you to bark, he was transferring some kind of pigment from his hands. Surely that's how those red moles got onto each of you . . ." When he reached this point, Li Ren could only stare at everyone with a look of wonderment on his face. His voice, which was trailing off, now stopped altogether.

"Why did the false Mutao bother to put red spots on their ears?" Lu Bi'en then asked Li Ren.

"You're pretty dense," said Li Ren. "What he clearly wanted was for us to accuse each other, so that we would eventually hand our valuables over to him!"

Bi'en stomped his foot in self-disgust. "You're right. You're right. We were thinking that one of us guests had to be Lu Ping in disguise. It never occurred to us he could pass himself off as the host! That's why he turned his face each time a servant brought in a dish of food. Too bad none of us made anything of that."

"But if he was concerned about a servant seeing through him, why wasn't he concerned about us doing the same thing?" Yang Guodong wondered. "Aren't our eyes as sharp as those of the servants? After all is said and done, Lu Ping's ability to disguise himself is simply uncanny. Even if he were to make himself over as one of our parents or siblings, we would still be taken in!"

"What's all this talk?" the officer then chimed in with a smirk. "I'll never believe anyone can disguise himself as an acquaintance and then fool the people who see him every day. That's just so much nonsense scribbled down by some writer of crime fiction. How can we take it as true? Lu Ping succeeded today because all of you had your sunglasses on half the time, and you couldn't make anything out clearly. Then he took advantage of your drinking, which made you all addlebrained. It's because you were far from your best that he could have been so casually confident he wouldn't be found out. As for me, I'd had no acquaintance with the host here, nor have I ever seen Lu Ping's face. So of course I was hoodwinked. Under different circumstances . . ."

Seeing the officer give such elaborate excuses now that the robbery was over and the thief had gotten away, Lu Bi'en could hardly contain his disgust. "Officer, sir," he interjected, "why are you still standing here? Please don't pass the blame onto us. You know, don't you, that it's *your* job to solve robberies and apprehend crooks." Embarrassed, the policeman left, his spirits greatly dampened.

After that, everyone steadied themselves to confer with each other.

"The loss from this caper amounts to about fifty or sixty thousand dollars," they calculated. "Can we hope to recover it?"

"It's hard, hard, hard," said Xu Mutao. "Lu Ping getting his hands on valuables is like a greedy official stuffing bribe money into his wallet. In either case, there's no way in the world to recover any of it." At this, the people couldn't help putting blame on Li Ren. Had he not boasted at the last gathering, the jewelry would not have fallen into Lu Ping's hands.

But Li Ren was unrepentant. "I still believe that my eyesight's keener than any of yours," he said seriously. "I would guess that even now, none of you know who Lu Ping actually is."

This startled one and all. "The one who pretended to be our host, wasn't he Lu Ping?"

"How could he have been?" said Li Ren. "He was only Lu Ping's henchman. The real Lu Ping was the police officer." No one could wait to ask the reason for this conclusion. "It's because I found a pair of real red moles on his ears when I looked at them closely," Li Ren explained. "Think about it. Had the supposed secret tip been phoned into the police station, the place would have been in a tizzy. Why then would they have sent just one person here to investigate? Isn't this suspicious in itself?"

The guests then rushed to call the police station to ask whether an officer had been sent to their address. Sure enough, they were told that nothing of the sort had occurred.

Now everyone was upset at Li Ren. "Once you figured out that the officer was Lu Ping," they shouted, "why didn't you blow his cover immediately? Why did you let him carry on his mischief?"

"Blow his cover? For one thing, we were all empty-handed. There was no chance we could have stood up to him," said Li Ren. Even if we'd managed to apprehend him, he'd likely break out of jail in no time. Why would I want to make an enemy of this crazy individual? Then again, he did realize at the time that I'd seen through his ruse. It was for that reason that he kept those formidable eyes of his on me all the while. He seemed to be warning me with his stare to look out, that he'd retaliate should I sound the alarm. Just think. Can anyone who's the subject of Lu Ping's ire avoid ultimate calamity? For these reasons, I thought I'd rather cut my losses and sacrifice my two diamonds, one of which was genuine. I'd never have dared to cry out."

— 1924

The Ghost in the Villa

. . . .

Cheng Xiaoqing

I. *Ghost Story*

O ne afternoon in early spring, our former servant Shi Gui brought in a visitor. The man was past fifty, with a short, broad face. His nose was flat and his eyes large. He wore a light-gray silk brocade robe with small circular patterns and an inner lining. On his left ring finger was a diamond. Overall, he looked extremely well-heeled. He swaggered when he walked, very much in the manner of a so-called revered member of the merchant class. Only after the customary greetings did I learn that the man's surname was Hua and his given name Bosun, and that he was the manager of the Colorful Threads Silk Factory in Shanghai. Then he explained his reason for coming.

He said: "Mr. Huo, I have long held you in the highest regard and known you to be a great detective, with phenomenal abilities. I have also read the case notes recorded by Mr. Bao here . . ."

Huo Sang's face betrayed his impatience. He held up his right hand. "You need not stand on ceremony, Mr. Hua. Whatever it is you want, please tell us directly."

The mild rebuke caused Hua Bosun's face to flush with embarrassment. He shifted his body on the couch before proceeding hesitantly.

He said: "What I . . . uh . . . what I need to ask you is to use your great talents to help me find the solution to a very difficult matter."

He was still not coming to the point, even though Huo Sang had so urged him. He riveted his gaze on Huo Sang's face, as if waiting for a reply. Huo Sang, his eyes shut, slowly puffed on his cigarette, absolutely refusing to take up the cue.

Huo Sang had this trait: Whenever he got insincere or formulaic blather from someone, he would invariably become annoyed. Here was a person who, on first encounter, appeared to be a bit highbrow. That alone was sufficient to trigger Huo Sang's impatience. In this case, however, I could see that the worry on the man's face was not pretense, and I felt a little bad that Huo Sang's cold and detached attitude toward our guest left the latter no room to avoid embarrassment.

I therefore interjected: "Mr. Hua, can you explain your difficulty? Were you robbed? Did you lose track of someone?"

Hua Bosun turned toward me and waved his hand. "No, no. If it were just a robbery or a missing person, the Shanghai police could handle the investigation; I would never dare to trouble the two of you. I'm here because . . . because . . ."

Again, he hesitated and stopped before getting to the point. Huo Sang's eyes remained closed. He seemed to be paying no attention. Oblivious as a slug in a windstorm, the man seemed too dense to ever get to the heart of the matter.

I tried again to draw him out. "What really is the problem, then? Please don't just talk around it."

The visitor blushed again. Then he said: "All right. I came especially to seek your advice because a ghost has appeared in my new villa."

Huo Sang's eyes popped open. "Bao Lang," he turned to ask me, "when did I hang out any sign about catching ghosts? Did you put out any advertisement for me saying I was some kind of exorcism expert?"

Another rebuke! The redness in Hua Bosun's cheeks spread to his ears.

He stammered: "Mr. Huo, please don't make fun of me. I worked up the courage to come to you because I had no other recourse. I've often heard people say you are not only an expert detective, but someone who can solve all mysteries. This case is really extremely bizarre. Other than you, sir, there is no one I can go to. You've just got to help me!"

His tone was sincere and desperate. His large eyes were wide open. Huo Sang did not show he was paying attention. He threw away the butt of his cigarette, took out another, and lit up once more.

I spoke for him: "Since this is the situation, please make clear to us the strange particulars. My friend here can perhaps be of some assistance then."

Huo Sang let out an unexpected chuckle. "Heh, heh. Bao Lang, you're really a great schemer. You just want to hear a ghost story free of charge!"

Hua Bosun raised a hand and spoke with a stern expression on his face: "Mr. Huo, this is in all seriousness a bizarre actuality; it's not some made-up ghost story. Please don't misunderstand."

Looking directly at the visitor for the first time, Huo Sang nodded. "In that case, let's first hear about it from you. How bizarre can it be?"

Hua Bosun rolled his eyes, as if somewhat comforted; then he gathered himself to speak: "My villa was built in rural Zhenru. The construction began in September of last year and took six months altogether. It was completed only at the end of last month. My intention in building it was to go there for a few days of restful peace and quiet enjoyment during summer and other vacations. That's why I deliberately picked a secluded spot far away from the village; I wanted to avoid being bothered. How could I have known that less than two weeks after the completion of the construction, rumors of the villa being haunted would begin?" With fear all over his face, he paused again to look at Huo Sang.

Huo Sang retained his cool detachment. "What sort of rumors?"

Hua Bosun said: "The first time, according to what was passed around the people there, the mournful sounds of a flute issued daily from within the villa, just before and after nightfall. Since the completion of construction, the villa had been locked and unoccupied. So the people naturally became astonished over the sudden occurrence of the sounds. The suspicion arose that maybe some sort of demons or ghosts was making mischief inside."

Huo Sang drew back his lips. "After hearing that, you just went ahead and believed it?"

"No. At first I absolutely did not believe it, since in our time superstitions about ghosts have all been shown to be groundless. I thought that the sounds of the flute could not have come from within the villa, that perhaps they had been carried from elsewhere by the wind. One rumor breeds another, and this kind of talk is typical of country folk."

"That's right. This is the only reasonable explanation. So what happened subsequently?"

"The rumor persisted. At first, it was only passed around among the people there. But later, my younger brother made a special trip to Shanghai to tell me about the matter."

Huo Sang interrupted him: "You have a brother in the country?"

Hua Bosun replied: "Yes. His name is Boyang; he lives in the town of Zhenru."

"How far is the town from your villa?"

"About a mile."

Huo Sang nodded his head. "Go on."

Hua Bosun picked up the thread again. "Boyang was deadly serious when he came to see me. He, too, had thought it was nonsensical gossip at first and gave no credence to it. After that he purposely went out to the villa for an inspection. He saw that the back door was locked up as before, that nothing at all appeared out of the ordinary. But sure enough, just as he was leaving, that heart-rending wail of the flute assaulted his ears. He felt certain that the sound came from within the house. Amazed, he didn't want to hesitate and came right to Shanghai to report to me. Even though I half believed him, I retained a basically rational attitude and did not become concerned at all. But after some time, matters grew more and more strange." His complexion was turning pale as he spoke.

"So what happened?" It seemed that Huo Sang's interest was piqued.

"Time and again, there appeared to be fires burning on the upper story of the building. Toward dusk one day, a mail carrier passed the front door and suddenly, through a window, saw flames leaping upward, as if the place was on fire. The carrier ran off in a panic, shouting for help. The townspeople became alarmed and dragged a water hose to the villa to put out the fire. But they found the doors and windows shut up tight and the whole place deathly quiet. Nothing seemed to be amiss. After this incident, the villa's reputation for being bizarre spread even more rapidly."

The visitor paused to catch his breath. Huo Sang, silently puffing on his cigarette, made no comment.

I interjected once more: "That is truly peculiar. What was actually going on?"

Hua Bosun said: "It wasn't all that peculiar. What was really peculiar occurred later. Because these things happened one after the other, I couldn't help feeling a little apprehensive. I was deeply concerned that were I to ignore everything that had gone on, the place might really catch on fire and the results would not be inconsequential. So I went out and hired a Shandong watchman, a big fellow named Lin Shangzhong, to guard the building. This would stifle rumors of the villa being haunted. Moreover, any unexpected calamity would also be prevented. How could I have foreseen that three nights after the man took up his watch, he would run off, never daring to go back to the place? When I asked why, he, too, said the place was haunted!"

Huo Sang put down his cigarette. "Oh? Really haunted? What all did he tell you?"

Hua Bosun said: "He said that on his first day in the house, the night passed without incident. The second evening, however, he saw a fireball rolling downstairs from the second-story window. He was so startled he shouted out, but on closer inspection, he saw that the fire had died out completely. He then went upstairs. The windows were shut up as before, with no trace of anything unusual. So even though he'd been unnerved, he as yet felt no fear. Then came the third night, during which he was sure he fell asleep on his bed. When he awoke in the morning, however, he was sleeping *under* it!"

II. *The Ghost-Summoning Spell*

There was a tremor in the visitor's voice. I, too, was mesmerized by the baffling account. Huo Sang had both his eyes wide open and rolled his eyeballs several times. It seemed his curiosity had been roused.

"Do you think that watchman was telling the truth?" he asked.

Hua Bosun said: "How could he not be? I was paying him to watch the place, and at a very good salary. There was definitely no reason for him to lie, especially after he voluntarily quit the job."

Huo Sang let out a puff of cigarette smoke as he thought things over. Then he asked the visitor: "That man from Shandong, did you hire him from the town of Zhenru or from some other place?"

"I hired him from Shanghai."

"Before he was hired, had he heard anything concerning the bizarre happenings in the villa?"

"Not at first. But I thought that once he got there, he would learn about it sooner or later. So I thought it best to explain everything to him beforehand and to ask him whether he was willing to go. He was—without hesitation. Moreover, he told me he'd never believed in ghosts in his life, much less been afraid of them. How was I to know that four short days after he got to the villa, he'd be running back to me?"

"After he ran out, did you go to see the villa?"

"I did, yesterday. A person there told me that when he passed the place the day before, he, too, saw a fireball flying through the air. Don't you think that's odd, Mr. Huo?"

"Mmm. It is indeed very odd. Yesterday, did you go upstairs to look?"

"I went up with my brother to examine everything. Whether there had been fireballs or no, nothing in the house showed any trace of tampering."

"Nothing was missing?"

"I looked over everything carefully. Nothing at all was missing."

Huo Sang nodded, then smiled in my direction. "Bao Lang, this case is even more interesting than those ghost stories in the old anthologies."

This quip showed that Huo Sang was remaining cool and aloof. Evidently, the uneasiness in the visitor's voice and his serious demeanor were not sufficient to earn his true regard. These days, when scientific thinking was becoming more widespread, it was of course not easy for any tale of ghostly phenomena to be immediately convincing to an intellectual. Still, the case itself was without question highly intriguing and definitely worth looking into. Huo Sang's attitude of casual detachment was not necessarily appropriate.

Huo Sang then broached another topic. "Mr. Hua, tell us something about the circumstances before and after the building of the villa."

Hua Bosun said: "I've already talked about it. The work was started in September of last year, and it continued until—."

Huo Sang stopped him right there. "I'm not asking you about that. I mean, who sold you the land the building is on? Was the land vacant, or had there been a building on it previously?"

"The land was originally an ancient burial ground. It was sold to me by a person named Cui from Zhenru. It is said that one of Cui's ancestors was a general during the Ming dynasty. For this reason, when the rumors began, everyone thought it was General Cui making the trouble."

"After the villa was built, did you ever live there?"

"I never did. The day the construction was finished, my brother and I and Hu Junqing, the owner of my factory, did spend some time there."

Huo Sang lowered his head, then threw away his cigarette butt and stretched. "What do you plan to do now?" he asked.

Hua Bosun said: "I think it will definitely turn out badly if things go on like this. That's why I've come today to beg you in all sincerity to find a way out of this difficulty."

Huo Sang was less than straightforward in his reply: "So you want a way out. I have a way out for you, but I don't know if you'd be willing to follow it."

Hua Bosun was quick to respond: "Please. Please tell me. If your plan is workable, there's no reason for me not to follow it."

"What I mean to say is that since this villa has gotten such an unsavory reputation, you should just sell it off and be done with it."

Unexpectedly, Hua Bosun showed a certain hesitancy in his expression. He opened his mouth, then shut it. For a time, he made no reply at all.

Huo Sang asked him: "What about it? You don't agree?"

Hua Bosun said: "Mr. Huo, please forgive me. It's because the villa is located in such a restful place, where I need not be bothered with neighbors. Also, it's so convenient to transportation. I hardly need mention the railroad. Behind the place is a navigable river; I can go there directly by steamboat. When the highway is built, coming and going will become even easier. I really love the locale for these reasons and don't want to give it up to someone else."

Huo Sang nodded. "Mmm. I understand now, and I can't blame you for feeling as you do. Then why don't you first rent the place out for a time. You can perhaps let your renter be your exorcist."

Hua Bosun's eyebrows remained knitted. "I'm not willing to do that, either. I've taken a lot of care and trouble to see that the furnishings and decor are exactly as I want them. If I rent it to other people, they may not treat my things with care. The best way is still for you to go there. Look it over, and think up a positive solution to save the place for me. I will not be stinting in my compensation."

Huo Sang gave me another smile as he stood up. "Bao Lang, you like to listen to old-fashioned ghost stories. Since this matter still lacks a conclusion, I can at least take up the role of Priest Zhang, the Imperial Daoist."

The following day, March 26, Huo Sang came back from his morning stroll and downed his bowl of rice gruel. He then changed his clothes, picked up his suitcase, and headed for Zhenru by himself. I had originally wanted to go along, but Huo Sang considered this a minor case that required his attention only, not worth both of us making a trip.

"You rest up," he said. "I'll surely be back by evening. I can tell you everything then."

The promise was not kept. After 7 P.M., Huo Sang still had not returned. Since he had missed the appointment, I thought that there must have been unforeseen difficulties connected with this unusual case. He'd probably thought it would be rather simple and had then found out it was not so. That's the only reason he could have miscalculated. When one approaches a task with a flippant attitude, one can often fall into careless neglect and as a result be unable to avoid ultimate failure.

Two days later, on the evening of the twenty-seventh, Huo Sang was still away. I could not prevent my initial unease from turning into full-blown concern. He had been gone for two days. Why had there not been a smidgen of news? Possible failure aside, could he have met up with some accident, perhaps? I thought about rushing to Zhenru myself, but then I was afraid he might return in the meantime, and the trip would have been for nothing. So I did not act on the impulse.

It wasn't until almost noon of the twenty-eighth that I saw Huo Sang stagger back, suitcase in hand. He looked extremely exhausted, his complexion a pale yellow, dark circles under his eyes. I couldn't help being quietly shocked. Had he actually failed this time? After a bath, Huo Sang's spirits were revived somewhat, and he began his explanation.

He said: "Bao Lang, this matter was really beyond my expectations. From now on I won't dare to be so cavalier."

I asked him in surprise: "Did you go for nothing? Were there any results?"

Huo Sang did not answer. He fished out a piece of red paper from his coat pocket and handed it to me. "Take a look at this first."

I took it and spread it out. It appeared to be an advertisement. The following was written on it:

The house has sixteen Western-style bedrooms, all completely furnished. It is ringed with flowers and shrubs, giving it an elegant appearance. It is perfect as a primary residence, or as a country retreat. The owner has agreed to lease or sell the entire estate. All interested parties please proceed to the residence of Mr. Hua Boyang in town.

—The owner

I was amazed. "What does this mean? Did the fellow want to sell the house on the sly after all?"

Huo Sang said: "No. This is my ghost-summoning spell."

"Ghost-summoning spell? Well, did you succeed in capturing the ghost?"

"Not only did I succeed, I've already set him free."

I was overjoyed. "Ah! In that case, you've already finished the job. But this ghost, what was he really like? Why did you stay around there for two days?"

Huo Sang's face turned somber. "He was a devil. You should be frightened just hearing me tell about him."

Was he joking? He couldn't be. He looked very solemn. There was no lilt to his voice.

I said: "What was it all about, really? Come now, tell me quickly."

Huo Sang nodded: "All right. I know you are impatient to hear the ending to this ghost story. Well, bear with me for now and let me tell it from the beginning. When the case started, even though there were a few puzzling things that were not immediately understandable, I nevertheless held to my belief that all phenomena in the universe can never go beyond the parameters of natural cause and effect. No matter what, the idea that there can be real ghosts had never entered my brain. Because of the situation, I hypothesized that someone or other wanted to attain ownership of that villa, or else, for whatever reason, desired the land on which the villa was built. But if the person were to try to buy it, he'd know that Hua Bosun would never agree to sell. So he made all kinds of surreptitious mischief in order to get what he wanted."

I nodded repeatedly in agreement. "Not bad. Your hypothesis is indeed reasonable. I, too, thought the same way in the beginning. But who was the person making that mischief from behind the scenes?"

Huo Sang said: "The one I suspected in the very beginning was Hu Junqing, the owner of the silk factory. He had been there once and could have concocted the plan because he liked the house. But then I met Hu on the morning of the twenty-sixth while I was taking a stroll. Right then, I realized I was off the mark. He really had no connection to the case. The other possible culprit, I surmised, could be Hua Bosun's brother Boyang. When I got to the countryside and met him face-to-face, however, I felt that my own imagination had been working overtime. He turned out to be a proper and contented rustic who managed the Jiangnan Dry Goods Store in town. As soon as the matter of the villa was brought up, trepidation appeared on his face. There was absolutely nothing to indicate that he could have wanted the place for himself. These two setbacks made me see that I had been taking the case too lightly. I needed to come up with a different approach. So I told Boyang everything I was thinking and concocted this plan with him. We hung the spell on the villa's front door, then waited for the ghost to come to the trap. I quietly went inside to make my own inspection. At night I also went there to stake it out."

"What did you manage to see?"

"First, I heard the *yoo yoo* sounds of the flute."

"Oh, so there really was a flute."

"Yes indeed. After that I also saw a fireball coming straight down from upstairs."

"How strange! Are you sure?"

"How could I not be sure? I heard it with my own ears and saw it with my own eyes."

"Oh, but did you find out what was causing all that?"

"Of course. But at the time I did nothing about it at all. It wasn't until the afternoon of the next day, the twenty-seventh, that the ghost's representative actually appeared."

I could not wait. "What kind of a person was he?"

Huo Sang steadied his gaze and answered: "The representative was very elegantly dressed. Now, I had arranged ahead of time for Hua Boyang himself to meet with anyone who turned up; I would hide myself in order to watch what transpired. The person said he wanted to rent and not to buy. When Boyang mentioned a rental price, he accepted it without bargaining. As to the matter of a guarantor, however, he said he didn't have any but was willing to put down a sizeable deposit right away as proof of good faith. At the time, I couldn't figure out why he wanted to rent the villa. I thought at first that since the place was an abandoned ancient cemetery, someone might want to excavate the graves for their contents. But no one could predict what might be in them, and it did not seem plausible that the man would be willing to risk so much money just to find out. So when he left, I quietly followed to see what he was really up to. Now, Bao Lang, what kind of person do you suppose the man was? What do you imagine he wanted to do with the villa?"

"Could he have been a shady dealer of some sort, with one scheme or another for selling black market goods—or illegal narcotics perhaps?"

"No."

"Did he want to use the place to organize the transportation or manufacture of military hardware?"

"No, again."

I shook my head. "I'm out of guesses."

Huo Sang said: "Don't you recall what has been in the papers a number of times recently, that a Five Blessings Gang has been active all over Manchuria? The person who wanted to rent the villa was one of the members. They recognized that it was located in a secluded spot convenient to transportation. So they cooked up a secret plan to make it their headquarters for the expansion of their activities in Shanghai!"

This was not something to be taken lightly. Naturally, I was beside myself. "Isn't that the gang that specializes in kidnapping and extortion?"

"Yes."

"Did you find out what they were really doing?"

"At the moment, they're housed in temporary quarters on a fishing boat not far from Zhenru Village. I've been to their boat and have also met one of their lieutenants. I've learned that they have five leaders, and that their chief is known as Hairy Lion. As yet, he has not come to Shanghai."

"Did you arrest this lieutenant?"

"What's the good of that? I learned their secret plans from eavesdropping on them. Up to now, they haven't done anything. And even though all this business at the villa is their doing, I have no proof and so could not just detain him. All I could do was drop hints, to warn them in a polite way of possible troubles ahead of them, so that at least they'd pull back before daring to operate in Shanghai."

"Did you succeed?"

Huo Sang's reply was full of uncertainty: "I don't know. That fellow seemed to have been taken aback upon learning who I was. When he found out later that the reason I was there was to look into the problems at the villa, he indicated indirectly that they would not carry on the monkey business anymore. As for whether they would disband or even do away with their plans for Shanghai, I am unable to say."

He pulled out a Golden Dragon cigarette, lit it, and went over to the open window, seeming to breathe in the warm, intoxicating air. He stood there for a while and sighed. I was also silent.

Maintaining his solemnity, Huo Sang said: "You know, Bao Lang, the livelihood of all the people becomes tougher and tougher each day. We don't know what a mess our society might turn out to be in the future. But even with the double whammy of domestic disorder and foreign aggression, we have to struggle on, haven't we?"

After a period of silence, I broke in with a question: "Huo Sang, you still haven't given a clear explanation for the flute and the fireballs in the villa, you know."

"That's easy. They were merely taking advantage of the weakness of country folk—their superstitious belief in ghosts. At dusk every day, they'd hide themselves behind the villa to blow the flute. Then they'd climb onto the rooftop to toss down burning rosin, which from a distance looked like fireballs. When I went to inspect the place, there were quite a few traces of rosin left on the flagstones."

"One more thing. That Shandong fellow winding up underneath his bed—did that actually happen?"

"That actually happened. I examined the window to his bedroom. It was evident that someone had tampered with a pane. We can surmise that while the man was asleep, a gang member got in by jimmying the window. Then he probably ignited some kind of anesthetic incense to render the man unconscious before moving him underneath his bed."

"Hmm. Everything seems to be rather simple once you've explained it. Before the truth's revealed, though, a person could easily have suspected the phenomena to be the work of ghosts or spirits."

From the window, Huo Sang turned his head to me. "That's right. Most everything that occurs on earth is like this. But now that you've gotten to the end of the ghost story, you'll have to give Hua Bosun a phone call. Don't let him go on wearing himself out with anxiety."

— *1947*

V. Satire

. . . .

IT MIGHT BE LESS THAN appropriate to characterize any of the "Saturday" stories, including the three here, as social satire. The problem does not lie with their social consciousness, which is amply evident. Rather, it lies with the very concept of satire, which in both China and the West has always consisted of (direct) morality presented through (indirect) wit.[1] Even though it is dated, the wittiness of a story like "Men's Depravity Exposed" should be clear even to a reader at a great geographical and cultural distance from its original point of publication. The moral point it seems to be making—or not making—is a different matter. For, with all three stories, a good case can be made that whatever they may be saying, their overriding aim is to provide the reader with the pleasure of escape from immediate reality, not to persuade him to become concerned over the social ills they expose. In each of the stories, in fact, wit so overwhelms morality that true satire is only minimally present. At most, the reader is expected to shake his head, not really to thrust his fist in the air.

This is evident in "In the Pawnshop," a well-crafted tale that could be instructively read with one of the first truly "modern" Chinese short stories, Lu Xun's "Kong Yiji,"[2] published just four years earlier. The narrator in "Kong Yiji" is a young lad in a wine shop, someone far less mature—and far less humane—than Manager Ma. Each, though, observes and interacts with particular customers who represent segments of society—an anachronistic literatus in the one case, the family of an urban profligate in the other—suffering from modern realities. Like so many of Lu Xun's characters, the young lad is unaware of social realities and unconcerned with Kong Yiji's plight. Just as Kong, crawling to the wine shop with his legs broken for stealing books, is the embodiment of China's crippled traditions, the lad's lack of sympathy for him is a sure indication of Lu Xun's condemnation of the inhumanity infesting all of Chinese society. It is all but impossible to read "Kong Yiji" without at least being affected by Lu Xun's unswerving message and wanting to make things better. "Pawnshop," in tracing the deterioration of a young couple owing to the husband's addiction to gambling and whoring, seems at first to follow the same path. But the difference is quickly evident. Manager Ma is both wise and humane. The Chinese society portrayed here, troubled as it is, is not utterly reprehensible. Ma the protagonist is, moreover, no social constructionist. Saddened as he is at the husband's demise, he quickly recovers. "I simply don't have enough grieving in me to pass around," he says as he returns to his *status ante quem.*

This refusal to grieve over victims or the social ills that bring them down is characteristic of all Saturday stories in this category. The resultant endings very often contradict the beginnings, greatly diluting whatever satirical (i.e., socially critical) sentiments were conveyed at the start. "A Writer's Tribulations" begins by satirizing Shakespeare East, the writer who manages through his popularity to earn an enviable income from his "curiously assembled manuscripts." Especially because the story then proceeds to tell of his troubles and tribulations, the reader is led to expect his demise. Toward the end, though, the story's satirical barbs abruptly change direction, pointing themselves now at the antagonists who bring him the troubles presented earlier as his proper deserts. Being for or against him leads in the end to a kind of moral confusion: The story loses any thematic point beyond perhaps that the writer and his readers are both reprehensible self-seekers *and* victims.

Likewise, sympathy for Qin Shuzhen, the "Mud Dolly" in "Men's Depravity Exposed," constitutes the major thrust of the first two-thirds of the story. Given the title, a reader might well expect it to be a sustained exposé of male depravity toward a hardworking but physically unattractive girl out to find a husband. The plot achieves a balance with a clever twist: She becomes rich through an unexpected inheritance, whereupon those who earlier rejected her now come to call on her. If social criticism is the aim, the story can surely end there. But the opportunity of detailing her revenge is too tempting to resist. Mud Dolly's decision to use marriage as revenge knocks her right off her moral perch. Her eventual cruelty to Minsheng, while amusing and perhaps viscerally satisfying, cannot but bring her down to his level. After all is said and done, the story is clearly one that prefers old-fashioned retribution to making a point about men's inhumanity to women.

Notes

1. See my book on an eighteenth-century Chinese satirist, *Wu Ching-tzu* (Boston: G. K. Hall & Co., 1978), especially chap. 2, pp. 40–59.
2. Included in *Diary of a Madman and Other Stories,* trans. William A. Lyell (Honolulu: University of Hawai'i Press, 1990), pp. 42–48.

In the Pawnshop

. . . .

Zhao Jiaokuang

Manager Ma of the Beneficial Pawnshop was an old gentleman who had been there since he was a student in elementary school. He had gradually worked his way up to his present position of head manager, which had taken him over ten years. For more than another decade since then, he had been transacting business behind the main counter. In spite of his advancing age, he remained young in spirit, continuing to carry out his duties with great conscientiousness. He brought a cheerful disposition to his job. Seated on his high stool each day, he very much enjoyed watching the people come in and out. Each one, among the many who did so, appeared different; to him none fitted any sort of stereotype. From his vantage point he would regularly make guesses as to each one's circumstances, each one's immediate good or bad fortune. He never wanted to force his conclusions on anybody, yet he was confident that, even if he were to miss the mark, he would not be all that far off. In this way, he was secretly rather pleased with himself.

On this particular day, the manager, atop his stool as usual, was taking care of business. It was a slow time, and he was rather relaxed. His eyes wandered outside the shop, where he noticed someone who looked like an old amah standing in front of the door. She stuck her head inside several times before slipping in. He surmised that the woman had probably never been in a pawnshop before; she was showing the obvious timidity of a neophyte. Even as he sat pondering, the amah approached the counter. She hesitated a second before pulling out a pair of diamond-studded bracelets from her blouse. "Mister, is this a place where people hock things?" she asked as she laid them on the counter. "I want to hock these."

The manager gave her a smile as he picked up the bracelets to assess their value. He saw that they were worth four to five hundred dollars, but he would have to knock down the price by quite a bit. "How much do you want for them?" he asked.

"My master has told me to ask for four hundred dollars," she said. "But a little less would not matter."

"Four hundred? That's impossible," Ma said. "I'll give you three."

The old woman nodded her assent without protest, and the transaction was swiftly completed. After she left, Ma passed the bracelets around to his several coworkers to ask whether anyone had seen them before. Upon learning that none had, he concluded that it was the first time the items had been brought there, and hence more than likely the first time that particular family had had to pawn anything. Whoever the people may be, he sighed to himself, it was never a good thing for them to have to do business with this place. For certain they would be coming in with increasing frequency and never be able to extricate themselves from having to do so. On the other hand, the shop had now added another client and significantly increased its business prospects. At this thought, a trace of a smile crossed his face.

Sure enough, from that day on, the amah came with great regularity. She would be there five or six times a month, sometimes with bracelets or with various gold trinkets, pawning them for tens of dollars each time. On occasion she did come with cash to redeem one object or another, but these times never equaled those when she came to pawn. Ma often talked to the others in the shop about what was happening, concluding that the family must have enjoyed good circumstances in the past and was now on the decline. Perhaps it had a prodigal son.

Strangely enough, Ma always seemed to be able to guess the day the amah would visit. Every so often, he would say to the others, "The old woman will probably come today." Then, in no time, she would actually be there, just as he'd predicted. Since this happened time and again, many of his mates began to wonder. Could the old man foretell the future? Why was it that his spoken guesses always came true? One evening, when everyone was at leisure, they gathered around to demand he reveal his secret. The manager pulled on his whiskers and smiled. "There's nothing difficult about this," he said. "You simply have not been paying attention. Now, let me ask you this: On which days does the woman come to hock her things?" At this the people looked at one another, unable to come up with any answer. Ma smiled again. "You see, you are not observant enough. I'll just have to tell you. She comes here either on the days of the horse races in Jiangwan, or on the first or fifteenth of the month. This is why I can always tell."

"In that case," said his mates, "the master in the family must love betting on horses. But why the need to hock things on the first and the fifteenth?"

Ma chuckled. "She doesn't come on those days because of the races," he said. "She comes because of another kind of expense. According to the practice of the city's brothels, regulars who have special ties to a particular girl must host dinner parties for her in the beginning and middle of each month. The money's probably going for that."

"But at the end of each month, the family must have all sorts of expenses," one of his fellows pointed out. "If the household's short of funds, she'd be coming here about that time. Why does her master wait for the very day when he has to play host for his lady before thinking of how he'll pay for it?"

"From that, you can see how messed up the man is," said Ma. "He likely never concerns himself with the other expenses, figuring that he can always owe a little here and there. The races and the whores, on the other hand, are necessities to him, and so he racks his brains for a way to pay for them. That's probably the only reason any of the other bills get paid at all. His devil-may-care attitude, moreover, can be said to have gotten out of hand. Just think: He always waits until the very last minute to get his money each time he wants to bet on the horses or party with the ladies. Never have I seen him prepare a day ahead."

"You talk as if you really knew him," another fellow said with a smirk. "You're so certain that he goes to the horse races and to brothel parties. But isn't it possible you could be wrong, that you've just jumped to those conclusions? Let's take a step back and reconsider. Even supposing what you say is so, I would still like to ask you this: In betting on horses, wouldn't there be days when he'd win? Why does he have to resort to coming here each and every time?"

"Those are very good questions," said Ma, smiling. "A person who gambles may lose on certain days, but there will also be days when he wins. He couldn't just lose all the time. But you don't realize that this kind of person is worse off after winning than after losing. When he wins a dollar, he thinks he's won ten; when he wins ten, he feels he's won a hundred. So he throws yet another dinner party for his girl, or sends her an extra present. Then he has to ingratiate himself with his wife by ordering her some clothes and getting some of her things out of hock. Only in that way will he have room to maneuver in the future. So think about it. Doing all this, wouldn't his winnings disappear in a wink? How could he possibly leave himself enough to bet on the next race? In fact, if he spent a little too much now and then, his winnings might not even cover his expenses. He'd have to dig further into his own resources."

This explanation brought one nod after another. The person who'd spoken up earlier was nevertheless unconvinced. "What you've been saying surely takes us to new depths of understanding," he said. "You have thoroughly described the mentality of a profligate. But your points are, in the final analysis, nothing but speculations. Before we are actually shown proof, we cannot, after all, consider them to be factual."

"So you're still skeptical," said Ma cheerfully. "If you want to learn the truth about him, that won't be difficult at all. Just wait until the amah comes. We can ask her then." Everyone indicated their approval as the gathering broke up.

A few days after that, the old woman appeared again. This time, rather than gold trinkets, she was pawning a leather overcoat and several fox furs. As they negotiated, Ma took the opportunity. "Your young master likes the horses, I suppose," he said to her. "He's going to Jiangwan again with this money, isn't he? And doesn't he also enjoy his dinners with the ladies?"

The woman gave him a stare. "How in the world would you know about that?" she said.

Ma let out a guffaw. "I can of course find out," he said as he felt around a side pocket of the overcoat and actually pulled out a roll of racing tickets. "And what a coincidence we have today," he continued as he waved it about. "I've got the proof right here! Isn't this a roll of tickets from the horse races? It's just that I've yet to find anything concerning those banquets." Looking down, he then unrolled the tickets, only to discover a printed invitation to a brothel party. Delighted, he held it up and waved again: "The proof of those banquets is now here as well. This is an invitation from the Golden Hunan Jade. Lots of names are printed on the back, in groups of four or seven. Looks like these have been prearranged for mahjongg or poker. From the list we can see that up to thirty people were expected—three tables at the minimum. Your master surely puts on extravagant shindigs!"

The old woman was quickly losing her patience. She shot Ma an angry glance. "Sir!" she said. "Why don't you just take care of what concerns you here at the pawnshop? Why bother yourself with someone else's business?"

"I mind my own business—and also other people's," said Ma, grinning. "I'm an old man and have to amuse myself this way in order to get through a day without being bored to death. Don't you see that, ma'am?" The words brought a smile to the old woman's face as she finished her business and departed. A few of Ma's coworkers were nearby and witnessed the entire episode. In no time at all, they were relating what they saw and heard to others. Now all the pawnbrokers were talking about Ma's uncanny ability to figure things out.

From then on the amah came frequently to the shop. What she now had to hock was clothing. A time or two, apparently out of desperation, she even brought in cotton-padded stuff worth hardly any money. Some of the pieces of jewelry she'd pawned earlier were nearing their expiration date, and she came to extend that by adding more interest. She also redeemed several items, which were then not seen again, unlike previous times when she would pawn and redeem certain things over and over. Manager Ma thought they must have been sold.

More time passed, and then the old woman was not seen anymore. Ma was just asking himself why the amah had not been back when he saw a twentyish young woman enter with a bundle under her arm. She was wearing old clothing, and her hesitancy—repeatedly leaning in and pulling back—was several times worse than that of the old amah on her initial visit. As for Ma, he was merely thinking to himself when he saw her that he was about to have a new client, by which time the young woman had gotten herself to the front of his counter. She handed him the bundle with great uncertainty, her face puffed up and crimson, not saying a single word. Ma opened up the bundle to find a few pieces of the clothing brought there by the amah before. Instantly, everything became clear. The family's situation had surely worsened; the old woman had had to be let go. With no more servants, the person standing there now must be none other than the young mistress. At this realization, he could not help losing himself in thought for quite a while. He never expected the young woman to misinterpret this reaction as an unwillingness to accept what she had brought because they were well-worn. "These pieces . . . you won't take them?" she blurted out, blushing with anxiety. This shook Ma out of his reverie. "Not at all. We'll take them," he said quickly as he smiled at her. Then he wrote out the ticket, handed her the money, and sent her on her way.

After that, the young woman became intimate friends with the floor tiles in the shop, visiting them without fail every few days, each time with something under her arm. Other than the few pieces of clothing she absolutely could not do without, everything she brought simply remained there; the shop did not add any interest for keeping them past due. There was no reason even to mention the word "redeem." Toward the end, she dug up clothes that were torn or thoroughly frayed to bring in. Seeing how bad off she was, Manager Ma gave her no trouble, sending her off each time with some cash. Her face, though, appeared more gaunt and dispirited by the day. Each successive time she entered the shop, she looked more and more decrepit. In the end, she became so emaciated that she seemed to be a different person. Seeing this, Ma departed from his normal optimism. "*Ai!*" he sighed to himself. "This woman is really pathetic and can't be long for the world. Isn't it her husband who's brought her to such straits?"

Then one day, as Ma was thoroughly occupied at the counter, someone suddenly lifted a bundle up to him. He untied it without thinking, then felt his heart thump as he looked over the contents. The few pieces of clothing were like old acquaintances, instantly recognizable to his eyes. First that old amah and then the young woman had brought them there before. Only, early on, they had been spanking new, before wearing down progressively. Now they were in an utterly dilapidated state. Ma steadied himself before turning his eyes to the person who'd handed him the bundle. He saw a young man in his twenties with a sullen expression on his haggard face. With his slovenly coat and hat, he presented the ghastly appearance of someone near the end of his rope. Upon closer inspection, however, his features were not at all common or unattractive. Dress him up and fill out his face with a few good meals and he could very well turn out to be handsome. "This has got to be the husband," Ma thought. These last several years, he had repeatedly speculated about what the man must be like, but it wasn't until now that he'd had the chance to see his face. This was a fateful meeting, indeed! A fateful meeting! "How much do you want for these things?" he asked, setting aside his thoughts.

"I want to pawn them for ten dollars," said the man.

"These things are worn through," said the manager. "How can they be worth so much?"

"Give me a little break, will you?" the young man said as his eyes welled up with tears. "My wife has died at home and I'm just short that much to pay for her funeral."

Ma's heart skipped a beat. So the young woman was really gone—just like that. "Your wife's dead?" he asked without betraying any emotion. The young man nodded ruefully. As Ma pondered the transaction, the woman's pitiful, careworn face passed before his eyes. He quickly gave the man what he wanted.

From that day on, the young man followed in the footsteps of the amah and young woman, becoming a regular at the pawnshop. But the things he brought were all worthless. Sometimes he would exchange one piece of clothing for another. The days he would show up, moreover, neither coincided with those of the horse races nor with the beginning and middle of each month. This schedule, not followed since the young woman first came by quite some time ago, had now definitely been discarded. His straitened situation, it goes without saying, precluded his participation in brothel parties. Nor did he have any more spare cash to bet on the horses. Every bit of money he took away from the pawnshop had to be used to stay alive.

Things went on that way for quite a while. Then, before anybody was quite aware of it, winter was again upon them. During a big snowstorm one morning, someone said that a person had frozen to death in front of the shop. Ma hurried out with a group to look. *Aiya!* The person, lying stiff as a stick in the snow, was none other than that young man! Heartsick at the sight, Ma went back into the shop with his hands over his face. He got back on his high stool and sat as if in a trance. Although he'd never learned his name, Ma was thinking, he had witnessed with his own eyes the man's slow descent into this abyss. How really tragic to end up like this! How could anyone not feel for him?

After some time, though, Ma's sanguine disposition got the better of his grief. "Oh, I'm just too much of a chump," he chided himself. "Of all those people coming in here, is there even one who's not living in pain? If I'd pay careful attention, I'd probably find quite a few others with stories even more tragic. Even if I were so inclined, I simply don't have enough grieving in me to pass around."

—*1923*

A Writer's Tribulations

. . . .

Fan Yanqiao

Over the past ten years or so, the reputation of the writer Shakespeare East had truly risen like the sun. Those publishers of magazines and daily newspapers—the people with their ears open but their eyes shut, their purses filled but their sensibilities drained—had one after the other borne the pain of exchanging shiny silver dollars for his curiously assembled manuscripts. Typesetters would simply leave the three leaden characters of his name stuck together, since they were needed so often that taking them apart and then putting them back would have been wasted effort. He employed two secretaries at home to help him copy out manuscripts and draft responses to letters. He also had a bookkeeper who, at the end of each month, counted the number of words he'd written and filled out the bills to send to various parties for payment.

Each evening the venerable writer would venture out to the highways and byways to gather material for his stories. Some days, street people would come around for the express purpose of providing him with material—in exchange for a bit of drinking money. Even if no transaction took place, they always enjoyed the cup of tea offered them. To the writer, however, what he heard from others could never be as meaningful or engrossing as what he saw for himself. For that reason, he would on occasion sally forth personally to gather the stuff.

To do that, though, brought on a number of difficulties. For one, the material was of varying quality, necessitating preliminary choices and classifications. The more revolting the account or repulsive the content, the sharper its impact and the more unforgettable it became. But stories with too many twists and turns of plot were difficult to follow. Then, too, the material came in different lengths. Short accounts had neither peaks nor valleys and invariably needed elaboration. Longer ones could not be read in a limited time span and often lacked proper openings or closings. Waiting around for real events to play out, moreover, could prove to be somewhat embarrassing. On two occasions he had encountered trying situations that had stopped him from being open and direct during his forays. Now he only relied on his sharp eyes and sensitive ears, picking up a little of this and that as he strolled along.

What were the two occasions?

The first was when he had to describe the life of prostitutes as part of a long novel he was writing. Even though writings on the demimonde were numerous, they were all concrete descriptions, none engaging in abstract generalizations of any sort. After careful preplanning as to exactly when and where to go, Shakespeare East made up his mind to take a pedicab to the red light district to see for himself. When he got there, the area was already all lit up. He went into a teahouse across from one of the brothels to sip tea and to observe at leisure both the physical surroundings and what really went on in them. Three ladies of the evening were sitting behind the gate of the brothel. The evident difference in their ages showed that they were of three separate generations. The heavy rouge and powder they had on, however, pretty much broke down the categories of senior and junior by blurring distinctions in their appearances. Many people went by on the street, including youths with their chests puffed out. The women knew full well they wouldn't be getting a second glance from people like them. The standard come-ons they were voicing were just perfunctory. Then a group stumbled by, mumbling to each other. They were all managerial types and good targets for solicitation. The three women tried hard, putting on their most seductive poses, but their efforts netted only jeers from several hoodlums. They were reeling from mortification when their six eyes converged on the odd fellow staring covetously straight at them from the teahouse across the way. Figuring they had spotted an easy mark, they scrambled over to plop themselves down on a wooden bench not five feet away, then proceeded to bombard him with all sorts of sweet-talk. Our great novelist took the opportunity to note their modes of speech. He also analyzed and examined their psyches in his own mind, with no idea that he was himself the object of *their* experiment. Seeing how oblivious he was, they began a concerted attack, dragging him out of his seat and inviting him to enter into hell with them, so that he could experience nirvana for once in his life. Realizing that he was under a heavy siege from which he could extricate himself only with difficulty, our writer wound up having to sacrifice his frayed leather wallet, which held seven small silver dollars, thirteen tiny cents, and two calling cards. With shoulder blades aching from a dozen punches and ears ringing with curses, he managed to leave behind his tormenters and regain his freedom. But the adventure left his literary mind befuddled for a full twenty-four hours.

The second occasion was when he visited a small street market to observe the bustle of morning shoppers. He'd thought that if he could only describe the many bizarre faces and modes of speech, his story would surely become a masterpiece of social commentary. On the appointed day he got up at the crack of dawn to get to the market. Now, the place was not a specially constructed building but merely a double row of vendors and peddlers in front of the shops. With breaks here and there, the row stretched as far as fifty or sixty addresses. Uncomfortable just stopping and staring, he slowly made his way down the middle, looking over everything as he went along. Coming one after the other and from every direction were cooks, mothers, aunts, amahs, professional women—all moving at a snail's pace and each carrying a small steelyard a foot or so in length—who began to haggle over prices and weights with the sellers on either side. Just as he was getting to where there was a barrel of mullet on the one side and a basket of shrimp on the other, a rickshaw happened on the scene. The puller kept ringing his bell and shouting to be let through. But the street was narrow at this point—less than ten feet across. The counters of the shops on either side took up at least four feet, and with the addition of the barrow, the basket, and three or four people, there remained in the middle a space of no more than three feet. Our great writer knew that he had to give way. He hurriedly retreated to the left, never expecting that he would then be stepping on an impeccably dressed lady in white stockings, leaving a large splotch of mud and morning dew on her leg. In his haste to pull back, he then stepped unthinkingly on that basket of translucent shrimp, transforming its contents into a pile of mush. The shrimp peddler seized the woman and demanded restitution. She in turn had no choice but to grab hold of our novelist. "It's all his fault," she declared. "He's even messed up my new stockings. Drat the luck. Why should I be paying you, besides?"

"It was the darned rickshaw," said our author. "The puller has now gone off without so much as a backward glance. So let's all just forget the whole thing." But that hardly mollified the shrimp man. In the end, the people there proposed a solution: The writer had to pay for half the loss, in the amount of fifty coppers. He also had to put up with both cold contempt and heated reprimand before the matter was at last considered settled. This time, though, he became especially distressed. Henceforth, he would never again leave home to gather his own material.

The stories he turned out were thoroughly dominated by actual facts, whether the topic dealt with family, society, love, or comedy. For the past twenty years, just about everything concerning his relatives, friends, or neighbors had been co-opted. Even though he tried to cover things up here and there, changing all the names, he invariably left detectable traces. For this reason, many more tribulations lay ahead.

On this particular day, he received a letter written as follows:

To the kind attention of the dishonorable novelist Shakespeare East:

The portrayals of societal situations in your work can be said to be vivid as the sketches of an imperial artist. But you put them into the form of street gossip in order to make a perfidious living for yourself. In your pointless scribbles, you cover up nothing. All those you portray receive derision and scorn from their acquaintances and can no longer show their faces to relatives and friends. Don't you think you deserve eternal damnation for such transgressions of the pen?

It has come to my attention that your work "Binoculars" is about a slovenly youth who considers girls' schools to be places for voyeuristic activity. This matter had not been common knowledge. But now that your story is receiving wide circulation, it is pored over by troublemakers and taken as indisputable fact. The youth involved has subsequently been expelled from his school. He wanted to vent his anger on you with his fists. Although I calmed him down and dissuaded him from seeking vengeance, I nevertheless felt it incumbent upon me to convey to you my true feelings. If you recognize your past, you can then change your future. Please cast no more aspersions on others for the sake of filling your own rice bowl. Then you will be able to avoid bitter repercussions on your person. I address you as "dishonorable" to catch your attention, so that you won't be ignoring this letter.

Sincerely,

Cool Eyes, Warm Heart

One after another, he received over thirty such letters. Some asked him to change the names in the story to the actual ones, others to announce openly the events the story was referring to. Some upbraided him for the utter heartlessness of his portrayal, others pointed out his oversights. A few of the letters were properly polite, but others caused him to tremble from threats to his physical well-being. Didn't all this amount to some kind of literary inquisition? He did, nevertheless, take note of the return addresses and, with care and courtesy, write a letter of regret and contrition back to each one. For letters signed with pseudonyms, all he could do was take out advertisements in different newspapers and magazines to express his abject apologies to one and all. When nothing more came of the matter in the several months that followed, he was finally able to breathe a sigh of relief.

How then was he to foresee that a very attractive and ferocious woman would come to him, the scandal magazine in her hand opened to the first page of "The Romantic Kiss," a story by Shakespeare East? Her claim was that the woman portrayed was exactly herself in character and behavior. The dozen lovers she'd had, moreover, were identical in names and occupations to those in the story, even though the order was jumbled. Most threatening to her reputation was that the clothing and jewelry of the woman matched what she really owned. She would have to seek redress from a court of law. The accusations brought fear to his heart and sweat to his brow. Shakespeare East, the man of words, became wordless, utterly unable to verbalize anything in his own defense. After negotiating for several hours, he ended up accepting his punishment. He would write another story, "The Chaste Kiss," to supersede "The Romantic Kiss." In it he would characterize the woman's previous romantic involvements as self-sacrificial experiments that resulted in her personal enlightenment and subsequent virtuous behavior. He also had to present the accuser with a basketful of eau de toilette before the matter could come to a peaceful resolution.

Another day he was visited by a private investigator who wanted him to delete an entire portion of a crime-case story concerning a detective who dealt in blackmail. Otherwise, the man would instigate a lawsuit, on the grounds that the story brought irrevocable harm to his means of livelihood. Fortunately, that particular issue of the magazine was not quite fully ready for release. So our writer rushed over to the circulation department and asked the manager to hold off. In the meantime, he added a paragraph praising the investigative profession, printing it on a separate sheet for insertion into the magazine. The whole process required extra funding from both the printing and circulation departments, necessitating the further loosening of their moneybags.

Finally, he was simply dragged into a local court for a lawsuit demanding payment for damages to a person's reputation. The summons from the bailiff that day took him quite by surprise. Until the opening of the trial, he had not known that the plaintiff was someone named Wu Lian. The case involved the story "The Sins of a Family: A History," which Shakespeare East had authored. In it was the character Wu Lian, who doted on his concubine while neglecting his wife and abusing his children. The story even included a love poem clearly written by the plaintiff at the time he received *his* concubine into his home—incontrovertible evidence that the defendant had intentionally sought to ruin his reputation. There was no way he could escape a guilty verdict. Our writer had thought that he could deal with legal disputes, as opposed to personal grievances where reason was replaced by barbarism. "Those of us who write fiction largely make up everything from nothing," he protested. "How then can a far-fetched connection like this be made? The names may be similar enough, but they belong to two different people. How can what is fictional be equated with what is actual, even though there may be coincidental similarities?"

"But every word of the poem is identical," said the plaintiff. "How can you explain that away?"

"If the story is taken to be something imaginary, then there is no problem," said our novelist. "But if it is considered actuality, then the plaintiff has himself admitted to favoring his concubine while neglecting his wife and abusing his children. Are these matters not against the law?"

The plaintiff was somewhat taken aback. He replied that this constituted a separate matter, one for which evidence must be gathered in order to proceed with legal charges. Reluctant to prolong the case and widen the dispute, the judge intoned the following verdict: "Fictional writings are analogues to actual fact. It is therefore difficult to treat them as material evidence. The charge of the plaintiff is judged to be without merit, and the suit is accordingly dismissed."

The writer also had to suffer severe reprimands from his aunt. "Having read your piece about 'A Devoted Couple or a Squabbling Couple?', your young girl-cousin has come to me with a frown on her face to demand freedom to choose her own husband," she told him. "Every day now she dresses herself up like a butterfly and cavorts around the entertainment district. We've received serious marriage inquiries from the families of Qian the rice merchant, Wang the lawyer, Gu the scholar, Fei the department store magnate, and Mao the police captain. But no matter what, the little wench refuses to consider any of them. She's in love with some destitute artist and not at all concerned about her own future. Just think of what you're doing to me. Your uncle died so young, and our son your cousin spends his time whoring and gambling as if there's no tomorrow. The fifty thousand he inherited should be gone before long. Who can I depend on for support and happiness in my old age if not my daughter and my future son-in-law? So haven't you made a mess of all our lives with that pen of yours?" She began to sob. Out of deference to her seniority, he did not care to defend himself; he simply tried to comfort her with a few muttered words of apology. He also accepted the responsibility of finding an opportunity to talk to his girl-cousin—to try to get her back on track—before escorting his still-fuming aunt out the door.

In short order, a lecture also came from a distant uncle. "Our clan has always accorded great attention to rules of behavior," he was told. "In the last few years, however, everything bizarre that could happen has happened—even second marriages. Now, don't you think a practice like that would be utterly disgraceful to our ancestors? I hear it was all the result of one of your stories." Shakespeare East was stopped short. He could not think of which story. "Didn't you write something called 'Twice a Bride in One Lifetime'?" his uncle demanded to know.

His memory was suddenly jogged. "I did write that," said Shakespeare East. "But how is it that it had any influence?"

"That woman who got herself remarried knew how to read," his uncle said. "It was in coming across this evil idea in your writings that she became tempted. As a result, she left a sixteen-year-old son and a seventy-nine-year-old mother-in-law and married a doctor."

"New ideas such as this did not originate with me," said Shakespeare East with a sneer. "I don't know how many millions of people have expressed it before I did. How then can you attribute everything to my one little story?"

This made his uncle furious. "The very, very bottom line," he said with venom in his voice, "is that fiction writing is outside the literary mainstream in the first place. To write that kind of preposterous fiction goes even further from propriety. Your guilt cannot be denied!" He left, shaking with rage.

The writer was not discouraged in the slightest, in spite of the many vexations that came his way. He continued assiduously to pursue his craft. Only, he now did his writing behind closed doors. Inevitably, the day came when he'd exhausted all his material and was at the end of his literary wits. He even took what his wife did as material for his fiction. In "Flirtatious Eyes," he portrayed a virago who ruled over her husband as a boss would over a hireling. The characterization was extreme. Parts of the story were based on fact, including the account derived from what went on between him and his wife. When his brother-in-law read it and told his sister, she was beside herself. Without so much as asking for an explanation, she proceeded to file for a divorce. In great trepidation, our writer made endless apologies, knocking his head on the floor in fifty or seventy kowtows. In the end, he had to rely on the good offices of the same brother-in-law who had brought on his troubles in the first place. From then on, he had to abide by a special agreement to let his wife censor everything he wrote. Should she find anything objectionable, he was not to submit it to the publisher. If he ever sent it off on his own, she would surely initiate divorce proceedings as soon as she found out.

After reading his love stories, many readers came to him to request that he reveal the actual names and addresses of the characters so that they could communicate their feelings to them directly. Some were more directly aggressive. With neatly composed missives, they unabashedly requested that Shakespeare East forward what they'd written to the persons concerned. A few of these were young men and women who were undecided and worried about getting married, having children, or falling in love. They, too, came around to ask this man of experience for answers. Even though he usually fended them off with a smile, the trade-off was still a lot of expended time and attention. Every contact of this sort, no matter how brief, proved to be very draining. Most annoying were those who, bearing him some grudge, mailed him letters from the post office without putting on stamps. He would then be fined the postage before he could open his mail, and be berated afterward. It came about eventually that he couldn't even leave his house without someone spotting him and insulting him with derisive laughter. Thoroughly fed up with literary fame—and the problems it brought—he wound up burning his manuscripts and discarding his writing instruments and inkwells. It was only then that he experienced a sense of peace and quiet—and learned that literary talent could prove to be detrimental to well-being.

—*1923*

Men's Depravity Exposed

. . . .

Xu Zhuodai

I.

When the bell sounded at five in the afternoon, all of the 120 or 130 workers of the Nova Factory rushed out at once, some clutching little packages, others holding on to umbrellas. Women workers made up roughly a third of the total. Exiting with the men, their voices blended into the general din as they chattered and joked along the way. Even as the mixed crowd emerged more or less together, a short, plump female worker seemed to cower by herself to one side, like a wild goose flying out of formation, staying away from the rest of the blue-collars. Within one of the clutches were several men who kept their eyes on her. "Why does the big Mud Dolly* walk with her head down?"one of them asked with a snicker.

"She's probably watching her own feet, so she won't step into a puddle," another said. "Water can turn mud into sludge, you know." The remark was greeted with a burst of derisive laughter from six or seven others as they again shot glances in the direction of the stubby girl.

---

*The Chinese term is *A-fu* (literally, Ol' Lucky), which refers to a type of roly-poly clay figurine still bought and sold as curios in cities and towns around the Yangtze delta. *Trans.*

Knowing full well the remarks and sneers were directed at her, the girl became even less inclined to lift her head and take notice. She merely quickened her steps. In short order, everyone was outside the main gate, heading home—in threes and fours, or fives and sixes—in different directions. Seemingly relieved that there were no more factory people around her, the girl went off by herself.

Now, this short, plump girl was called Qin Shuzhen. While her father was still living, her situation had been rather tolerable. He was an elementary school teacher. As the only child of her parents, she attended school for quite a few years. The meager salary he earned was at least sufficient to keep the family going, since prices were lower a decade ago. But Shuzhen's father died from a sudden illness the year she turned fourteen. Then, again, her mother was a sickly person. What savings her father left them were just enough to take care of his funeral expenses. Other than a monthly ten-dollar supplement from one of Shuzhen's paternal aunts, there was no other means of meeting their living expenses. Still, were it simply a matter of survival, the two of them could have just about managed. The monthly medical expenses for the mother, however, proved to be a huge drain on their resources, and they'd had to find a solution. So during the second half of Shuzhen's sixteenth year, her maternal uncle got someone to place her in the Nova Factory.

Now that she was twenty-three, Shuzhen had been working there for going on eight years. During the first four or five, she had been extremely innocent. All she had wanted was to do her work, earn a little money, and provide for her sick mother. She had been rather happy at the job. In the most recent two or three years, however, she had undergone a sudden change. For her, the factory had become irritating, a place where she could no more relax sitting down than she could standing up. Were it not for the need to meet her mother's medical expenses, she would have long since quit. How could she have had such a sudden change? Well, she was associating with a lot of men day in and day out at an age when she had become attracted to the opposite sex. The physical and emotional changes she was naturally undergoing were propelling her toward romantic attachments with the men she encountered daily. Yet, alas, Shuzhen's body was stocky, her face narrow in the upper portions and broad in the lower, with a purple birthmark the size of a grape to the left of her nose.

That she was physically unattractive had not been a consideration for a couple of reasons. First, she had still been a child when she first entered the factory. And second, the majority of employees never stayed on for more than three years. Because of her very early entry, she became one of those with the greatest seniority. Had she suddenly come on the scene at this point, that face of hers would have instantly attracted notice and been the topic of everyone's conversation. Still, even though everyone ordinarily paid no attention to Shuzhen's looks, as soon as she felt attracted to a man in that workforce, the person would inevitably find her face all the more frightful and repulsive. He would not only reject Shuzhen's advances; he would also make fun of her, thus adding insult to injury. The first time she was hurt that way, she quickly resolved to find another man within the factory, both to salve her wounded spirits and to "show" the original person. But she struck out with the second man, then the third, the fourth, the fifth, and on and on. No matter how many times she tried to swap someone new for someone old, she never once succeeded.

That was not all. Those in the factory who despised Qin Shuzhen increased by the day. The harder she tried, the more she became a pariah. Everyone was allied against her, it seemed. Her mortification soon turned to anger. She became even more anxious to succeed in her quest, so that she could wreak a kind of moral vengeance on them all. She no longer took time to learn about a man's character or background. So long as the person was a member of the male sex, she wanted him—both to ward off her crisis and to make of him a kind of advertisement. In that way, she could wipe away the humiliation she suffered from all the others. Her targets, therefore, included not just workers. Even staff members came to be considered as falling within the realm of possibility. But all her efforts went for naught. She did not get so much as a single positive response. Consequently, her heart was always pointing to one male objective, then changing to another as soon as she missed out. She thus remained in a state of flux, never able to settle down for any length of time. What she reaped was the nickname Mud Dolly—known throughout the factory—along with an endless amount of ridicule. That was all. In recent years, she had become isolated. Even women workers could not help resenting her as an indiscriminate hunter, out to capture for herself the men that rightfully belonged to them all. Deep revulsion and anger came down on her from every side, so that she dreaded coming to the factory as she would to a prison. Nonetheless, she was determined to provide her mother with the money for medical treatment and drugs, and so she had no recourse but to go into that prison house day after day.

II.

Even so, among the scores of male workers in the Nova Factory, there was one who provided a measure of comfort to Shuzhen's spirits. Yet this was also the same person who brought her the most grief. The man's name was Zou Minsheng. He was about Shuzhen's age and was decent looking. But he was an extremely devious sort who loved to make mischief above all else. He usually considered it his role to play practical jokes on everyone, constantly stirring up one kind of trouble or another. Upon discovering that there was a girl as sincere and fervent as Shuzhen looking for a boyfriend, he thought he would at least be good material. Most definitely, he would go and present himself to her. But it was not to be so easy. Even though Shuzhen's naive eyes could not discern Minsheng's cunning, she nevertheless felt he was too flippant and not a person she could probably rely on for an entire lifetime. So initially she brushed him off as she continued to seek fulfillment from a host of others. But then she was rejected as she headed east, turned away from the west, and bounced around in different directions until all alternate paths were cut off. Flippant or not, she just had to give this one a try.

Who would have known that once Shuzhen made the effort, good things would follow? Zou Minsheng had been waiting for Shuzhen to cast her affections his way. He was even becoming rather anxious. Now that it was actually happening, he naturally began to play out the different schemes he'd been preparing. It was the first time the innocent Shuzhen had ever experienced favors from a man. Individuals with feelings did exist in the world, she discovered. Even within this factory, there was someone who loved her. How could she have been so blind as to have ignored him before? Thus mesmerized by the honeyed attentions of the opposite sex, Shuzhen could never have detected Zou Minsheng's false pretenses.

Aware that Qin Shuzhen was thoroughly oblivious of the wicked play he was just starting to act out, Minsheng brought even greater energy to his task. He appeared to be in dead earnest, spending his every spare moment at Shuzhen's side, engaging her in intimate conversation. Seeing them together, workers all over the factory could hardly refrain from chuckling under their breath. Shuzhen, however, was overjoyed. She deliberately displayed her apparent closeness with Minsheng for all to see, partly to vent her own spleen. Minsheng regularly presented her with food; she became his personal seamstress. In the evenings after work, Minsheng would visit Shuzhen at her house, where, since her mother was bedridden, they could be by themselves. On Sundays he even took her out to the movies and for fastfood. Realizing that her initial goal had now been reached, Shuzhen was truly overjoyed. It shouldn't be long before the relationship would advance to the marriage stage.

That Qin Shuzhen had become so vulnerable was not lost on a crafty person like Zou Minsheng, who couldn't refrain from taking increasing advantage of her. He developed the cruel feral mentality of stalking the weak, fully intending to make Shuzhen's body his temporary plaything. To him it wasn't a matter of loving her, but a chance to take advantage of her through deliberate deception. Whether Shuzhen was attractive or otherwise was not at issue. He merely wanted to toy with her to the extent possible. But then the situation turned sour. Everyone in the factory thought at first that Minsheng was just playing around, never expecting to see him become as ardent as he eventually became. Inevitably, everyone's suspicions were raised, and the factory buzzed with derisive talk about his behavior. This brought Minsheng up short, quickly causing him to alter his plans. Three days later, a new girl named Qiaozhu came to work in the factory. According to common gossip, this person had been Minsheng's girlfriend. Sure enough, Qiaozhu began to spend time with Minsheng, who then no longer bothered with Shuzhen.

The shock of this nearly made Shuzhen ill. From that time on, the look of triumph of past days was wiped from her face. Her distress exceeded anything she had previously experienced. Whenever she went into the factory, it seemed that each word and gesture of everyone there was directed to mocking her. But for the fact that she had a mother living at home, she would surely have put an end to her own life. Noting that Minsheng had undergone a swift change of heart and that Qiaozhu was evidently not his new acquaintance, she realized that everything he had previously done had been pretense as well. Thenceforth, Shuzhen would no longer dare throw her affections unthinkingly at those of the male gender. She had no other wish than to get away somehow from the factory that had brought her such emotional turmoil.

III.

Then Shuzhen's fortunes took another abrupt turn. Her paternal aunt was a widow with an only son who turned seventeen that year. The four of them, in their two households, constituted the remaining members of the Qins' extended family. But because the two families were actually no more than distant relatives, they had been rather cool toward each other. Now, this aunt, having inherited an estate from her mother's relatives, was very wealthy. Still, she had done nothing for Shuzhen's family other than provide them with a bit of extra cash. Quite unexpectedly, the seventeen-year-old cousin fell ill with smallpox and died. Then the aunt, having grieved to excess, developed a serious heart ailment. In less than half a year, she joined her son in death, leaving behind an estate worth $130,000. Because her mother's relatives were long dead and gone, she made out a will on her deathbed to leave everything to her niece Shuzhen. Getting such an unexpected windfall was, to Shuzhen, like getting struck by a lightning bolt on a sunny day. She dutifully arranged for her aunt's funeral, at the same time entrusting her mother to the care of a hospital.

The story of a female factory hand abruptly attaining a fortune of $130,000 made good newspaper copy, and it was soon spread with great excitement all over the country. After settling the affairs of her aunt and her mother, Shuzhen began to ponder her own future and the proper disposition of her newfound wealth. After all was said and done, she was an educated and prudent person. "There must be many who admire the fact that I, a poor hapless waif, could have come into such a fortune," she thought to herself. "But, without doubt, there will be others who would be envious. Anything I do from now on will inescapably bring on criticism. I must therefore exercise great care. Whatever status I attain in the future, some people will say I was a former worker at the Nova Factory who climbed up through serendipitous wealth. That's probably inevitable. What then should I do? Frankly, for me personally, it makes little difference whether I have the estate or not. I really wouldn't know how to spend all the money on myself. So I might as well continue doing what I've been doing. I'll go on working at the Nova Factory. What could anyone say, then? I'll just leave my aunt's estate intact. Other than taking care of Mother's medical expenses, the money it earns will be put into the bank, to await the day when I think through what I should be doing with all of it. I'll be earning my own keep at my job. That's the way to go." Having thus come to her decision, she went to the supervisor to explain herself and returned to work right after the funeral. Not only did the supervisor not try to dissuade her, but he was unusually polite to her. Every request she made met with a positive response. He almost gave her the impression that he was sorry she was asking for so little.

The following day Shuzhen again put on her cotton blouse and skirt and went as usual to her job at the appointed time. The atmosphere inside the factory was greatly different, however. The workers, both male and female, came up with smiling faces to welcome her and to make friends. The women, who had been highly prone to jealousy, did not seem envious at all over the rise in her fortunes. They evidently understood that envy would get them nowhere, that nothing could beat amiability for attaining beneficial results. The men were more changed still. Underlying the greetings and the proffered friendship was the intention of using masculine charm to bring about a lasting, close relationship with her. Before this day, all that had entered her ears was "Mud Dolly! Mud Dolly!" Now she kept hearing everyone say, "Much felicity! Much felicity!" Shuzhen remained as detached as ever. Observing how quickly everybody had changed, she could not help smiling to herself.

Everyday thereafter, she unflaggingly reported to work on time, giving no indication she would slow down. The men, who used to shake their heads whenever they saw her, now vied with each other to present themselves to her. Shuzhen was kind enough to treat each one equally, without the slightest bias: She rejected them all. She also told them straight out that she wanted a husband whose physiognomy suited her fancy in every way. And what kind of looks would that be? The kind with enough indications of good fortune to make him the master of a $130,000 estate. In this way, those men who had turned Shuzhen down in the past were now, one after the other, turned down by her. They were not aiming to marry *her*, since Shuzhen was still herself—still a big Mud Dolly. Her physical self had not changed, with the exception of her hands, which now held on to money. They were really aiming to marry that money. That was the reason for the quick turnaround. Before, when she had gone to them, they had all avoided her. Now they hastened to satisfy her every whim, to flatter her with what each one considered his own brand of charm. By responding with her statement about wanting someone with the physiognomy of a rich tycoon, she was only giving them proper medicine. She was also thinking of how incredibly shameless these men were. Could the worth of a woman change so quickly? The love bought with material goods—could it ever be true love?

Those who were proposing marriage to Shuzhen at the time, moreover, were not just the ones she'd paid attention to before. Nor were they just people from the factory. Even young men from outside, the ones she had not dared so much as to look at, were now playing up to her. Among these was an especially ludicrous individual who had studied abroad. He was a person so westernized that he accepted even the superstitious practices of Europeans and Americans. About the time he set out to court Shuzhen, someone tried to dissuade him by telling him she was unlucky. Didn't he believe that thirteen was an unlucky number? Well, the fortune she held was thirteen times ten thousand. Why would he want anything to do with a jinxed sum like that? "You only considered one side of the question," he answered. "It's true that the sum is unpropitious. But once she married me, the money would belong to both of us, meaning that each one would be holding only six and a half ten-thousands. So there wouldn't be anything unlucky about it."

Having been subjected the last several days to such nonsense from men both inside and outside the factory, and having seen the facades so many of them put up, Shuzhen could not suppress a sigh: "The depravity of all members of the male species has been utterly exposed by such representatives as yourselves!"

IV.

So it came about that Qin Shuzhen saw through to the true mentality of the human male. "As a woman, there has to come a day when I'll be getting married," she thought to herself. "Since the world is populated with such brazen males, where can I find a suitable husband? Then again, since all the men in the world are depraved and dirty, I may as well stay single. Otherwise, I won't be able to escape being the wife of someone unscrupulous. As long as that's the way it's going to be, though, why don't I just sacrifice my life and marry the most unscrupulous of men? As the wife of such a man, I could then use the power of my money to subjugate him. What happened to him could then become a warning to all others of his ilk, and perhaps be a source of enlightenment to them. As for me, I would then be taking revenge on behalf of countless women who suffer as a result of men courting them for their money."

Now, Qin Shuzhen was basically very decisive. It took but a second for her to make up her mind. Right away, she set out to look for that supremely unscrupulous individual. It seemed at first that she might have trouble picking him out among those within her immediate purview. Then it occurred to her that she didn't need to look very far: Zou Minsheng was already well-qualified. Why couldn't she just proceed with him? It just so happened that Minsheng, learning recently that she'd become rich, had quickly tossed Qiaozhu aside and come running back to her, wanting everything to be as before. What had been pretense was now to be actualized. The pursuit, however, was now directed toward her wealth, not her body. If she played along, she would instantly be able to attain her objective. So, having thus made the grand decision to give herself up to avenge the majority of womankind, she again took up with Zou Minsheng, and subsequently accepted his marriage proposal. Once the matter was settled, everyone in the factory was amazed. Both admiration and criticism were directed at Minsheng. The criticism, however, probably derived from the admiration, so that one can say that the men in the factory were all green with envy.

Three months later, Shuzhen and Minsheng were married. The event astonished the great majority of the people, because the wedding celebration was not at all typical of those worth $130,000. The couple had a most simple ceremony in a small hotel. Only their very close friends were invited, to a banquet of three or four tables. The groom and the bride each had on formal wear that had already been worn. Total expenditures could not have exceeded a hundred dollars. Rich people were all skinflints, someone said. How could these two have learned to be like that so quickly? No one, however, was disappointed for Zou Minsheng over the shoddiness of the party. After all, he had become the master of $130,000.

"Did you want to marry me because you love me, or because you love my money?" Shuzhen asked Minsheng on the very night of the wedding.

"Of course it's because I love you," Minsheng was quick to respond. He was thinking that telling this lie would not make the money disappear. He had put on his most sincere expression.

"Very well, then," Shuzhen said. "You ought to know that I really don't care to touch my late aunt's estate. Since it's not the money you care about, the two of us will just make a simple little home from now on, as I told you a couple of days ago. We both ought to continue working at the Nova Factory. Only, now that I've become a housewife and must take care of hearth and home, I won't be going there anymore. You'll be working at the factory every day. When you get home, I'll have the house all neat and tidy. You'll be able to enjoy a domesticated existence. The money you earn will be used to cover our living expenses. That's the proper responsibility of a husband, one you cannot shirk." Minsheng could only voice his assent.

After three days, Minsheng went back to work at the factory, as he did every day after that. For him, nothing at all was different from before. Shuzhen alone underwent a huge change. The gentle disposition that was originally hers had swiftly vanished. Her temperament now became truly nasty and volatile. If Minsheng came home a little late, she would curse at him harshly. Under her invisible but strict control of the money, Minsheng dared not utter a sound in response. Should he even attempt any kind of answer, Shuzhen would say she wanted a divorce. So what became of the domestic bliss Minsheng was supposed to have when he came home in the evening? It consisted of no more than cold rice and cold vegetables. When his pants had too many rips to wear in public and no money was available to buy new ones, this is what Shuzhen said: "Since you are the breadwinner, you ought to take care of your own appearance. But there's hardly any money left after our living expenses. It's a good thing I don't go out. Just let me have your torn trousers. You can take mine for your own use." The following day, everyone in the factory was quietly chuckling at the pants Minsheng was wearing. There was, however, nothing he could do.

It was raining cats and dogs one Sunday, flooding the yard, while Minsheng was home for the holiday. He caught a mudfish in the water and, with great excitement, brought it to show his wife. Shuzhen happened to be in an unusually good mood that day. "That must've been a lot of fun," she said with a smile. "There's nothing great about just catching it, though. You've got to take this live fish and swallow it whole for a real kick."

The suggestion brought him up short. Not daring to protest, he could only stand there shivering. "So you're not willing to do that?" Shuzhen said as her face instantly stiffened. "Aren't you going to listen to what the person dearest to you tells you to do? *Ai!* If my husband won't even listen to me, is there anybody on earth I can rely on?" Then she began to weep.

"But . . . but this is a live thing, and so long . . . ," Minsheng muttered hesitantly.

"I'm not blind," said Shuzhen angrily. "Don't I know it's alive? I just never thought you could treat me this way. I was a fool to have married you. I can see now that you were anything but honest with me. I'll just have to get a divorce!"

Once the word "divorce" reached Minsheng's ears, all color drained from his face. He shut his eyes and shoved the mudfish down his throat. At that, Shuzhen clapped her hands and let out a hearty laugh. "You do have a bit of a conscience after all!" Minsheng, choking and gagging, fought off repeated attacks of nausea while she prattled and giggled, not paying him the least attention. Even though he had married her for money, poor Minsheng never received a red cent. All he netted was Shuzhen's abuse, meted out under the tyranny of all that money.

So many interesting incidents went on in their home that I can hardly recount them all. Suffice it to say here that in the end, Shuzhen wound up treating Minsheng as a large wild beast would treat its tiny prey. She would toy with him or torture him—amusing herself by doing with him anything her heart desired.

— *1923*

Afterword

. . . .

What's in the Name?

THE STORIES GATHERED HERE represent a type of fiction belonging to the "Mandarin Ducks and Butterflies School," a largely pejorative label attached to writings which, beginning in the 1910s, achieved sustained popularity, spurred on by the development of modern journalism in Shanghai and other urban centers in China.[1] By the 1920s, when most of these stories were first published, the prominent establishment of the magazine *The Saturday* (*Libai liu*), begun a decade earlier, had already added another designation to them. The Chinese scholar Fan Boqun, from whose collection many of the stories were taken, suggested in the early 1990s that after considering the facts, "It's [now] best for us to give to this school of literature a name that places it in literary history," and that, in his opinion, "the designation of 'Mandarin Ducks and Butterflies–"Saturday" School' appears to be the most appropriate."[2] Significantly, a number of writers of such fiction also referred to it as "old style," in contrast to the "modern" fiction written, in the words of the revered writer Lu Xun (1881–1936), "to change the spirit" of the Chinese people, whom he pictures, in a much-cited preface, to be fast asleep in an iron house, stubbornly oblivious of the pressing problems besetting their nation.[3]

It is in fact the steady refusal of Butterfly-Saturday authors to take up the moral burdens expected of all serious literature in both traditional and modern China that kept their writings outside the respectable mainstream and that brought on the low regard, if not the utter disdain, of many early-Republican intellectuals. The designation "Mandarin Ducks and Butterflies" came into vogue partly as a critical reaction to the maudlin love tales that followed in the wake of Xu Zhenya's (1889–1937) *Jade Pear Spirit* (*Yuli hun*).[4] Lu Xun's drippingly sarcastic description, written in 1931, is right to the point:

> These days, new stories of "talented lads and lovely maids" [*caizi jiaren*] have become popular once more. But the lovely maids are now from good families and are hardly distinguishable from those talented lads with whom they fall in love. Under the shade of willow trees and among the flowers, they are coupled like butterflies or paired off like mandarin ducks. But sometimes because of stern parents or because of their own misfortune, they encounter tragedy in the end and so no longer turn into immortals. We cannot say—can we?—that this is not great progress.[5]

As widely recognizable as the label was, and still is, it fitted such stories as "The Bridal Palanquin" in this collection, but hardly any of the others. For by June 1914, when *Saturday* began publishing the first of an initial hundred weekly issues, the stories were not at all limited to those of forlorn lovers. They now included, among others, scandal (*heimu*), martial gallantry (*wuxia*), crime detection (*zhentan*), and social satire (*shehui fengci*), none of which pushed hard for social change. In terms of discerning the nature of the stories the magazine made popular, a quick review of its founding and naming is informative.

In dynastic China there was of course no such concept as the work week. Sunday, based on the Judeo-Christian idea of a seven-day cycle, was introduced as an official holiday only a decade or so after the turn of the century, at about the same time these stories became popular reading fare.[6] In Shanghai from the 1910s on, people still went to work on Saturday morning, but the practice of having Saturday afternoon off as a prelude to a holiday the following day had clearly taken hold. Saturday, or even half of it, as time off from work was still a new concept for the working man and woman. But especially in Shanghai, the practice of seeking escape, if only vicariously, from the sometimes harsh realities—or just the humdrum boredom—of the workweek quickly caught on. In an era when new and cheaper methods of printing and a rise in the literacy of the urban populace came together, the idea of producing reading materials to provide that escape had all the makings of immediate success.[7] The unmistakably lighthearted and playful tone of the opening preface, "Remarks on the Publication of *The Saturday*," by its founding editor, Wang Dungen (1888–1950), makes clear the fiction's purpose and appeal:

"May I ask you why, in setting up your weekly fiction magazine, you're not calling it *The Monday, The Tuesday, The Wednesday, The Thursday*, or *The Friday*, but insist on calling it *The Saturday*?"

Say I: "People are all occupied with work on Monday, Tuesday, Wednesday, Thursday, and Friday. It's only on Saturday and Sunday that they have the leisure to read fiction."

"Then why not name it *The Sunday*? Why must it be called *The Saturday*?"

Say I: "On Sunday, businesses are mostly shut down. So we're distributing the magazine on Saturday afternoon in order to give people a headstart on their day off."

"But there is so much available to amuse oneself on a Saturday afternoon. Wouldn't people rather go to a restaurant for wine, or to a brothel for women, or else to a theater for song? Why would anyone prefer to seek amusement alone, venturing out by himself to buy and read your stories?"

Say I: "Not so. Brothels cost a good deal of money. Drinking is hazardous to health. Popular music can be loud and boisterous. None can compare with fiction for economy and calm relaxation. Wine, women, and song are moreover amusements which fade away in a blink; none continues to give pleasure the day after. It's different with stories, which can be purchased by the score for a single silver dollar. When you get home, tired and beat, you can turn on a light and open up the magazine.

Then you might have a spirited discussion of a story with a buddy, or read a selection together with your darling wife as you sit shoulder to shoulder. According to your mood, you are free to put aside for another day what you don't feel like reading. With the sunlight from the window, with the scent of flowers about your chair, all your cares disappear as you hold an issue in your hands. After a week of exhausting work, to be able to rest and relax on this one day—isn't that just grand? That's why there are those who do not care for wine or women or song, but none who don't like to read this kind of fiction."[8]

The stories to come in *The Saturday* were, as promised, directed much more to disengagement than to commitment, to friendly discussion and personal enjoyment than to revolutionary zeal, to whiling away a free afternoon than to picking up a political poster, a sword, or a gun. Though none of the stories translated here were ever published in *The Saturday,* all are very much a part of the plethora of pleasure fiction that was prevalent in Beijing, Tianjin, Guangzhou, and, especially, Shanghai for the larger part of the twentieth century, with notable downturns during the Second World War and for the first twenty-five years following the establishment of the People's Republic in 1949.[9] For this basic reason, they all fit properly into what came also to be called Saturday fiction.

The Problem with Saturday Fiction

But *The Saturday,* along with the kind of fiction it popularized, achieved its great popularity during the 1910s and 1920s, at a time when China was in the throes of trying to modernize.[10] Those serious writers who, like Lu Xun, were looking to fiction as a means of changing attitudes quickly, saw such stories as greatly subversive to their efforts and went out of their way to train their critical barbs on their essentially self-effacing fellow authors, who never really fought back. Bao Tianxiao (1876–1973), the grand old man of Butterfly-Saturday fiction, declared as an aging exile in Hong Kong that he never wanted "to wear that kind of hat." And Zhou Shoujuan (1895–1968), the "steadiest contributor" and a later editor of *The Saturday*, was adamant about *not* being of the Mandarin Ducks and Butterflies School, which he insisted on distinguishing from its Saturday counterpart.[11]

What many serious writers saw as the shallow and formulaic escapism of Butterfly-Saturday fiction looked even more reprehensible when one considers the commercialism that seemed to have motivated the authors. Mao Dun (Shen Yanbing, 1896–1981), perhaps the most prominent of China's literary critics of the time, minces no words in pointing this out:

> To put it indelicately, [Butterfly-Saturday writers] have been poisoned by the worship of the almighty dollar, which is the enemy of true art. No attitude of disloyalty toward art can be worse than this. From their perspective, fiction is a commercial product. As long as there is some place to peddle it, they will turn it out in a hurry. And as long as it meets the psychological needs of society, they are willing to accept any alteration in what they write.[12]

It is clear that, to Mao Dun as to Lu Xun, commitment to literature is inseparable from commitment to truth, commitment that is serious, moral, and not for sale. It remained for the scholar-critic Zheng Zhenduo (1898–1958), a man who, following Mao Dun, promoted realism in fiction in order to make it "a literature of blood and tears," to sum up the opposition of his colleagues for what amounts to fiction as a commercialized plaything:

> The Mandarin Ducks and Butterflies School . . . sees literature entirely as a game. . . . just as it sees human life itself. The people in it regard weighty national matters as minor and trivial and take a condescending attitude towards them. They lack the slightest hint of passion, the slightest bit of empathy. All they want is to meet the basest, the most transient desires of their immediate society. They engage in petty gossip; they play the clown; they go for laughs. They write mostly of scandals and other kinds of Butterfly stories in order to maintain their decadent and hedonistic way of life. They seem almost oblivious of the kind of world in which they live.[13]

We can understand from such scathing criticism why leading Butterfly-Saturday writers such as Bao Tianxiao and Zhou Shoujuan took so little pride in their own writings. As importantly, we can also see why so many recent studies, from both China and the West, sought to raise the status of the School not by considering what it was in its own time and place, but by rationalizing its worth in terms of truth or morality —values Zheng Zhenduo insists are alien to its character. Even though Butterfly-Saturday stories are a twentieth-century product, they show themselves to be direct legatees of traditional Chinese fiction, which began as entertainment and which has had to stand up to critical standards derived from theories demanding serious truth or morality in any type of literature.

The Connection with Old Xiaoshuo

From dynastic times to the present, the Chinese have called their fictionalized stories *xiaoshuo*, a term explained by two prominent translators as originally standing for "chit-chat of no great consequence."[14] The term has of course connoted as well as denoted changing concepts through the centuries. Nonetheless—and the different reasons need to be explored well beyond the scope of this brief essay—it is clear that traditional Chinese themselves never considered writing or reading *xiaoshuo* a praiseworthy activity. *Xiaoshuo* is, after all, "talk [*shuo*]" which is "minor [*xiao*]," and hence quite separate from the mostly Confucian literary canon that merged weighty morality with aesthetics. When modern anti-Confucian intellectuals such as Lu Xun or Mao Dun or Zheng Zhenduo condemned Butterfly-Saturday *xiaoshuo* for its commercialized hedonism and noncommitment to morality and/or truth, they were taking exactly the same official position the Confucian literati of the past took toward *xiaoshuo* before the nineteenth-century entrance into China of Western ideas on fiction: They kept it outside the literary mainstream for being itself, for remaining minor when all literature was expected to deal with matters of major import. So even though Butterfly-Saturday stories have also been accused of being products of Shanghai's "extended foreign mall [*shili yangchang*]" and even though their plots refer overwhelmingly to their immediate present and not to their more distant past, their fundamental link is much more to China's *xiaoshuo* tradition. Those Butterfly-Saturday writers who would rather be known as old-style fictionists should therefore be taken at their word. It is clearly this link with the past that accounts for the appeal of the Butterfly-Saturday stories, and that explains why they offered what Perry Link calls "comfort" to urban dwellers confronted with a bewildering array of newness and change in their daily lives.[15]

For readers without knowledge of China or concern for Chinese traditions, however, these stories may prove as difficult to evaluate as their better-known predecessors. Even though literary art may be held by some to deal more with medium than with message, there is little doubt, even with *xiaoshuo,* that a seriousness of purpose, when personally felt by a talented writer, can raise the level of the total effort. That is surely why defenders of either traditional *xiaoshuo* or Butterfly-Saturday fiction, working under heavy influence from the rise of the Western novel since the eighteenth century, have tended to attribute to them one sort of high purpose or another, without considering entertainment or escape as acceptable in itself.[16] That is surely a major reason why looking at either old or old-style Chinese fiction on its own terms—something first articulated as worthy of inquiry only in the early 1970s—has proven to be far more difficult than anyone had at first envisioned. Precious few critics—including Chinese critics—in the twentieth century would agree to look at *xiaoshuo* as *xiao.* If traditional Chinese fiction is to be respected, goes the consensus, then it must be concerned with something of greater consequence than momentary pleasure or respite from care—never mind what *xiaoshuo* really was or is. The result is a regrettable loss of identity of the native *xiaoshuo* tradition, one which flourished in the imperial past as well as the commercialized present simply because its writings, with whatever changes, did not deviate from its original nature as purveyors of escape.

The Appeal of Butterfly-Saturday Fiction

As students of literature, we ought not to dismiss even what has been regarded as minor in the great literary traditions that were China's. This is especially so when we consider that fiction was widely loved in spite of the sharp distinction the Chinese have always drawn between fiction and histories, philosophical writings, and classical poetry. What complicates matters is the parallel existence, under the modernizing influence of Japan and the West, of the "modern" fiction developed with the deadly serious purpose of waking up readers to what writers saw as imminent threats to the nation's very survival. Wei Shaochang—without question the single most important figure in reviving the current interest in Butterfly-Saturday writings—tells us that even by the roughest estimates, "the total number of publications of this type of fiction has been much, much greater than the publications of [this] 'modern literature' " that have dominated the attention of scholars and critics in and out of China.[17] If only to understand China of the past and present, we need to understand not only the "new" fiction literature it produced when, under great political stress, writers took on values once foreign to the genre; we need also to understand the fiction China enjoyed when it was culturally confident and secure, and what made this old fiction continue to appeal to its readers when it changed into modern dress. The value of seeing *xiaoshuo* as an essentially unbroken tradition is enormous if we want to consider *China's* experience—in literature as well—as an alternative to the experience in the dominant modern West. At the very least the consideration should yield an appreciation of different literary possibilities.

An important indication of what this tradition was can be found in the article "The Principles of Fiction" ("Xiaoshuo yuanli"), published in 1903 by the pioneering journalist and reformer-intellectual Xia

Zengyou (1863–1924).[18] Xia, who tellingly begins by focusing on readers rather than authors, draws a sharp distinction between those who read for a serious purpose—religious, moral, scientific—and those who do not. The former read "for the sake of their character development, their intellects, reputations, or education." The latter, however, are those who read various kinds of *xiaoshuo*. They do so in defiance of "the censorship of their fathers and elders, the criticism of their Confucian teachers," but with neither plan nor direction. To procure their texts, they would exhaust every effort rather than pursue any other form of amusement as they are traveling or resting from their daily routines. Most importantly, those who formally disapproved of such literary purposelessness were really no different. "While these fathers and elders invariably criticize such fiction in public," Xia tells us, "they, too, enjoy such fiction when they are alone." Even more than his friend Liang Qichao (1873–1929), whose recognition of *xiaoshuo*'s power to mesmerize readers led to his influential suggestion that it be used to educate his countrymen to an understanding of modern realities,[19] Xia attributes to traditional fiction an irresistibility tied to human instinct, which draws people to fiction as surely as it does to food and sex.

The stories in this collection would suggest that the use of *xiaoshuo* to change the nation was alien to the larger tradition of fiction in China, even though modern studies of that tradition, which tend to focus on the few "literati novels" that appear to present serious personal visions of their various authors, have preponderantly assumed otherwise.[20] The stories here, far from presenting any socially constructive ideas or personally felt truths, are undeniably inattentive to any such purpose. Instead, in aiming to give their intended readers respite from their daily cares, they were written and read for quite an opposite reason. As Xia Zengyou saw, just as food and sex are necessary to human existence, so is the opportunity to fictionalize in the fundamental sense of removing oneself temporarily from the pressing concerns of life. Surely the extraordinary appeal of Chinese fiction

—the enchanting power it wields over its readers—must be tied to its ability to do so successfully.

A Fiction of (F)actuality

The stories here are but a very limited sampling of a twentieth-century variation of the kind of fiction that achieved popularity in the written form only in the later Ming dynasty—really after 1550. What this fiction might be fundamentally, or how and why it attracted readers, are questions that have rarely been asked, in China or elsewhere. But within the blend of factuality and imagination that make up all narratives, we can say with validity that traditional Chinese writers past and present have largely hidden themselves behind the factuality, while modern writers and critics have generally valued authorial imagination. In his widely cited study of traditional Chinese novels, C. T. Hsia admits to this even as he betrays a certain frustration with what he finds.

> Even judging by its finest titles, [old Chinese fiction] differs from the modern Western novel not only because it shows no comparable concern with form but because it represents a different conception of fiction. A modern reader regards a novel as fiction whose truth can be vindicated by the author only through an elaborate process of demonstration. In Ming and Ch'ing [Qing] China . . . author and reader alike were more interested in the fact in fiction than in fiction as such. The barest story would do as long as the fact contained therein proved sufficiently arresting.[21]

There is no doubt that this "different concept of fiction" characterizes these Butterfly-Saturday stories as well. The obsessive interest in accounting for fact that Hsia finds in earlier *xiaoshuo* is almost certainly the result of its extension of history, of turning the focus from morally consequential events to chit-chat. We know that as modern journalism began to appear in China in the first decades of the twentieth century, it also brought on Butterfly-Saturday fiction, which pays close attention to actual fact, extended or otherwise. Almost without exception, the early writers of Butterfly-Saturday fiction were also pioneering journalists. With the commercial need to popularize, their native inclination to amaze immediately became as natural (or even more natural) as their new-found directive to inform. The result, then, was the easy blending of fiction into fact, to make fact more interesting, if not always more "arresting." In essence, the stories are not different from those which now appear in tabloid journals in news stands all over China, as well as Europe and America.

The effort to mesh fantasy and fiction, which pique the reader's interest, with actuality and fact, which retain the reader's faith, has been characteristic of all traditional *xiaoshuo*, past or present. The faith is a basic need, in a situation where a fiction-making author's personally felt truth is not respected. This is evident, for example, in the three stories under the "Scandal" rubric, all of which refer to people and situations readily recognizable to middle-class urban dwellers in the 1920s. Lest there be lingering doubt about the staggering stakes in the mahjongg game the story recounts, the author of "The Red Chips" separates himself from the narrator to assure the reader in a postscript that "this news story was spread with great excitement from the north to the south during the fall of 1921" and that it is "absolutely factual." Stories that are by nature fantastic, such as the *wuxia* tales dealing with all-but-supernatural physical feats, are nevertheless careful to retain believability with such actualities as particularized time and place, as well as familiar objects. In "Thistle Town," for example, the heroine appears to the student Xu Gongmei "like one of those fashionable models on a calendar [with commercial advertisements], with a form-fitting embroidered jacket, a short skirt, and long silk stockings." And in "The Windmaster," the reader is assured that everything "happened between the twelfth and thirteenth year in the reign of the Qing dynasty emperor Guangxu," which corresponds to the years 1886 and 1887.

Why Read Xiaoshuo?

While the expected focus on factuality may indeed be detrimental to an author's presentation of any personal vision, it allows the intended reader (though not all readers) to quickly identify with the characters and the situation, and thus entices his imaginative participation in the plot. Persons living in Shanghai in the early 1920s, for example, would, upon reading "The Confidence in the Game," quickly recognize a Sanxin or a Miss Zhou, whether or not they ran around in similar social circles. Their sense of "comfort" would kick in with the factual references to Sanxin's Snow Blossom facial cream, to the New World Cinema and the Second Theater, the Hotel Europa and the domino games, to the First Class Fragrance Restaurant, to the different locales of the city, even to Miss Zhou's cheap and combustible "imported gold" bracelet. Whatever happens to Sanxin or Miss Zhou then takes on an aura of actuality that covers over anything made up.

For the sense of actuality, of the story *not* being made up, has been a crucial element of Chinese storytelling since premodern times. All the stories collected here strive to convey the same sense. Whether they succeed or not, it is important for us to see that the essence of their appeal to their original Chinese readers consists of cloaking the remarkable or extraordinary happenings they relate—even in the *wuxia* stories—with the feeling that these happenings really occurred. Because of this, readers were easily able, if not to identify with the characters totally, at least to participate very personally in the plot, to ride what is ordinary and familiar to what is interesting, extraordinary, remarkable, even fantastic. Whatever readers today expect of their fiction notwithstanding, this is surely why traditional *xiaoshuo* stories exercised such a grip on readers, as Xia Zengyou and Liang Qichao testify. A well-cited preface to an early collection of short stories, published in 1621, tells us that oral storytellers could "bring on gladness or astonishment, grief or tears, singing or dancing" on the part of their listeners.[22] The enthusiastic words of a young man extolling the virtues of *The Saturday*, within a story labeled as "comical" in the inaugural issue, essentially echoes this preface:

"Ah, mister, don't you really understand what we call *The Saturday*? Listen, mister: *The Saturday* is an unmatched feast for our eyes as well as our greatest hope . . . *The Saturday* treats all of us equally, without distinguishing between the rich and the poor, the high and the lowly; it gladdens everyone. *The Saturday*'s general advocacy is universal love. It specializes in appealing to human nature to advance human knowledge, to bring life to the human heart. It takes as its heavenly charge to sympathize with and soothe human dejection over injustice. It is moreover *The Saturday* . . . which provides every kind of recreation. It's *The Saturday* which directs us to enjoy life. It's also *The Saturday* that makes a tiny profit seem like a largesse from the god of wealth."[23]

For some of today's readers, these stories will appear both foreign and dated. But, partly because of their factuality, they do give us an experiential glimpse of a faded era (mostly the 1920s) in places (principally in Shanghai) that have gone through staggering changes. Most importantly, through their clear connection with *xiaoshuo* of the past, they remind us of the need to explore Chinese fiction on its own terms, if only to understand why something could have been so captivating to the same readers who considered it minor and insignificant.

Notes

1. The pioneering study of such fiction in English is by Perry Link, *Mandarin Ducks and Butterflies: Popular Fiction in Early Twentieth-Century Chinese Cities* (Berkeley: University of California Press, 1981), pp. 7–23. See also Liu Ts'un-yan, "Introduction: 'Middlebrow' in Perspective," *Renditions*, nos. 17 and 18 (spring/autumn 1982), especially pp. 30–35.

2. See Fan's introduction "Yuanyang hudie–'Libai liu' pai xinlun" (A new discussion of Mandarin Ducks and Butterflies–"Saturday" School) to his two-volume collection *Yuanyang hudie–"Libai liu" pai zuopin xuan* (Selections

from the Mandarin Ducks and Butterflies—"Saturday" School), vol. 1 (Beijing: Renmin wenxue chubanshe, 1991), p. 23.

3. See, for example, Zheng Yimei's "Guanyu 'Libai liu' zhoukan" (Concerning *The Saturday* weekly), included as a preface in the 1987 photolithographic reprint of all two hundred issues of *The Saturday* magazine by Guangling guji keyin she in Jiangsu, vol. 1 (hereafter, *LBL*), pp. 1–3. Lu Xun's famous preface to his short-story collection *Nahan* (Call to arms), translated by Yang Hsien-yi and Gladys Yang, is included in Kirk A. Denton, ed., *Modern Chinese Literary Thought: Writings on Literature, 1893–1945* (Stanford: Stanford University Press, 1996), pp. 238–242.

4. Link summarizes the plot of this work and discusses its author in Link, *Mandarin Ducks*, pp. 40–54. See also C. T. Hsia, "Hsu Chen-ya's Yu-li hun: An Essay in Literary History and Criticism," in Liu Ts'un-yan, ed., "Middlebrow," pp. 199–240. See also Fan Boqun, *Xinlun*, pp. 19–21.

5. See "Shanghai wenyi zhi yipie" (A glimpse at the literary art of Shanghai), included in Wei Shaochang, ed., *Yuanyang hudie pai yanjiu ziliao* (Research materials on the Mandarin Ducks and Butterflies School), vol. I (Shanghai: Shanghai Wenyi chuban she, 1984), pp. 2–5.

6. See Lien-sheng Yang, "Schedules of Work and Rest in Imperial China," in *Studies in Chinese Institutional History* (Cambridge: Harvard University Press, 1961), pp. 18–42.

7. Link, *Mandarin Ducks*, pp. 79–124. See also Leo Ou-fan Lee and Andrew J. Nathan, "The beginnings of Mass Culture: Journalism and Fiction in the Late Ch'ing and Beyond," in David Johnson et al., eds., *Popular Culture in Late Imperial China* (Berkeley: University of California Press, 1985), pp. 360–395.

8. *LBL*, vol. I, p. 1. Cf. the translation by Gilbert C. F. Fong in Denton, *Modern Chinese Literary Thought*, pp. 243–244.

9. Perry Link, *The Uses of Literature: Life in the Chinese Literary System* (Princeton: Princeton University Press, 2000), pp. 106–107, 220–222.

10. The magazine continued to be published for a total of 200 issues, the initial hundred from June 1914 to April 1916, and the latter hundred beginning from March 1921. It was the best-selling periodical of its time. Perry Link estimates its circulation at 20,000 to 30,000 during 1914–1916, and "about 50,000 during 1921–1923." See Link, *Mandarin Ducks*, pp. 253–254; see also Zheng Yimei in *LBL*, vol. 1, new preface, pp. 2–3.

11. Wei Shaochang, *Wo kan Yuanyang hudie pai* (My view of the Mandarin

Ducks and Butterflies School) (Hong Kong: Zhonghua shuju, 1990), pp. 1–5.

12. Quoted in Wei Shaochang, *Wo kan*, p. 8.

13. Quoted in Wei Shaochang, *Wo kan*, p. 9. Mao Dun's brief essay on "Literature of Blood and Tears," first published in 1921 under another pen name, is reprinted in Rui Heshi et al., eds., *Yuanyang hudie pai wenxue ziliao* (Materials on the Mandarin Ducks and Butterflies School of literature), vol. II (Fuzhou: Fujian renmin chubanshe, 1984), p. 733.

14. See Yang Hsien-yi and Gladys Yang's translation of Lu Xun's (Lu Hsun) *A Brief History of Chinese Fiction* (Peking: Foreign Languages Press, 1964), p. 1.

15. Link, *Mandarin Ducks*, pp. 20–21.

16. For a recent example of this, see Thomas Barthlein, "'Mirrors of Transition': Conflicting Images of Society in Change from Popular Chinese Social Novels, 1908 to 1930," *Modern China*, vol. 25, no. 2 (April 1999): 204–228. Cf. Rey Chow, *Women and Chinese Modernity: The Politics of Reading Between East and West* (Minnesota: University of Minnesota Press, 1991), pp. 34–83.

17. Wei Shaochang, *Wo kan*, p. 1.

18. The essay, first published in the early fiction magazine *Xiuxiang xiaoshuo* (Illustrated fiction), has been conveniently reprinted, under Xia's pseudonym Bieshi, in Chen Pingyuan and Xia Xiaohong, eds., *Ershi shiji Zhongguo xiaoshuo lilun ziliao, 1897–1916* (Theoretical materials of Chinese novels in the twentieth century), vol. 1 (Beijing: Beijing daxue chubanshe, 1989), pp. 56–61.

19. Liang's much better-known essay "*Lun xiaoshuo yu qunzhi zhi guanxi*" is reprinted in Chen and Xia, eds., *Ershi shiji*, pp. 33–37. For an English translation by Gek Nai Cheng, see Denton, *Modern Chinese Literary Thought,* pp. 74–81. See also C. T. Hsia, "Yen Fu and Liang Ch'i-ch'ao as Advocates of New Fiction," in Adele Austin Rickett, *Chinese Approaches to Literature from Confucius to Liang Ch'i-chao* (Princeton: Princeton University Press, 1978), pp. 221–257.

20. See Andrew H. Plaks' study, *The Four Masterworks of the Ming Novel* (Princeton: Princeton University Press, 1987), especially pp. 3–52.

21. C. T. Hsia, *The Classic Chinese Novel: A Critical Introduction* (New York: Columbia University Press, 1968), p. 16.

22. See the preface by Lutianguan Zhuren (The Master of the Azure Sky

Studio), in *Gujin xiaoshuo* (Stories old and new), collected by Feng Menglong (1574–1646). Later, the collection was renamed *Yushi mingyan* (Clear words to instruct the world). See Ding Xigen, ed., *Zhongguo lidai xiaoshuo xubaji* (A collection of prefaces and postscripts from traditional Chinese fiction), vol. 2 (Beijing: Renmin wenxue chubanshe, 1996), pp. 773–774.

23. *LBL,* vol. I, third selection, p. 2.

Publication Notes

The Confidence in the Game *(Cizhong mimi)*
This story appeared in the fourth issue (February 1922) of *Kuaihuo* (a.k.a. *Happiness*), which was published every ten days from January to December of 1922 by the World Book Company in Shanghai. In spite of the magazine's popularity, it ended publication when its editor Li Hanqiu (1874–1923), once praised as the premier fiction author of early Republican China, abruptly resigned over an editorial dispute.

The Red Chips *(Niehai hongchou)*
"The Red Chips" was published in November of 1922 in *Hong zazhi* (a.k.a. *The Scarlet Magazine*), then under the editorship of Yan Duhe (1889–1968) and Shi Jiqun (1896–1946). The magazine was another effort by the World Book Company to compete with the Great Eastern Company in Shanghai's burgeoning fiction market in the early 1920s.

Rickshaw Man *(Zhu gongguande baochefu)*
This story was first published on February 7, 1923, in vol. I, No. 4 of the magazine *Xinsheng* (Heartbeat), a bimonthly edited by, among others, Wang Dungen (1888–1950). At one time or another, Wang was also editor of *Shen Bao,* Shanghai's second largest newspaper of the time, as well as the pivotal fiction magazine *The Saturday* (see Afterword). *Xinsheng* was in circulation from December 1922, through August 1924.

The Bridal Palanquin *(Hua jiao)*
Just as *Hong zazhi* was one of the World Book Company's most successful fiction publications, *Banyue* (The semi-monthly), in which this story was published in October 1921, was an equally successful venture of its rival, the Great Eastern Book Company. *Banyue* was edited by Zhou Shoujuan (1894–

1968), who took over the editorship of *The Saturday* from Wang Dungen. *Banyue* was published continuously from September 1921 to November 1925.

For the Love of Her Feet *(Jiao zhi aiqing)*
This story is also taken from *Hong zazhi* (see under "The Red Chips," above). It is included in issue no. 25 of that publication dated February 1923.

So Near, So Far *(Zhichi tianya)*
Written more than two decades after most of the others in this collection, this story was published in February 1949, in issue no. 32 of *Cha hua* (Tea talk), a post–Second World War reincarnation of the old fiction periodicals. The monthly magazine, begun in June 1946, ceased publication after April of 1949, a victim of the economic inflation and political turmoil that devastated all of Shanghai.

On the Road to Thistle Gate *(Jimen daoshang)*
"Thistle Gate" was published on August 9, 1924, in the second issue of *Hong meigui* (a.k.a. *Red Roses*), which replaced *Hong zazhi* beginning July 2, 1924. Yan Duhe (1889–1968) continued as "honorary editor," while Zhao Tiaokuang (see About the Authors) handled the regular editorial chores. *Hong meigui* did not cease publication until January 1932, one of the longest runs of any fiction periodical.

The Windmaster *(Feng xia)*
This story was included in the August 16, 1924, issue of *Hong meigui,* its third to appear. The magazine was a weekly until 1928, when it began to be published once every ten days.

From *Marvelous Gallants,* Chapter 40 *(Jianghu qixia zhuan)*
Even though the story related here eventually became a chapter in *Marvelous Gallants*—generally regarded as the most popular martial arts fiction of its time—it was first published as part of a serialization that began in *Hong za-zhi* in 1922 and continued in *Hong meigui,* its successor, from July of 1924 (see under "Thistle Gate," above). Xiang Kairan, the principal author, stopped his serialization in that magazine just five chapters later, and much later gave up writing *Marvelous Gallants,* after chapter 95 of the 134-chapter work.

The Black Cat *(Hei mao yu qi'an)*
This is yet another story from *Hong meigui* (see under "Thistle Gate," above); it appeared in the twenty-first issue, published on December 20, 1924.

The Sunglasses Society *(Yanjing hui)*
The story originally appeared in *Banyue* (see under "Bridal Palanquin," above), vol. 3, no. 18, published on June 2, 1924.

The Ghost in the Villa *(Bieshu zhi guai)*
The story was not initially published in a magazine, but in a collection of detective fiction entitled *Huo Sang tan'an* (Cases investigated by Huo Sang), published by the World Book Company in February of 1947. Subsequently, it was reprinted in at least two other collections, including vol. 4 of *Cheng Xiaoqing wenji: Huo Sang tan'an xuan* (Collected works of Cheng Xiaoqing: Selections from the cases of Huo Sang), published by Zhongguo wenlian chuban gongsi (China United Publishing Company) in 1986.

In the Pawnshop *(Dian dang)*
The story was included in vol. 2, no. 1, of the weekly *Xiaoshuo shijie* (The world of fiction) on April 6, 1923. The magazine is the successor to the well-known *Xiaoshuo yuebao* (a.k.a. *The Short Story Magazine*), a pioneer venue for Butterfly literature from the important Shanghai Commercial Press (Shanghai shangwu yinshuguan). *Xiaoshuo shijie* was published for six and a half years, beginning in January of 1923.

A Writer's Tribulations *(Xiaoshuojia zhi fannao)*
The story first appeared in *Xiaoshuo shijie*, vol. 1, no. 5, published on February 2, 1923.

Men's Depravity Exposed *(Chiluoluode nanzi choutai)*
Another story originally in *Banyue* (see under "Bridal Palanquin," above), this was published on November 22, 1923, in vol. 3, no. 5.

About the Authors

Bao Tianxiao (1876–1973) was, despite his own disclaimers, one of the two or three most important contributors to Butterfly-Saturday fiction. Born into a literati family from Wu county in Jiangsu, he began translating and writing fiction soon after the turn of the twentieth century for the highly influential late–Qing dynasty newspaper *Shibao* (a.k.a. *The Eastern Times*), founded in 1904. In a long career as a *ranzhi* (jack-of-all-trades), he worked as a copyist, tutor, translator, news reporter, novelist, school administrator, calligraphy instructor, and organizer of literary societies. He is best known for his fictional writings as well as for his editorship of such journals as *Xiaoshuo Daguan* (Grand magazine, 1915–1921) and *Xingqi* (Weekly, 1922–1923). He resided in Hong Kong during the latter part of his life.

Cheng Danlu (1879–1943), a native of Suzhou, Jiangsu province, was a teacher in various secondary schools in his hometown. He frequented storytelling sessions at teahouses, sometimes taking copious notes. As a writer, he was said to be especially adept at humorous portrayals of common folk. His fiction appeared regularly in Shanghai's periodicals as well as in the publications of such prominent firms as Commercial Press and Zhonghua shuju. He enjoyed great popularity and was known as a writer who exercised great care with his manuscripts.

Cheng Xiaoqing (1893–1976) was born in the Old City (Nanshi) district of Shanghai, where he remained until his move to Suzhou for a teaching job in 1915. From the 1910s through the 1940s, Cheng was highly active in Shanghai's literary circles, translating Western crime fiction, editing magazines such as *Zhentan shijie* (Detective world), and writing screenplays for the city's cinema industry. He is best known, however, for his highly popular adaptation of Arthur Conan Doyle's stories of the London detective Sherlock Holmes and his partner Dr. John Watson, who became Huo Sang and Bao

Lang of Shanghai. A recent biographer claims that Cheng eventually authored over seventy such stories, making him the undisputed "Grand Master" of Chinese detective fiction.

Fan Yanqiao (1894–1967), a native of Wujiang in Jiangsu province, was an early contributor to the seminal literary supplement of *Shibao* entitled *Yuxing* (Surplus Spirit). An avid—some say addicted—reader of traditional fiction in his youth, he became a leading writer of popular fiction in Shanghai beginning in the 1920s. In that capacity, he became a founding member of the Southern and Star literary societies and edited such magazines as *Xingguang* (Starlight) and *Shanhu* (Coral). Like many others in his avocation, he was a teacher and administrator in various elementary and secondary schools. As a writer, he worked with prodigious speed, reportedly churning out stories at the rate of a thousand ideographs an hour. Of all the defenders of Saturday fiction, he was the most instrumental in linking it to its tradition in premodern China.

Feng Shuluan (dates unknown), originally named Feng Yuanxiang, was a native of Yangzhou in Jiangsu. He became well-known as a drama critic in Shanghai after starting out as an actor. He worked as a reporter for *Zhonghua Xinbao* (New China news) and *Dagong bao* (*L'Impartial*), for which he edited the literary supplement *Xiao gongyuan* (Little park). In writing fiction, he was careful not to overproduce, saying that many of the best traditional authors wrote no more than a single book. Especially after the Republican Revolution of 1911, he became a political commentator for various newspapers. He often said that he never sought to make his name as a fiction writer, and so used the pseudonym Ma'er (derived from the ideograph "Feng" of his surname) in his stories. His published fiction includes, notably, *Shuluan xiaoshuo ji* (Collection of Shuluan's fiction).

He Haiming (1887–1944), a native of Hengyang in Hunan, was born in Kowloon, Hong Kong, well after the peninsula officially became part of the British colony. Nevertheless, he reportedly expressed time and again his patriotic desire to see it become Chinese soil once more. After leaving a teachers' college in Hubei because of a lack of funds, he entered military school, where he organized a literary society. He went to prison for three months as a result of his editorship of the revolutionary *Dajiangbao* (Great Yangtze news) and then became an advisor to the government at Hankou subsequent to the Republican Revolution of 1911. Eventually, he severed his relationship with the military and took up the cause of the overseas Chinese. In his leisure time, he was nonetheless fond of writing entertainment fiction, which he submitted to various magazines. As a writer, he was especially known for his portrayal of courtesans. His major works include *Qinma xiaozhuan* (A brief account of a lute-playing madame) and *Changmen honglei lu* (A record of courtesans' heartfelt tears).

Sun Liaohong (1897–1958), whose original given name was Yongxue, was a descendant of Ningbo natives who emigrated to Shanghai during the later Qing dynasty to set up a shop selling clocks and watches. Although his stories of the master thief Lu Ping, taken directly from Maurice Leblanc's Arsène Lupin, numbered far fewer than his friend Cheng Xiaoqing's detective stories, he will be forever remembered as Cheng's obverse double in his portrayal of a clever and noble thief essentially similar to Cheng's detective Huo Sang. One biographer noted the casualness with which he regarded his own writings, which he loaned to anyone who wanted them, so that not a single manuscript remains of what he wrote. He is said to have treasured friendship over material gain throughout his life, which was plagued with illness and poverty.

Xiang Kairan (1890–1957), a native of Pingjiang in Hunan, is widely known by his self-deprecating pen name Unworthy Son of Pingjiang (Pingjiang buxiaosheng). The name, many believed, was a reference to his years studying abroad in Japan, where he whiled away his time in the demimonde without regard to his schooling. He did, on the other hand, write a satirical account of what he saw and heard, entitled "An Unofficial History of Studying Abroad in Japan" *(Liudong waishi),* which was well received. But Xiang will always be remembered for his tales of *Marvelous Gallants (Jianghu qixia zhuan),* which he began serializing in *Hong zazhi* (a.k.a. *The Scarlet Magazine*) in January of 1923. These loosely connected stories achieved high popularity in the 1920s and were eventually published as a 134-chapter novel, with Xiang authoring the first 95 chapters. Even though their element of fantasy was unprecedentedly strong, these tales are a clear link to the martial arts fiction of the Qing dynasty, whose tradition they have maintained so successfully that, in both print and film, the popularity of marvelous gallants with fantastic physical abilities continues to our own day.

Xu Zhuodai (1880–1958), originally Xu Fulin, was from Wu county in Jiangsu. Somewhat unruly as a child, he was raised by his mother and grandmother in the absence of his father, who died when he was just seven. After studying abroad in Japan, he became a pioneer in establishing physical education back home, setting up a highly influential school that helped spread physical training to various secondary institutions. He was also interested in modern drama, for which he was a successful advocate in the *Shibao*. Later he turned his attention to writing fiction and became known for his comic wit and ability to surprise, even though his literary fun was always directed to presenting some truthful point. He edited the magazine *Xin Shanghai* (New Shanghai). Among his best-known writings are *Li Amao waizhuan* (The unofficial biography of Li Amao) and *Feijia tongmenghui* (The anti-marriage society for women).

Yan Fusun (b. 1901), whose family was from Tongxiang in Zhejiang, began writing Butterfly-Saturday fiction at the young age of fourteen, publishing his works in the first series of the magazine (*Libai liu*). While still a teenager, he founded three different periodicals of his own, each of which failed quickly because of the lack of funds. Along with some two hundred short stories, he is also the author of three popular novels. In 1922 he founded the short-lived Green Society in Shanghai, gathering together some two dozen of the leading Butterfly-Saturday writers of the day.

Zhang Biwu (b. 1897), was born to a Yizheng (Jiangsu) family in financial decline. Before he could complete his education, he was forced to seek his own livelihood. Through the help of Bi Yihong (1892–1926), a relative who wrote fiction for *Shibao*, Zhang got his start translating English stories. His own fictional writings became popular subsequently, even though two newspapers he edited in Wuxi quickly failed. He returned to Shanghai, still a young man of twenty-two, to work on other fiction publications as editor and translator. From then on, his stories appeared in many of the city's publications. His major novels include *Shuanghong douzhi ji* (Cerebral wars) and *Jiehou yushang* (Survival).

Zhang Mingfei (dates unknown), was a friend of Xiang Kairan and, like him, a writer of martial arts fiction. His stories appeared in the leading fiction magazine *Hong meigui* in the 1920s. He was probably a journalist on the staff of *Zhongguo wanbao* (China evening news). Other than passing mentions, biographical information on him has not been available in the standard sources on Butterfly-Saturday writers.

Zhao Tiaokuang (1893–1953), a native of Wuxing, Zhejiang province, was a quintessential Butterfly-Saturday writer in terms of personality, lifestyle, and productivity. It is said that he was fond of traditional fiction while still very young and took up writing it soon after finishing his formal education. He read ravenously, causing, some say, his severe nearsightedness. Like so many of his peers, he was fond of social gatherings and liquor. As editor of the prominent Butterfly-Saturday magazine *Hong meigui*, he reaffirmed on its fifth anniversary in 1929 that its "main principle" was "to always focus on the two ideographs *qu* and *wei* [which form the word for 'fun'], to make sure, as our fundamental directive, that all readers are entertained." Among his best-known novels are *Shiwai tanxian ji* (Adventures outside the world) and *Guai furen* (Oddball tycoon).

Zhu Shouju (dates unknown), also known as The Dream-Teller of Shang-hai (Hai shang shuomeng ren), was born and raised in Shanghai and was highly familiar with the contemporary social situation there. He turned out a series of carefully written "scandal" stories about this society, which he published in *Kuaihuo* in the early 1920s. But he is best known for his novel *Xie Puchao* (Dwelling by the Huangpu's tides), which he began serializing in 1920, and which was published in the following year by Xinmin tushuguan of Shanghai. The novel, which gave Zhu a measure of fame, deals with Shang-hai's modern social decadence, especially the demimonde. A fashionable dresser who enjoyed travel and the company of people from all walks of life, he was regarded as a leading Butterfly-Saturday writer throughout the 1920s and 1930s.

About the Translator

Timothy C. Wong is Professor of Chinese at Arizona State University in Tempe, where he teaches the language and literature of China. A former grantee at the East-West Center in Hawai'i, Wong received his Ph.D. from Stanford University in 1975. He was also on the faculty of the Ohio State University for ten years. Wong's major research interests lie in the tradition of Chinese fiction, which, he believes, has remained essentially unbroken from premodern to present-day China.

Production Note for Wong / STORIES FOR SATURDAY

Cover and interior design by April Leidig-Higgins.
Text in Monotype Garamond.
Composition by Copperline Book Services, Inc.

Printing and binding by The Maple-Vail Book Manufacturing Group.
Printed on 50# Glatfelter Hi-Opaque.